I Pucking HATE THAT You Love Me

DL GALLIE

Edited by **Karen Hrdlicka**, Barren Acres Editing

Man cover designed by **R.L. Kenderson**, R.L. Cover Designs

Main cover designed by **Kristie**, Vanilla Lily

Proofread by **Emily,** Lawrence Editing

Formatting and interior design by **DL Gallie**

I vowed I'd never give my heart to a man again. I learned my lesson the first time. But then Jameson "JJ" James came back into my life. When we started working together, he became a huge problem.

Not only is he on my "Don't fall in love with him again" list, but he's also sitting pretty high on my "I still hate you, but I also still want you" list. But I can't date him again.

It doesn't matter how good-looking he is with his green eyes, bitable ass, and heart of gold because when we were eighteen, he broke my heart. He smashed it to smithereens and left me to pick up the pieces. But now he's back in my life and wants another chance.

I pucking hate that you still love me, but I think I still pucking love you too … I'm so pucking screwed.

For Brooke.
Thanks for the laugh and for inspiring the golf scenes

PROLOGUE - JJ

"DR. KNIGHT, I NEED YOUR ADVICE," I SAY, NERVOUS AS ALL hell as I walk into his office at the hospital. I'm visiting him here because I need to talk to him where no one—aka Lexi—will interrupt us.

"What can I do for you, JJ?"

"As you know, sir, I got a scholarship to play hockey at the University of Colorado. I'm heading to Boulder in a few weeks and—"

"I never did pass on my congratulations. If anyone deserves it, it's you, JJ. Your dedication and tenacity to hockey is admirable."

"Thank you, sir, but I ... umm ... I have a dilemma." Taking a breath, I just spit it out. "I love Lexi with all my heart, but I think I need to break up with her."

"May I ask why?" His voice is low and menacing. If I were in his shoes, I probably would have grabbed me by the shirt and shoved me into the wall for even thinking about breaking up with his daughter, but Dr. Knight isn't a loose cannon, or an asshole.

"As you know, Lexi has always dreamed of being a physical therapist for a sports team. Her getting this late scholarship to study at USC in California is a great opportunity for her, but she's talking about turning it down. She's still coming to Colorado with me, but I can't let her do that. I won't let her give up her dream for me. She deserves to go to the best school and that's at USC, not UC. She has to follow her dream like I am, but how do I get her to do that without hurting her?"

"Have you tried talking to her?"

"Yes," I chuckle. "But she told me I was being ridiculous. That she can make her own choices, but this is the wrong one."

"UC is a good school, but I agree. USC is the better choice of the two when it comes to what she wants to do. I know she loves you, JJ. She has since you moved here, and a love like you two have doesn't come around often."

"I know that and I love her with everything I have. It's because of that love I can't let her follow me. She needs to follow her dreams, but how do I make her see reason? You've met her. She's headstrong and stubborn at times and when she's made up her mind, there's no changing it." I mean that. Lexi Knight is the most amazing woman I have ever met, but when her mind is made up, it sticks like superglue. I knew from the first moment I saw her up in that treehouse that I was going to marry her. And I still feel the same way now, but I also refuse to let her give up her dreams for me. She'd eventually resent me and I'd hate myself for that.

"Well, son, you just need to be honest with her. Honesty is the best policy. Lex isn't stupid. If you explain it to her like you just did to me, I'm sure she will see reason. You can always do the long-distance thing and when she finishes, you guys can meet up and go wherever you're drafted."

Nodding, I smile at him. "I hope you're right."

He stretches out his hand and I take it. "Good luck … with both my daughter and your career."

"Thanks, Dr. Knight, I appreciate your advice."

Walking out of his office, I take in all he said and head home … then I do the complete opposite of what he suggested.

1

JJ

RESTING MY HEAD ON THE WINDOW, I WATCH THE TREES PASS US by as Mom and I make the move from upstate New York—where I was born—to a place in the burbs of Chicago.

Mom got a new job with Luxe Resorts and she's going to be the manager of their new Chicago hotel. It's a great opportunity for her, but it means I'm leaving my friends and my hockey team. And yes, I know I'm being a selfish sixteen-almost-seventeen-year-old, but I was happy in Port Ewen. It was my home, and now we're moving eight hundred miles away ... midsemester ... just before my seventeenth birthday.

I'm going to be the new kid at school and at hockey.

It's not fair.

It's been Mom and me for as long as I can remember. My deadbeat dad took off when I was five and we haven't heard from him since. Mom and I are a team. I may only be sixteen, but the brightness in her eyes when she got the call to say the job was hers is just like the brightness I get in my eyes when I take the ice. How could I take that away from the woman who has been there for me from day one?

So here I am, in the car, moving cross-country.

I've played hockey since I could walk. The first time my dad put a stick in my hand, I knew I was destined to be a professional hockey player. One day, I'm going to play for the New York Crushers, and when I grow up, I'm going to be just like Maverick 'Rick' McQueen. He's a legend on the ice and he's my hero, alongside my mom. She's the real MVP and if I'm half as amazing as her, I'll be pretty awesome.

It's funny, the only thing I will ever thank my dad for is strapping me into a pair of skates and placing that stick in my hand, but really, I need to thank my mom. She's the one who takes me to all my early-morning practice sessions. She's the one who pays for all the training camps and equipment and new skates each season. She's the one who lines up sponsorship and donations for my team. She's done everything associated with hockey for me, and I will forever be grateful to her for that.

If it weren't for her support, I wouldn't be the player I am. I also wouldn't have met my best friend, Kallen Jones. Kal and I met at a junior hockey camp a few years back. He's my brother from another mother, and country. He lives in Vancouver, but from the moment I met him, we clicked. Kal is an amazing goalie and, one day, he and I are both going to play for the Crushers. But before we get there, hopefully, both of us will be attending college together.

Mom pulls into the driveway of our new house, and I sit in the car and stare up at our new home. I haven't even gone inside yet, but a sense of belonging washes over me. This is where Mom and I are meant to be.

She's rented a small two-bedroom cottage, which has a bright blue door—Mom's favorite color—and a front porch complete with a bench swing. A white picket fence lines the property and the path leading up to the porch is lined with daisies.

Already I like the place.

After climbing out of the car, Mom and I head inside. Pushing the door open, I look around and smile. You enter into the living room and off to the right is the hallway leading to the bedrooms. Behind the living room is the dining area and kitchen with a freestanding island counter. The kitchen leads out into the small backyard, complete with a gazebo and grassy area.

"Can we get a dog?" I ask Mom as I push open the back door and step into the backyard.

Giggles from next door garner my attention and when I turn my head toward the sound, I see a treehouse. This tree-house is a mini mansion up in a tree. It has windows with curtains, a ladder, and a fireman's pole.

A girl pops into view and she looks out the window. A smile appears on her face and when she yells out, "Hello" and waves at me, I'm instantly smitten. A grin takes over my face and I lift my hand to wave back, but before I can sing out to her, she yells, "Stop it, CJ. Ugh, you are so annoying," and then she's gone.

Only one word has been spoken, but something inside me is calling to this girl. I have a feeling she's the one I'm going to marry when I grow up.

As time went on, I learned her name is Alexis Knight, or Lexi for short. Her dad is a doctor and her mom is a stay-at-home mom, looking after her younger sister, Pepper, and brother, Clay, or CJ as everyone calls him.

Lexi and I become friends, best friends in fact.

Where she goes, I go.

I'm harboring a massive crush on her, but the shy side of

me doesn't want to ruin our friendship. However, the more time I spend with her, the more I fall for her. Miller Wentworth, a guy from school and fellow puckhead, keeps telling me to put on my big boy panties and take that final step, but what if it changes us?

I don't want to ruin what we have.

Just before her eighteenth birthday and a year after first laying eyes on her, I pluck up the courage and decide to ask her out on a date ... after I check with her dad first, because manners are always a good thing to have when it comes to the girl you're lusting after.

With Dr. Knight's blessing, I climb up the ladder of the treehouse and before I climb in, I balance on the last step and stare at the girl I've been enamored with from the moment I moved in next door over twelve months ago.

"Are you staring at me?" she asks from her spot on the beanbag in the corner, reading. No doubt a smutty book.

"Maybe ... so what if I am?"

"It's creepy," she says.

She sits up and crosses her legs. She taps the floor next to her and with a nod, I climb into the treehouse and shuffle over beside her. I'm getting too big to be in here with her, but there's no place I'd rather be than by her side.

"Lexi?" Her name comes out more like a question and I can't help the nerves building inside me.

"JJ," she says back and I smile.

"Go out with me on Friday night?" I ask, eagerly awaiting her answer.

Silence envelops us and I have no clue what she's going to say. Then after what feels like an eternity, when in fact it was only a few seconds, she answers.

2
LEXI

Holy shit, JJ is asking me on a date ... I think. "Are ... aaaare you asking me on a date?"

Nodding, he takes a deep breath, reaches over, and laces our fingers together. "Yes, Lexi, I'm asking you to go out with me, but as more than just friends. I ... I also want you to be my girlfriend."

He stares at me.

I stare back at him.

Neither one of us speaks.

The air around us thickens. I thought that was only a thing that happened in the smutty books I read, but right now, I'm living in one of my smutty books ... just without the kinky sex. Hello, I'm only seventeen.

My heart is racing. It feels like it's going to burst through my chest. I've wanted more with JJ for months now, but I was too scared to make the first move because if he didn't feel the same way, I'd be embarrassed. Plus, I didn't want to risk our friendship, but it seems we both want the same thing.

He's still staring at me and I realize I haven't answered. My head starts moving of its own accord and I whisper, "Yes, JJ, I'd love to go out with you and be your girlfriend."

"Good, because I couldn't go another day without making you mine, Lexi Knight, and now that you're mine, I'm never letting you go."

Then something even more magical happens. He kisses me.

Lifting himself up, he leans over and presses his lips to mine, but he quickly pulls back. From the look on his face, he's sorry for what he just did, but I'm not. I've imagined what it would be like to kiss him many, many times before. And since he made the first move, I make the second and instigate another kiss.

Leaning over, I press my lips to his. He's frozen and I think maybe I overstepped, but then he forces his tongue into my mouth and starts to kiss me back.

Holy.

Kiss.

Batman.

And it only gets better when he reaches out and grips my cheeks in his palms. Deepening our kiss, our tongues slip and slide in and out of each other's mouths. Gently, he pushes me backward and I fall onto the beanbag I was sitting in. He covers my body with his and we continue to make out.

I'm cocooned under his body and I've never felt more safe and cherished than I am right now, but the most perfect of perfect first kisses is broken when my sister, Pepper, yells from beside us, "Daaaaaad! Mooooooom, JJ and Lexi are kissing."

"Ewwww," CJ sings out from beside her.

My eyes widen at the sound of my siblings and I push JJ off me with an almighty shove. He lands on his ass with a thud, and to be honest, I'm impressed with my strength. He scrambles to his feet and whacks his head on the ceiling of the treehouse as he stands up and shuffles backward ... right out of the treehouse entrance.

With his arms flailing about, he falls out of the treehouse and lands on the grass below with a thud.

"JJ," I cry out as I shuffle to the doorway and look down at a winded JJ lying at the base of the treehouse ladder.

"I said you could ask her out, not kiss her," my dad growls as he offers his hand to JJ to help him up.

"I ... I ..." JJ stammers.

"You okay?" Dad asks JJ. Even from up here, I can hear the concern in Dad's voice, he used his doctor voice.

JJ lifts his gaze to me, smiles, and nods. "I'm better than good. She said yes and I kissed her, and then she kissed me back."

Dad snaps his gaze to mine. "You kissed him?"

My eyes widen, but before I can answer, he shakes his head and rubs his temple. "Cress, it's started."

"What's started?" Mom asks as she joins us and takes in the scene before her.

"Our little girl is growing up."

"Dad," I hiss, "I'm seventeen now."

"Doesn't matter if you're seven, seventeen, or seventy. You will always be my little princess who loves *My Little Pony*."

Smiling down at my dad, I can't help but feel loved and cherished, even if he probably wants to kill JJ right now. My dad, Preston Knight, is the knight in scrubs, who rescued my mom and me from the clutches of my evil bio dad when I was little. He stole my mom's heart and she got the happy ever after she deserves.

Creed Dawson was—past tense—a monster, plain and simple. When I learned the truth about my bio dad, I was devastated for my mom. Had the asshole not been dead, I would have killed him myself and that's saying a lot because I'm a lover, not a fighter. As she told me the story about him, I vaguely remembered bits and pieces about him, but I seem to have blocked him out. As far as I'm concerned, Preston Knight is my dad. I even have the paperwork to say he is.

When he married my mom, he officially adopted me too. From that day forward, I was a Knight. And just like him, I want to save people. Well, I want to work with sports people and aid their recovery and help prevent further injury.

Watching JJ play this past year has opened my eyes and when I grow up, I want to be a sports physical therapist and, hopefully, work for the team JJ signs with. Then we can work together, him on the ice and me behind the scenes.

Shuffling out of the treehouse, I climb down. When I reach JJ, Mom, and Dad, I slide my arm around JJ's waist and he winces. "Are you sure you're okay?"

"Never better," he replies. "You're going on a date with me this Friday and next week, I'm off to hockey camp. My life is fudging great."

"Language," Dad berates him.

"Fudging isn't a bad word, sir."

"I'm second-guessing you dating my daughter."

"Preston," Mom scolds him. "JJ is a lovely young man and our daughter is an amazing young woman. They are both sensible and they both know that I'm too young to be a grandmother—"

"Moooom," I interrupt her, "how did we go from a first date to me having a baby?"

"I was your age once," she says. "River Pinkelman asked me out when I was sixteen, and well, that night I became a woman."

"Moooom," I complain, while Dad growls, "Cressida, don't give them ideas."

"Ohhh, you got full named," I tease my mom. "But for the record, I won't be getting pregnant this Friday. It's just dinner and a movie. Besides, I'm still a virgin."

"Shoot me now," Dad complains.

"Sir, as I told you when I asked for permission to date your daughter, I really like Lexi and I have ever since I moved in next door and her head popped up in the tree-house window. I will be nothing but the gentleman my mom raised me to be."

"And you remember what happens if you hurt her?"

"Yes, you know how to inject me with something that will kill me and it won't show up on an autopsy report, allowing you to get away with murdering your daughter's boyfriend."

"Daaaaaad," I berate him, while Mom says, "You did not threaten him like that," and she smacks him in the arm.

"I'd do anything for my princess, even murder a boy."

Smiling at my dad, I can't help but feel safe. Then I look at JJ and another feeling washes over me … I wonder how much longer I'll be a virgin because Jameson "JJ" James is the man I want to lose my virginity with.

3

JJ

Not being able to see Lexi for the next two weeks is going to be torture. We're banned from seeing one another because we fell asleep in the treehouse together after our amazing date. If Pepper hadn't ratted us out, we would have spent the day together in said treehouse.

Thankfully, I'm off to hockey camp tomorrow, so I won't even be here for the ban, but it still means two weeks away from Lexi.

Normally, I'm super excited for camp, but this time, not so much because of Lexi and my new relationship. I'm going to miss her, a lot.

Grabbing my phone, I shoot her a text.

JJ

I miss you already

Immediately those three bubbles appear and my heart races.

LEXI

I miss you too ... I wish I could kiss you goodbye.

I know :(

Two weeks is a long time without seeing your gorgeous face

I'll send you a selfie every day you're gone and when you get back, you can take me to Navy Pier again

It's a date

I'll hold you to that

You can hold me to more than just that **wink wink**

Jameson James, who knew you were such a dirty boy?

You clearly don't know me well enough to not know that

PS. There's a difference between dirty and diiirty ... and for the record, I really like getting diiirty with you

I really like getting diiirty with you too ... and when you get back maybe we can discuss further what we were discussing last night

Holy shit, this woman is going to be the death of me.

A part of me wishes we had done it the other night, but I also know it's best we wait, and I know the perfect moment ... and how I can make it special for us.

You + Me + Prom **wink wink**

> You mean it?

I wouldn't joke about that

> Then you have yourself a date ... guess I better go dress shopping

> ... and lingerie shopping

You can't say stuff like that to me. My mom is sitting next to me and that image has given me a semi

> Oops, my bad

> **picture**

I groan as I stare at a picture of Lexi. She's on her bed in a sexy pink cami and she's blowing me a kiss.

> Nite nite, JJ

Nite nite, you minx ... dream of me

> Always

Before I embarrass myself in front of my mom, I say good night and race up to my bedroom. After stripping off my clothes, I sit on the edge of my bed and jerk off to the image she just sent me. Spilling my load all over my fist, I let out a contented sigh before I drop back to the mattress with a smile on my face.

Jumping up, I climb into the shower and when I start to think of a naked Lexi and water cascading over her body, my dick hardens and I need to jerk off, again.

After washing myself, I dry off and then hop into bed.

Resting my hands behind my head, I stare up at the ceiling and realize that for the first time ever, I'm excited for a school dance, well, prom, 'cause I'm going to have the hottest date there and afterward, I'm going to have sex for the first time.

The two weeks away at camp flew by, but at the same time, the fourteen days crept by ever so slowly. I learned so much there and it was great to catch up with Kallen again.

An NHL scout was there and he said to me and Kal that if we keep up the good work, we will make it to the big league. I hope he's right and one day, I make it to the NHL. If, know when, that happens, all my dreams will have come true.

There's still one day until I can see Lexi—stupid ban for falling asleep in the treehouse.

This ban totally sucks. When I was away at camp, it was easier because there was a couple hundred miles between us, but knowing she's just next door now is torture.

JJ

Just got home … can't wait to see you tomorrow

LEXI

Tomorrow is forever away. It was so much easier when you weren't next door … knowing you're home and I'm here, it's torture

I laugh that she said what I was thinking. Just proves the two of us are meant to be together.

> Maybe we can chat over the fence? That's technically not seeing one another, right?

> You're a genius. Meet me at the fence

Jumping off the couch, I race out to the back and when I look over, Lexi is already standing there. She's grinning at me and I return the sentiment. If I thought she was beautiful when I looked over here when we moved in, I was wrong. Because right now before me is an angel. Lexi Knight is perfect in every way, and she's mine. All fucking mine.

"Hi," she nervously says in greeting with a little finger wave.

"Hey, babe, how you doin'?"

"Really, you Joeyed me?"

I shrug at her.

"How was camp?"

"It was amazing, but I missed you."

"I missed you too. So, so much."

Hearing her say she missed me is so different than reading it in a text. It feels realer—and yes—I know realer isn't a real word, but it's true. Hearing those three words come from her lips made my heart flutter, amongst other parts of my body. If there wasn't a fence and our grounding separating us, I'd race over and throw myself at her. I'd lift her up and she'd wrap her legs around my waist and grip my cheeks in her palms. She'd kiss me like her life depended on it.

"Where did you go just now?" she asks me.

"I was just imagining what I'd do if we weren't banned from seeing each other and there wasn't a fence separating us."

"Do tell," she commands.

"Well …" I proceed to tell her what I'll do when we are able to be together again.

"Maybe tomorrow we can make that happen." Then she adds, "In less than twenty-four hours, I get to feel your lips against mine again."

Silence falls between us and we stand here quietly, just staring at one another like lovesick fools.

"You can go next door," a deep voice rumbles from behind Lexi.

She turns her head and looks at her dad. "Really?"

"Really, really, go kiss your boyfriend."

My eyes widen at his words. She looks back at me, smiling.

"I'll come to you," I shout. Turning on my heel, I race next door and when I run through the house, I earn myself a "don't run inside" scolding from my mom.

"Sorry," I call out.

I swing open the front door, race down the stairs, and I jump the little fence separating our yards. Then I climb her front stairs, taking two at a time. Her front door flies open and my sandy-brown-haired angel slams into my muscular chest before we fall with a thud on our asses.

She stares up at me. I'm assaulted with her scent, and a shudder runs through me, but I shake off that thought. I need to make sure she's okay. "Shit, babe, are you okay?"

Nodding, she places her hand in mine and when our palms touch, a spark jolts up my arm. Pulling her into a standing position, she throws her arms around my neck.

Mine slide around her waist and I hold her tightly to me and, on her front porch, we kiss.

"Daaaaaad! Mooooooom, JJ and Lexi are kissing on the front porch," Pepper yells out from inside the house.

Breaking the kiss, I look over my shoulder at Lexi's younger sister and smile, but her sister scolds her, "You're such a snitch, Pepper."

"Am not," she hisses.

"Girls, cut it out," their mom scolds.

"Welcome home, JJ," Cress says. "You two head out back and help your dad set up for the barbecue."

"Yes, Mom," Lexi agrees, while I nod and smile.

"Sure thing, Cress, but do you mind if I invite my mom?"

"She's already on her way." No sooner does she say that and my mom appears. She walks up the front path with her famous cheese and bacon cob loaf in one hand and a bottle of wine in the other.

"Is that your famous cob loaf?" Dr. Knight asks at the doorway, his eyes lit up like a Christmas tree.

"It sure is. It wouldn't be a barbecue without it."

My mom is known for her cob loaf. It's this amazing Aussie creation a co-worker of hers from Australia introduced us to. It is basically a hollowed-out cob loaf that she makes from scratch, or if she's lazy—code for short on time —she buys French bread, but it's definitely better when she bakes a cob—don't tell her I said that. She then fills it with this creamy, delicious bacon and cheese mixture. Sometimes I think we only get invited because Mom always brings it. I remember one time, she made a charcuterie board and Dr. Knight pouted. He literally pouted when he realized she didn't bring her cob loaf. Ever since that barbecue, Mom always brings one for him. He's even conned her into making one just for him on his birthday each year for the rest of eternity.

We all head inside, and Lexi and I cannot keep our hands off one another. I guess we pushed him a little too far because for the rest of the day, he keeps Lexi and me apart, but one thing I do know, I'm happier than I ever have been before … and I cannot wait to sneak back over later tonight.

4
JJ

ONCE MOM TURNS OUT THE LIGHTS, I WAIT UNTIL I HEAR HER
snores—which she will deny—and as soon as I do, I climb
out of bed and sneak downstairs. Easing the back door open,
I step out into the cool night air and head next door.

Silently, I make my way over the fence, but with it being
the middle of the night, it sounds like an elephant
heffalumping around as I climb up the ladder and hoist
myself into the treehouse.

Soon, I will be too big to fit in here, but if it means I get to
spend time with Lexi, I will contort myself into any small
place. As long as she's there, so will I.

When my head pops into the entryway, a smile appears
on my face when I see Lexi is already here. She's lazing in
one of the beanbags and has her eyes closed.

She's wearing a sunset orange cami and boxer set. She
opens her eyes and they glow in the moonlight filtering in
through the window.

"Sorry to wake you," I whisper.

She just smiles at me. "You came."

"And I always will, Lex. Wherever you are, I'll be there."

"And wherever you are, I'll be there too."

We silently stare at one another. I may have only recently turned eighteen, well, in February I did, but I love this woman with every fiber of my being. I know we've decided to wait till prom to take that final step in our relationship. However, with her lying here like a goddess on that beanbag, it's going to be very hard to behave, but Lexi deserves more than a quickie in her childhood treehouse.

Lifting myself into the treehouse, I crawl over to her. Leaning above her, I lower my head and press my lips to hers to kiss her hello. She lifts her arms and places them around my neck. Pulling me into her, she deepens our kiss. Her tongue plunges into my mouth and I swallow down her moans.

My dick hardens against her thigh and the minx that she is, wriggles beneath me, causing it to harden further.

"JJ," she mumbles against my lips.

Pulling back, I stare down at her. Her cheeks are flushed and her eyes are filled with lust. "What's up?"

"I wanna …"

"Wanna what?"

"I want to suck your dick."

My body freezes and I mutely stare down at her. My head begins to nod of its own accord and my already hard dick hardens further at the thought of her delectable lips wrapped around my shaft.

"What can I do for you?"

"Just let me suck you. I … I need to replace *that* memory."

The other week, Lexi walked into the kitchen in the middle of the night and saw her Mom and Dad in a compromising position on their counter. She won't go into specifics, but she's been traumatized ever since.

"You know I'll do anything for you, but once you've sucked me, I want to go down on you too. Fair's fair when it comes to oral."

"And sharing is caring," she seductively whispers.

I know she was supposed to blow me first, but I'm a gentleman and it's only fair that she comes first. Nibbling and kissing down her neck and chest, I make my way between her thighs.

Kissing her mound through her clothes, I can smell her arousal and it's the ultimate aphrodisiac. Sliding my hands up her thighs and under her clothes, I rub her through her panties. She moans wantonly and it's music to my dick. Pushing the material of her panties to the side, I slide my finger through her folds.

"Yes," she mewls.

Pushing my digit deeper into her, she grinds herself against my hand and demands, "More." I begin to plunge my finger in and out of her. Lowering my head down, I pull my finger from her wet channel and lick her from taint to clit. Swirling my tongue around her clit. She swivels her hips, adding to the motion of my tongue circling her swollen nub.

Licking and sucking her clit, I press my finger back into her. She slides her hands into my hair and tugs on the strands before pushing my face deeper into her slit.

Her inner walls tighten around my finger and I know she's close.

"Jaaaaay-J," she draws out my name and I smile against her pussy. Sucking harder on her clit, I gently bite it and she cries out, "I'm coming."

Grinding herself against my face, she rides out her release, soaking my mouth and chin.

Her body goes limp and I pull my fingers and face away from her. Staring down at her, I lift my hand toward my mouth, but before I can lick them clean, Lex sits up and pulls my hand to her mouth. She wraps her lips around my fingers and licks them clean.

Hottest.

Thing.

Ever.

She removes my fingers from her mouth and purrs, "My turn."

5
LEXI

I DON'T KNOW WHAT CAME OVER ME, BUT I WANTED TO TASTE myself. Sucking on his fingers is not something we've done before, but then again, we haven't gone this far before either. Sure, JJ and I have fooled around over our clothes, but tonight when his head popped into view, I needed more.

It was supposed to start with me blowing him, but after that orgasm, I'm not upset that I got to come first.

With my eyes locked on his emerald green orbs, I lick his fingers clean. I've tasted myself on my own fingers before, but this time I taste different. I think it's because I came harder than I ever have before.

His fingers pop out of my mouth and I demand, "My turn."

With a nod, JJ pulls me upright so we can swap positions, but before we do, I grip his cheeks and kiss him. Tasting myself on his lips is hedonistic. Taking control, I somehow flip JJ onto his back and straddle his legs.

He's wearing a Crusher's T-shirt and athletic pants. I make quick work of freeing his dick. I've rubbed him through his pants before, but this is the first time I'm seeing one in the flesh. They aren't the most attractive appendage out there, but I don't have to look at it for long because the need to have his dick in my mouth overtakes me.

Leaning down, my tongue slides through the glistening slit at the tip. With my eyes locked on his, I hollow my cheeks and suck his shaft into my mouth. The tip hits the back of my throat and I gag a little, but having his dick in my mouth is empowering. Pulling back, I circle the head again with my tongue before I lick and suck down the side.

Taking it deeper into my mouth each time, I bob my head, grazing my teeth along his shaft, earning a hiss from JJ. He slides his hands into my hair and starts to guide my head up and down, taking control. He moans like the guys do in the porn I've watched and I inwardly high-five myself.

Lifting my hand, I cup and fondle his balls as I continue to suck him like a melting popsicle on a hot summer's day.

"Lex, I'm gonna come," JJ says from above.

"Do it," I mumble around his cock in my mouth. The vibrations of my words set him off and he spills his seed down my throat. It's saltier than I expected, but I drink every last drop down. His cock pops from my mouth and I wipe at the side of my lips where I spilled some.

"Holy puck," JJ pants. "That was—"

"Mmmhmpf," I confirm as I lie down beside him and snuggle into his side. "I love you, JJ," I whisper into the silence that befalls us.

"Love you too, Lex, and I cannot wait for prom. I'm going to make it a night you will never forget."

Lifting my head, I stare down at him. I know I'm only

eighteen and I have my whole life ahead of me, but JJ is where my world starts and ends. Where he goes, I go … or so I thought.

TODAY WE'RE TRAVELING TO SCOTTSDALE POINT FOR THE FINAL varsity game of high school. Going into the game, we are the favorites, but the Scottsdale Point Prep Sea Pups have really upped their game recently. The last time we played them, we only won due to a penalty shootout, but I refuse to let the final game end like that.

The atmosphere on the bus is electric, but I kind of wish I was traveling with Mom, Lexi, and her family. The Knights are coming along to support me as well, something they have not done before, but then again, Lexi and I only just started dating.

"You ready to play your heart out, James?" Coach Johnson asks as he drops into the seat across from me.

"You know it. The team's in top form and if we keep our heads in the game, we can win this."

"That's the attitude that got you your scholarship."

"You and your guidance got me the scholarship, sir."

"Not me, son, you. You are the one who is at the rink before everyone else. You're the one still at the rink after everyone else has left. You got it because of the effort you put in."

"Thanks, Coach, I appreciate it."

"You can thank me by winning this thing today. Give me another win before I retire."

"Retire?" The word comes out a little louder than I intended and then silence befalls the bus.

"Yep, today will be my last game coaching the Aviators. After twenty-six years, it's time to hang up the whistle."

One of the guys in the back starts clapping and soon after the whole bus is clapping and chanting, "Johnson. Johnson." Over and over.

We arrive in Scottsdale Point and make our way into the locker room to get ready for the championship game. Coach gives us his usual motivational speech, and then Miller, the team captain and our center, makes a speech and ends it with, "Let's win this for Coach Johnson and let him go out on a high."

We make our way down the tunnel and head toward the ice. We wait for the announcer to call us out, one by one. My name is called and before I step onto the ice, I close my eyes, take a deep breath, and let everything out of my brain. I focus on one thing and one thing only, winning this thing.

Stepping onto the ice, I'm met with boos from the locals and cheers from those back home who traveled to be here and support us.

Like a moth to a flame, my eyes lock onto Lexi. They are sitting to the left of our bench. Skating over to them, I blow Lexi a kiss and throw her a wink before I rejoin my team for our warm-up. We hit the puck around, tap our goalie on the pads for luck, and then it's go time.

The puck drops and we get possession. Miller passes it off just before he's slammed into the wall. Scott Wilson, our left wing, gets the puck and with a clear path to the goal, he takes off. I skate after him. He takes a shot, but the goalie blocks it and the puck is loose. I make my way down the ice and manage to steal the puck away from their captain. I pass it off to Miller, who came out of nowhere, and with a clean shot, he swings back and hits the puck with everything he has. It sails right into the back of the goal, lighting it up.

We all clap him on the back and cheer. We are off to a great start, but a few minutes later, the Sea Pups score, evening us up.

Up and down the ice we skate and the first period ends one to one.

Within the first ten minutes of the second period, we score twice, taking our lead to three to one. The Sea Pups are not happy and they start to play dirty. A fight breaks out at the end of the period and two of their players end up in the box for five minutes apiece.

The last period sees us keeping our lead, but with five minutes to go, the Sea Pups score twice, bringing the score to three all. Our boys are playing sloppy. Coach Johnson is losing it and me, well, I'm pissed the fuck off.

Miller and I are on the bench, eager to get back out there, and with a nod from Coach, we swap out.

He and I head straight into the action. The puck is flying back and forth, each team playing with everything they have. There's forty seconds left on the clock and Miller steals it away from the Sea Pups and breaks away. Their defense is hot on his heels, but he's faster. Just like earlier, he's once again slammed into the wall, but he manages to pass it off to me before he goes down.

With an opening, I swing and just as the puck leaves my

stick, I'm Kronwalled by two of their defensive players. I'm slammed to the ground. My head bounces off the ice and my body is crushed by two hulking hockey players. My vision dots.

My hearing muffles.

Vaguely, I hear the buzzer sound and then my eyes droop closed and darkness engulfs me.

Blinking my eyes open, I stare up at the concerned faces of my teammates, Coach, and a medic. "Did we win?" I ask, causing my coach and the medic to shake their heads and for Miller to chuckle.

"Yeah, it went in, James. The puck effortlessly slid between the goalie's legs and into the back of the net, securing us the win," Miller informs me, but rather than seeing excitement on his face, I see worry.

Pushing myself up into a sitting position, I hiss, "Awesome." Pulling my helmet off, I shake my head and a wave of dizziness takes over me and I fall back to the ice.

"I need a board," the medic calls out, but there's no way in hell I'm being stretchered off the ice.

"I'm fine," I growl. "I will be skating off this ice. I will not be stretchered off in my last varsity game." Looking at Miller, I plead, "Help me up."

He looks between Coach and the medic and when Coach nods, he leans down and helps me up.

The fans in the stadium begin clapping when they see me on my feet. Giving them a wave, I look to where Lexi and my mom were sitting, but their seats are empty. I'm guessing they're heading to the tunnel to meet me, so with the assistance of my coach and captain, I make my way off the ice.

The guy who hit me stops and outstretches his hand. "You good?"

"Yeah," I tell him with a nod, but nodding wasn't the best thing to do because a wave of nausea washes over me and I wobble on my feet. With what just happened, I'm pretty sure I have a concussion.

We exit the ice and before I make it to the dressing room, a sweet voice calls out my name and when I turn toward the sound, my girl comes barreling toward me. She stops and grips my cheeks in her palms. "Are you okay? That hit was …"

"Hard," I finish for her. "I'm okay, a little dizzy and nauseous but—"

"We're going to the hospital," my mom interrupts. "No arguments."

"I'm fine," I refute. "Dr. Knight can look at me when we get home."

"And Dr. Knight agrees with your mom," the doctor in question states as he and the rest of the crew join us.

"As do I," Coach Johnson says from behind me. "And you know the rules when it comes to a hit like that."

"Fine," I relent. I know they mean well and I do need to get checked on, but after our nail-biting win, I want to celebrate with my team.

A few hours later, like we all knew, it's confirmed that I have a concussion. I'm ordered to rest up and take it easy for a few days.

Lexi and I hang out on my sofa and we watch countless

movies and for the first twenty-four hours, my mom hovers, keeping a watchful eye on me.

Because I follow the rules, I'm cleared to attend prom and it's an evening I will never forget.

7
LEXI

"YOU LOOK BEAUTIFUL, SWEETHEART," MOM COOS. SHE'S smiling brightly as I stand in the middle of the dressing room at Fancy Schmancy. We're here for the final fitting for my prom dress. I'd always dreamed of getting my dress from here and Mom remembered.

A few weeks ago, she brought me here and I found THE perfect prom dress. It's a purple strapless gown with violet gold embroidery and a lace-up back. There's a thigh-high split that Mom says, "Dad is going to lose it over." But I feel like a princess in this dress, so Dad will just have to suck it up.

I stand here, staring at my reflection, and I can't help but swish my hips from side to side and the silky soft material swishes about my legs.

Looking up, I catch her gaze in the mirror and notice tears in her eyes. Spinning around, I step off the platform thingy and walk over to her. "Mom, are you okay?"

"I'm fine. It's just, you, you look so grown-up."

"I feel so grown-up in this dress. Do you think JJ will like it?"

"He's going to love it. Your dad, on the other hand ..." She just shrugs.

"You said that when I first found this dress."

She chuckles. "And I still stand by it. His little girl is growing up."

"I won't be his little girl forever."

"You always will be to him and me, Lex. We're so proud of the woman you've become. The world is your oyster, baby."

"Thanks, Mom. I wouldn't be who I am if it weren't for you and Dad, when he literally lives up to his last name."

"He is one of a kind," Mom agrees with that dreamy look on her face. Even all these years later, she's still head over heels in love with Dad. It's disgusting at times. "You know, JJ looks at you the way your father looks at me. That boy is gaga for you."

"And I'm gaga for him," I confirm, grinning when I think about what's going to happen after prom.

"Just tell me you're being safe. I'm too young to be a grandma."

"Mom," I scoff, "we can't discuss that here."

"Well, get dressed and we can go to that new donut place near home to discuss ... things."

"Ooookay," I draw the word out, not sure what 'things' Mom wants to chat to me about, but when donuts are involved, I'm down to chat about anything.

Changing into my regular clothes, I rejoin Mom and the saleslady. She takes my dress and pops it into a garment bag while the owner and Mom settle the bill for my dress and heels.

With our goodies in hand, Mom and I turn to leave when

the saleslady calls out to us. "Ohhh, and don't forget this." She hands me a small gift bag and when I peek inside, I smile. Mom coordinated with Lisa, and they have a matching tie and pocket thingy-ma-giggy in the same color as my dress for JJ. This way, he and I will be matchy-matchy for when he and I win prom king and queen. According to Serena, my best friend, she thinks he and I are a shoo-in to win because no one at school likes Mandy and Will. Mandy has been campaigning hard to win. Mandy and I have a hate/hate relationship. If I'm honest, beating her would be sweet, but deep down, I really don't give a shit about frivolous stuff like this.

With our decadent donuts in hand, Mom and I grab a table by the window and before we get to our 'chat,' we both devour our donuts. Each of us moan and groan as the donutty goodness explodes in our mouths. "Oh My God," I singsong when I finish my donut, "that was the best donut I've ever had."

"I'll have to bring your brother and sister here."

"So, what you're saying is I can't tease them that you and I had the best donuts in the world?"

"Exactly," she confirms.

"Fine, but can I come with you?"

"If you keep quiet, then yes."

Smiling at Mom, I pick up my drink and take a sip. "So, you wanted to discuss *things*?" I hesitantly ask. Mom and I have a pretty good relationship, but we've never spoken about 'things' before.

"As I said, are you and JJ being safe?"

"Mom, I'm a virgin," I honestly tell her, "and so is JJ."

"Ohhh, I thought all those times the two of you would sneak up to the treehouse that you were, well, you know?"

"You knew about that?"

"Yes, you know I'm a light sleeper. Every time JJ climbs over the fence, I hear it."

"Does Dad know?"

"Considering JJ is still alive and has all his fingers, toes, and appendages, what do you think?"

A laugh escapes me and I shake my head at Mom's statement. "Fair enough." Biting my lip, I'm nervous about what I want to say next. "Mom, I … I think I want to …"

"Want to what?"

"You know." I lean closer to her and whisper, "Sleep with him."

She doesn't say anything, just nods. "Are you nervous?"

Now it's my turn to nod. "I'm filled with nerves mixed with excitement and apprehension."

"Why are you apprehensive?"

"This is a big step. Not just in my life, but for JJ and me as a couple. What if we suck together? What if it hurts? What if—"

"That's a lot of what-ifs, sweetheart. Taking that step with someone is a big deal, but when it's with the right person, it's magical. When your fath—"

"Lalalaaaah," I interrupt, "I don't need specifics about you and Dad. I'm already traumatized over lollipops. I don't need to be traumatized over sex too."

Mom's eyes widen. "Fuck me. What? When? Where? Fuck."

"Mom, you just swore."

"Well, it's not every day you discover your daughter has

seen her mother and father getting kinky with a lollipop. Why didn't you say anything?"

"Because of this," I flick my finger between us, "it's awkward and uncomfortable and the repressed memories are resurfacing."

"I can't believe I'm asking, but what did you see?"

Thinking back on that night, I close my eyes and tell Mom what I remember ...

... It's the middle of the night and I wake up with a dry throat. Needing water, I climb out of bed and pad quietly down the hallway so as to not wake my siblings and head to the kitchen for a drink.

Getting closer, I hear Mom giggle and when I round the corner, I stop mid-step when I see my parents in the kitchen. Mom is sitting on the island counter sucking on a lollipop. Dad is shirtless in his sleep shorts and he's standing between her legs. He reaches up and takes the lollipop from Mom's mouth and pops it into his. He sucks on it and pushes Mom's nightie up her thighs. Mom widens her legs and Dad pulls the lollipop from his mouth and moves his hand between her legs. Mom's head drops back and she pants, "Ohh God, Preston, don't stop." She lifts her hands to her breasts and squeezes them.

"Come for me, Cress," he commands. At his demand, Mom squeezes her boobs again and then she moans in that 'I'm coming' way.

Dad pulls the lollipop and his hand from between her legs and pops the sucker back into his mouth and sucks. "Fuck, Cress. Your taste is so much sweeter mixed with this lollipop. A Cress pop is my favorite candy." Then he drops to his knees and places his face between her legs.

· · ·

"… That's when I turned around and headed back to my room. I was traumatized after seeing that, and I have not and will not ever touch a lollipop again. Ohhh, and now, I always take a glass of water to bed with me."

Mom is white as a ghost, but her cheeks are also stained pink, I hope with embarrassment and not anything else.

"Fuck me," Mom mumbles again. "Baby, I'm so sorry. Why didn't you say anything?"

"'cause it's weird and embarrassing … for all of us. I just pretend it didn't happen."

"I like that idea, but just promise me, when you and JJ finally do it, be safe." She pauses and then adds, "And I hear lollipops can be fun."

"Mooooooom," I groan and shake my head, "too soon."

"I'm sorry but, umm, let's just keep this between us. Your father doesn't need to know about this."

"That's fine by me. Recounting it once is enough."

"I promise never to have kinky lollipop times with your father again … in the kitchen anyway."

"Moooooom," I protest again, but when I look over at her, she's grinning and we both start to laugh.

"Come on, we better get going," Mom says.

On our way out, I convince Mom to grab a box of to-go donuts—not the lollipop one. With the box of donuts in hand, Mom and I head home and as we climb into the car, I realize I lost my chance to tease my siblings over the donutty goodness I just devoured.

We walk into the kitchen and Dad is cooking dinner. When he hears us, he turns to face us and he has a lollipop in his mouth. My eyes widen and when I look at Mom, her cheeks are pink … just like at the donut place, and I realize it's aroused pink and not embarrassed pink.

"Is that Cress-flavored?" I throw to my dad. Placing the

box of donuts on the counter, I quickly race out of the kitchen, chuckling to myself at the shocked expression on both of my parents' faces. ... However, it's me who is embarrassed a few days later when my dad catches JJ and me in a compromising position on the side of the house.

8

JJ

"OH MY GOD," LEXI COOS AS WE WALK INTO PROM. "THIS IS amazing. I was expecting something cheesy, but this, this is amazing."

"Helps that my mom works here," I tell her. "She pulled some strings and because of that we get a fancy prom."

"Complete with spiked punch," Miller says, joining us. He throws his arm around my neck, pulls me in, and ruffles my hair. Pushing him away, he looks at Lexi. "Damn, Knight, who knew you were so fine?"

"Back off, Wentworth," I growl.

"Down, boy." Lexi placates me, pressing her hand to my chest. "You don't look too bad yourself, Miller, but if you want to see graduation, I suggest you focus on Selene, you know, your girlfriend, and not me."

"If she was still my girlfriend, I would," he informs us, his tone subdued.

"What happened?"

"She dumped me. Some bullshit about us being on different paths and hockey will always come first for me."

"That's rough, man, I'm sorry," I tell him.

Lex reaches out and takes his hand, squeezing in that reassuring way she does. "Her loss, Miller. You'll find Mrs. Wentworth when you least expect it."

"It is what it is," he replies, but you can tell he doesn't believe what he's saying. Before we can say anything else to him, he takes off toward the spiked punch bowl and proceeds to chug back three glasses in quick succession. Then he lets out a "WooHoo," and beelines for the dance floor.

"Care to dance, Mr. James?" Lexi asks.

"I'd love to." Lacing my fingers with hers, we make our way to the dance floor. We dance for a few songs before the prom committee takes the stage. Margaret, the Queen Bee of our year, grabs the microphone and begins her speech. That woman was built for public speaking and one of these days, she's going to be the Speaker of the House. I'd bet my left nut on that.

"Thank you for being here tonight. You all scrub up pretty well. Even you, Dash."

Dashiell Dash, yep, that's his name, is the person who no one wants to sit next to because not only is he weird, but he's feral by definition. His hair is knotted and long and scruffy. He always has horrendous body odor and stains on his clothes, but tonight he looks washed and put together. Margaret has been waffling on for ten minutes when finally she gets to the prom king and queen part.

Personally, I don't give a shit about this, but Lex is excited, only because she doesn't want Mandy and Will to win … actually, no one in our class does. "This year's Prom

King and Queen are … Jameson "JJ" James and Lexi Knight."

Mandy audibly groans, stomping her foot, and Will cups his mouth and bellows, "Riiiiiggged."

Lex and I make our way onto the stage where plastic crowns are placed on our heads. Taking Lexi's hand, I lift it in the air and then as per tradition, the two of us walk to the middle of the dance floor for our inaugural dance. I can't tell you what song we dance to, but all I know is I hold Lexi tight to me and we sway to the music.

Just as the song ends, I dip her backward and kiss her deeply. Everyone around us cheers and hollers, and when I bring her back up to her feet, her cheeks are flushed and she's panting.

"Want to get out of here?" I ask and she nods in reply, but before we can make our escape, we pose for the relevant photos.

As soon as the last photo has been snapped, I take Lexi's hand in mine. We exit the dance floor and make our way to the elevators. Pressing the call button, the car arrives immediately and we step in.

Pulling out the room key card, I swipe for our floor. The air in the small space is heated and bubbles with desire the higher we get.

The elevator dings on our floor and we step out. Hand in hand, we head toward our room. My heart races because this is it, this is the moment Lexi and I take our relationship to the next level.

9
LEXI

THE CLOSER WE GET TO OUR ROOM, THE FASTER MY HEART races. I'm nervous and excited and everything in between.

We reach the door and JJ swipes the card over the scanner thingy and the click of the lock disengaging echoes in the silent hallway. It feels like it's shouting, "These two are gonna do it!" and I chuckle to myself.

"What's so funny?"

Shaking my head, I lick my lips. "Nothing."

He nods and steps to the side, allowing me to enter before him. Stepping over the threshold into the room, my eyes widen when I see the scene before me. There are rose petals scattered all over the floor, leading a pathway to the living area. On the coffee table is a tray of chocolate-coated strawberries and in an ice bucket sits a chilling bottle of Diet Coke. An unladylike snort escapes me. Looking over my shoulder, I notice JJ grinning.

"Only the finest Diet Coke for my girlfriend."

"You spoil me," I voice.

Turning to face him, I stare at my boyfriend. At the man who stole my heart when I was sixteen and his family moved in next door. Standing here in the middle of the hotel room, all the nerves and fears I had in the elevator disappear.

All I see is JJ.

All I see is the love radiating in his eyes reflecting at me.

With shaking hands, I reach for the side zipper on my dress and lower it down. The sound echoes around the room and then there's a whoosh as the material slides down my body, pooling on the carpet at my feet. Leaving me in nothing but my purple strapless bra with matching thong and my heels.

"You're a vision," JJ huskily growls, his gaze roaming over my body. "How did I get so lucky to score the hottest chick in the world?"

"You moved in next door," I remind him.

"And I am thankful every day that Mom got that job … even if I was unimpressed to start with, but as soon as I saw you in that treehouse, I knew."

"You knew what?"

"That one day, you would be mine."

Lifting my hand, I beckon him toward me with my index finger. As he approaches me, he shucks off his jacket, kicks off his shoes, and untucks his shirt. Stopping in front of me, he stares into my eyes. I feel his gaze deep in my soul and even though I'm pretty much naked, I've never felt more powerful than I do right now.

Resting my hands on his chest, I trace my finger over his pecs and then one by one, I begin to pop open the buttons on his shirt. Once his shirt springs free, I slide my hands up his chest and slip the material down his arms.

His shirt joins my dress and soon after, so do his pants.

The two of us stand before one another in our underwear. Even though we've fooled around before, we've never actually seen each other naked. Nerves begin to build and as if he's in my head, he reaches up and cups my cheek. "There's nothing to be nervous about, Lex. It's just me."

Turning my head, I place a kiss on his palm and then reach behind me and unclasp my bra before dropping it to the ever-growing pile of clothes. Taking a nervous breath, I hook my fingers in the top of my panties, but before I can remove them, JJ covers my hands.

"Let me," he growls. Yes, he growls. If I thought I was aroused before, those two words uttered in that tone set my insides on fire.

Dropping to his knees, he presses a kiss to my stomach and then pulls my thong down my thighs, leaving him at eye level with my pussy.

"What happened to the hair?"

"I got a Brazilian," I tell him. Spreading my legs wider, I lift my foot and rest it on the coffee table. I don't know where this brazen version of me has come from, but I like her. "Do you like it?"

"I think I need a closer look." He leans forward, closes his eyes, and breathes in deeply. "Mmmmmmm," he groans. Opening his eyes, he lifts his gaze to mine and with his eyes locked on me, he sticks his tongue out and licks me from taint to clit.

My head drops back at the sensation and I close my eyes, focusing on the tongue-lashing he's giving me.

He pulls away and my eyes fly open at the loss of his tongue on my most sensitive parts.

"Eyes on me at all times, Lex. I want to see you come apart."

"Yes, sir," I cheekily reply.

"I like you calling me sir."

My legs feel wobbly at all this dirty talk. Dropping down to the sofa before I fall, I shuffle back into the cushions and get comfy. Spreading my legs wide, I trace my finger down my chest toward my pussy with my eyes locked on JJ. There's a hunger I've never seen before reflecting back at me, and I cannot wait for him to lick me again. "Well, then, sir, have at it."

"As you wish," he replies and in the blink of an eye, he moves himself between my thighs and lowers his head. Like the other night in the treehouse, he devours my pussy with his mouth and fingers, bringing forth an intense orgasm that has me crying out his name.

Thanking the heavens that I'm sitting down, I meld into the cushions and breathe deeply. JJ lifts his gaze to mine and I beckon him to me. Lifting to his knees, he leans up and kisses me. Wrapping my arms around his neck, I hold on tight. Breaking the connection, he stares into my eyes and I whisper, "Make love to me, JJ."

10
JJ

MAKE LOVE TO ME, *JJ*.

Hearing those words pass through her lips is more than I ever thought. Yes, actually having sex is the goal of tonight and one of the reasons we're staying here. Even if we don't take that final step, I'll be okay with that too. What Lexi and I have is more than just the physical side of a relationship. We have a deep connection that encompasses us as a whole. This is just the final part of what we are.

Nodding, I stand up and scoop her into my arms. She giggles and the sound is like an aphrodisiac. I was already aroused, but holding her naked in my arms increases that feeling tenfold. Carrying her bridal style, I walk around the sofa and over to the bed. Gently, I lower her down onto the mattress. She shuffles back to the pillows and since she's naked, I remove my briefs. My hard cock springs free, slapping my stomach. The tip is weeping and when Lexi sees the moisture glistening on the end, she licks her lips.

Staring down at the woman who owns my heart, I smile.

I cannot believe we're here. That we're about to take this final step in our relationship.

Miller always teased me over the fact Lex and I hadn't had sex yet, but I brushed him off each time. Lex and I have built a solid foundation and that's what counts. Sex isn't everything when it comes to a relationship.

Resting my knee on the edge of the mattress, I take her ankle in my hand and squeeze. "Lex, are you sure?"

She nods. "I've never been more sure." She bites her bottom lip. "JJ, I'm glad we waited to do this. Now feels like the right time, so get over here and kiss me."

"Just kiss?" I playfully throw back at her.

"Never said where you can kiss me, but for the record, I want your lips on my lips and your dick in my vagina."

"Yes, ma'am." With a salute, I climb the rest of the way onto the bed and crawl up her body. Dropping kisses and nipping her along the way, her skin breaks out in goose bumps. Cocooning her with my body, I stare down at her, admiring her beauty before I take her mouth with mine and passionately kiss her.

She runs her hands down my back, squeezing my ass before sliding them up and into my hair. She pulls on the strands and deepens the kiss. "Please, JJ," she mumbles against my lips.

Pushing myself up, I smile down at her. From the position I'm in, with a quick flick of my hips, I'd be inside her, but this is her first time. Our first time, and I don't want to hurt her.

Slipping the head of my cock between her folds, I circle my hips, but I don't push in. I'm ready to move in when she presses her hands to my chest, stopping me. I look at her with concern. "We need protection," she utters. "I'm too young to be a mom, and you have your career ahead of you."

Nodding, I climb off the bed and head over to our bags. I grab the box I bought earlier today and walk back to the bed. With nimble fingers, I grab out a foil packet. Tearing it open, I slide the rubber over my shaft and return to my position between her thighs. Lining my dick up, I begin to push in. No waiting this time.

It's tight.

It's hot.

It feels like I'm coming home.

Lexi scrunches her face up and I start to pull out. "No," she shouts, "keep going!"

"But it's hurting you," I protest. "I don't want you to be in any pain," I tell her. "This is supposed to be special between us."

"Look at me," she demands. Lifting my gaze to hers, I still see lust and desire in her eyes and her face is less scrunched up now. "It's a bearable pain, I promise. And I promise to tell you if it becomes too much." She reaches up and cups my cheek. "Please, JJ, keep going."

With my eyes locked on hers, I do as she asks and push in. I can tell it's hurting, but with her eyes, she silently encourages me to keep going. When my dick is all the way in, I hold still, letting her adjust to my cock filling her up.

"I need you to start moving," she says.

"I … I don't think I can. I … I don't want to hurt you."

"Let me go on top then. I can control the movements and stop if I need."

Nodding, I pull out and shuffle back. She sits up and we stare at one another. At the same time, we lean forward and start kissing.

It's hurried and frenzied, but at the same time it's soft and sensual.

Lexi pushes me to my back and straddles me. Our lips never break contact. We lie here, making out for a few moments. She pulls away and sits up. With her eyes locked on mine, she lifts herself up and begins to sink down on my shaft. She winces a few times, but eventually, her face morphs from pain into euphoria. Rocking her hips, she begins to ride me and never have I seen a more beautiful sight.

Lexi's head is thrown back and she's giving herself over to the pleasure. She's using me to bring herself to climax, and at the same time drawing me closer and closer to my own.

"JJ," she pants and then she lets out a guttural sound that has me coming alongside her. Together, we tumble over the edge and I explode into the condom. The only sound in the room is the hum of the air-conditioning and our deep breathing.

Lexi stares down at me. "That was …"

"Yep," I agree. There are no words for what we just experienced together, but I know one thing. I will always love this woman … and I cannot wait to do that again.

11

LEXI

...a few weeks later

I'M STILL IN SHOCK THAT I RECEIVED A LATE FULL SCHOLARSHIP at the USC Division of Biokinesiology and Physical Therapy in Southern California to complete my bachelor's. And if I so choose, this would then lead into their Master's of Science in Biokinesiology with the Sports Science Emphasis program that I have wanted to do for as long as I can remember. It's the one course I had my heart set on, but I missed out, so I applied at the same college as JJ so I could be with him.

Ever since I decided I wanted to be a physical therapist who specializes in sports rehabilitation, I had wanted to do my Master's of Science at USC, but it's tough to get into and when I missed out, I gave up that dream and I focused on UC and what they had to offer.

Some clerical error stuffed it all up at USC and now that it's been rectified, I have a choice what I want to do.

When Mom and Dad heard the news, they organized a

last-minute celebration dinner at Las Tapas 'cause Mom and Dad know their paella is my favorite and tonight is all about me. This restaurant also happens to be Mom and Dad's favorite too because he brought her here on their first date, way back in the Stone Age.

Dad taps the side of his glass and stands up, garnering everyone's attention. And I mean everyone. Every person in the restaurant turns their attention to him. "Your mom and I are so proud of you, Lex." He looks at me and smiles that dad smile of his. "You go after what you want with a tenacity that reminds me of your mother when I first met her." He glances at Mom and has that 'I love you so much' look on his face and I want to gag. "And you've grown into an amazing young woman."

"Clearly she gets it from her aunty Bay. I mean, I am fabulous," my aunt interrupts Dad, earning herself an eye roll from Mom, while Uncle Corey leans into her and growls, "Down, Kitten."

Aunty Bay being, well, Aunty Bay, just sticks her tongue out at him and pops a purple taffy into her mouth. I don't think I've ever not seen Aunty Bay eating taffy … or taunting my mom … or wearing any color that's not purple.

My mom and Aunty Bay are the definition of frenemies, like seriously, their pictures would be in the dictionary next to the definition of the word.

Aunty Avery, Baylor's twin sister and Mom's BFF, always jokes that CJ and Lily are going to get married one day, effectively binding the two of them together forever. Like that will ever happen, CJ and Lily are polar opposites. Where CJ is as quiet as a mouse, Lily is a lioness and queen of the jungle. She's literally a mini version of her mother. She'd eat my poor lil' bro alive, but it would be funny as hell if they did.

"As I was saying," Dad says, ignoring Bay—like Mom should—and he gets back to his embarrassing dad speech. "We are so proud of you, Lex, and we cannot wait to see you thrive as a sports PT." He pauses and raises his glass. "To Lexi."

Everyone raises their glasses and toasts me, my name echoing around the restaurant as everyone says, "To Lexi."

My cheeks darken because I hate being the center of attention, but then they darken for another reason. When JJ leans in and kisses my cheek, his hand beneath the table slides under my dress and he grazes his finger over my clit. "You and I will celebrate in private later, but for what it's worth, I'm so proud of you, Lex."

A shudder runs through me and then I freeze when Dad stands behind me and rests his hand on my shoulder. "What do you want for dessert, Princess?"

"Ohh—um, I'd—umm," I stutter, trying to answer my dad. JJ, the bastard, continues to run his finger over my clit.

"She'll have the flan. It's sweet, just like her," JJ answers for me.

Dad nods and walks over to my siblings to see what they want.

"I hate you," I hiss between clenched teeth as I remove his hand from my nether region and clench my thighs together to try to ease the throb that developed between them.

"No, you don't," JJ replies with an air of cockiness. "You love me."

"Right now I don't," I sneer, earning myself a chuckle. "Guess what?"

"What?" he asks.

Leaning into him, I kiss his earlobe and whisper, "I'm not meeting you in the treehouse later tonight. I'm going to stay in my bedroom and I'm going to slide my hand under the waistband of my pajama pants and I'm going to finish what you started. I'm going to circle my clit and squeeze my tits until I come all over my fingers. Then, I'm going to lick my juices from my fingers before I fall asleep, blissfully sated after my self-induced orgasm."

A throat from behind clears and when I look over my shoulder, I see my dad standing there. He looks traumatized and then I realize he heard what I just said to JJ. "They are, umm, out of flan. I wanted to know what you want now?"

"Ohhh, umm, I won't have anything then. It's flan or nothing here."

Without another word, Dad turns and walks away. My face is redder than a tomato and JJ, the bastard, is sitting next to me, chuckling to himself.

"What's so funny?" Aunty Bay asks.

"Nothing," I quickly answer. "JJ is just being a douche."

"You love me," he cheekily says, leaning in to kiss my cheek.

"Yes, I do," I tell him, "but right now I don't."

"You do," he states and he's right, I do love him. Even when he's being a douche, I love him because he's my person. JJ is the other half of me and I'd follow him anywhere.

"How will you two cope with not seeing each other every day?" his mom asks when dessert is served. "Boulder and Berkeley might both start with B, but they are several states away."

"We'll manage," JJ tells his mom while I just nod, but will we? I hadn't really thought about that. I've been so wrapped up with being accepted into my dream course that I didn't even think about the logistics of it all.

I'd resigned myself to the fact I didn't get in to USC, so I was moving to Colorado with JJ and I'd do a course there, but now, I have the chance to follow my dream. Where does that leave JJ and me?

The rest of the evening passes by without any more embarrassment or hard-hitting questions, but my mind is a mess. I can't stop thinking about Lisa's question. The more I think about it, the more I still want to go with him. I love JJ. Where he goes, I go, but when I tell him that, he doesn't react how I expect him to.

12

JJ

AFTER MOM FINALLY WENT TO BED, I WAITED UNTIL SHE WAS asleep and then I snuck over the fence to see my girl. I climb up the ladder and shuffle into the treehouse to wait. I don't have to wait too long and like every time I see her sandy-brown hair pop into sight, my heart skips a beat.

"Hey, you," I say in greeting.

"Hey, yourself," she replies, dropping into my lap and straddling my thighs. She leans in and presses her lips to mine. I'm going to miss kissing her whenever I want when she goes to SoCal.

"I'm going to miss being able to do this whenever I want, but then again, it will just make our kisses and time that much more magical when we get to."

"We won't miss out on them because I'm still coming with you. I'm going to turn down USC."

"What?" I screech at her. "You need to go to SoCal, Lex. That course has been your dream for as long as I can remember and to get a last-minute full scholarship, that's everything."

"It's not everything, JJ. You are my everything and I'm going to Colorado with you. It's all planned and I don't want to mess it up for you."

"Don't worry about me. Focus on you and your career."

She opens her mouth to protest, but I press my finger to her lips, silencing her.

"And before you come at me with 'it's selfish blah fucking blah' don't. It's not selfish to study the course that you have always wanted to study."

"But what about our plans together?"

"They'll just be on hold for a few years. We have forever to live together, Lex. For now, we each need to follow our dreams so we can have our forever."

"I guess," she reluctantly says.

"And in the meantime, we can stock up on kisses and spank bank memorabilia."

"I don't have a cock to spank," she says with a shrug.

"But you do have a bean to flick and since I'm an amazing boyfriend, I'll get you started."

Sliding my hand between us, I slip it under the waistband of her pajama pants and press the pad of my finger onto her clit.

"More," she pants, so I give her more, circling the sensitive bud of nerves with my fingertip. Moving my finger from her clit, I slide it between her folds and hook it inside her. In and out I thrust my finger and before long, she's crying out as she explodes around my finger.

Not being a selfish lover, she shuffles back and returns the favor. Sucking my dick and bringing me to orgasm.

When we're both sated, we say our good nights and part ways.

Lying in bed, I stare up at the ceiling, concerned that she really is going to turn down USC. I need to talk to her dad. He's the one person she will listen to. With that decision made, I fall asleep, but my dreams are plagued with night-mares regarding Lexi and me.

The next morning over breakfast, I text Dr. Knight to see if he's free. He tells me he has time at ten, so I quickly scarf down my omelet and then head to the hospital.

Sitting across from Dr. Knight is nerve-wracking. "Dr. Knight, I need your advice."

"What can I do for you, JJ?" He leans back in his chair, resting his elbows on the armrests, stippling his fingers like Monty Burns from *The Simpsons*.

"As you know, sir, I got a scholarship to play hockey at the University of Colorado. I'm heading to Boulder in a few weeks and—"

"I never did pass on my congratulations. If anyone deserves it, it's you, JJ. Your dedication and tenacity to hockey is admirable."

His words just now are what I would expect my dad to say to me, if he were still around and I guess in a way, he is. Dr. Knight will be my father-in-law one of these days, so I better get used to chats like this. "Thank you, sir, but, I, umm, I have a dilemma." Taking a breath, I spit it out, "I love Lexi with all my heart, but I think I need to break up with her."

"May I ask why?" His voice is low and menacing and the look he's giving me now is a protective dad one, and I start to think meeting here to have this conversation was a bad idea. Here he has access to that drug he always threatens me with, but then again, if I were in his shoes and we were discussing my daughter, I probably would have grabbed me by the shirt and shoved me into the wall for even thinking about breaking his daughter's heart.

"Lexi has always dreamed of being a physical therapist for a sports team and as you know, she got that scholarship to study at USC, but she's talking about turning it down and still coming to Colorado with me. I can't let her do that. I won't let her do that. She deserves to go to the best school, and for her to follow her dreams. That's at USC, not at UC. She has to follow her dream like I am, but how do I do that without hurting her?"

"Have you tried talking to her?"

"Yes, and she told me I was being ridiculous and she can make her own choices, but this is the wrong decision. She will regret it and one day resent me if she doesn't follow her dream."

"UC is a good school, but I agree, USC is the better choice of the two. I know she loves you, JJ. She has since you moved here, and a love like you two have doesn't come around often."

"I know that and you're right. I love her with everything I have, and it's because of that love I can't let her follow me. She needs to follow her dreams, but how do I make her see reason? You've met her. She's headstrong and stubborn at times and when she's made up her mind, there's no changing it."

"Well, son, you just need to be honest with her. Honesty is the best policy. Lex isn't stupid. If you explain it to her like you just did to me, I'm sure she will see reason." He pauses. "You do understand if you break up with her; she might never take you back. You have to be certain about this decision."

"I understand and as much as it pains me, it'd be worth it to see Lexi following her dreams. I love her too, more than anything, but I can't let her give up her dreams for me."

He nods. "You can always try to convince her to do the long-distance thing. Then when she finishes, you two can meet up and go from there. Think about it before you make a rash decision that you may live to regret. And if you break my princess's heart …"

A laugh escapes me. "I know what you will do. You remind me all the time."

"Good," he states matter-of-factly. "When you become a parent, waaaaay down the line, you will understand where I'm coming from but trust your gut, Jameson. I'm sure the two of you will get through this together."

Nodding, I smile at him. "I hope you're right."

He stretches out his hand and I take it. "Good luck … with both my daughter and your career."

"Thanks, Dr. Knight, I appreciate your advice."

And with that done, I leave him to it. On the drive back home, I process his words and advice. Just as I pull into the driveway, I make a decision about what to do.

13

LEXI

Sitting in my bedroom, JJ takes my hands in his. He seems nervous and seeing him nervous makes me nervous.

"What's up?"

"You need to go to USC."

"But I want to go to UC with you."

"And I'd love that, but, Lex, this amazing opportunity has fallen into your lap. A full scholarship at your dream school, doing the course you have dreamed about for as long as I've known you, it's literally your dream come true and if you turn this down, you will regret it."

"I won't. I want to be with you."

"And I want to be with you too but, Lex ..."

Silence falls upon us and it's awkward and uncomfortable.

"But what?" I growl at him, my hackles rising the longer we sit here in silence.

"You deserve the best."

"As do you and we can achieve the best together. In

Colorado."

"Lexi, it feels like suddenly we're on different paths. Yours is leading you to California at USC and mine is leading me to Colorado at UC. And … and when I get drafted, who knows where I'll end up. I want you to follow your dreams like I'm following mine."

"But you're my dreams too, JJ. My future is with you."

"I thought so too."

"What do you mean thought so?"

"Lex, babe, I can't let you give up your dreams for me."

"I'm not!" I shout at him. "The course in Colorado is good and I'm smart. I'll be fine."

"That course might be good, Lex, but you deserve the best." He pauses and inhales deeply. A feeling of unease washes over me and then he utters a sentence that changes my whole life. "With that in mind, it's over."

Sitting here, I mutely stare at him. My mouth opens and closes, but nothing comes out. "What do you mean it's over?" I air quote 'it's over' because surely he doesn't mean what I think he means.

"It means that you're going to USC and I'll go to UC."

"No," I snarl. "Where you go, I go. Like Jack and Rose in *Titanic*, 'You jump. I jump,' meaning we both go to UC."

"No, it doesn't." He drops my hands and stands up. "Lex, I turned down the apartment in Colorado and I'm going to be staying in the dorms now."

"Are you fucking serious?" I shout at him. "You just made that decision without me?"

"Yes, I did," he defiantly replies.

"Why?"

"Because you would have made the wrong one. I did this for us." He pauses and drops back onto the bed next to me. "I'm doing this for you."

"Well, I don't want you to. I'm a big girl. I can make my own fucking decisions and I'm going to Colorado with you and I'm attending UC."

"If you follow me there, it'll still be over. I ... I'm sorry, Lex, but I can't be with you anymore. You need to focus on your future and I need to focus on my career."

Without saying anything else, he stands up, kisses my head, and walks out, quietly closing the door behind him. Sitting here, I stare at the closed door, expecting him to come back and tell me it's a joke, but then I hear the front door close and I realize he left.

He dumped me and walked out. Just like that, he dumped me.

I let out a feral scream and slide off the bed, curling into a ball on the floor. I hug my knees to my chest and cry.

Tears cascade down my cheeks. Snot leaks from my nose and my heart shatters. I read about this in my spicy books, but I never thought I would feel the despair the characters do.

There's a knock on my door, followed by my mom's voice calling out my name.

"Go away," I tearfully shout, but my mom ignores my request and she opens the door. Stepping in, she looks down at me and when our gazes meet, I blubber harder. "Moooooom," I wail, "he ... he ..."

"Ohhh, baby," she coos.

Dropping down to the floor, she lies facing me and pulls me into her chest. Her embrace sets off another round of tears and I sob into my mom's chest.

I will never love or think about Jameson 'JJ' James ever again, but that's a bald-faced lie. Even though I hate him because he just destroyed me, I still pucking love him ... and I think I always will.

14

LEXI

…three years later

ANOTHER FAILED COFFEE DATE.

Another reason to hate *him.*

I don't know why I even bother dating anymore because every time I go on a date, I compare them to him, Jameson-fucking-James.

It's been almost three years now and he's still wedged deep in my psyche.

Whenever I go out with someone, no matter how amazing the first date is, it never lives up to my first date with *him* and the events that transpired in the treehouse afterward … that resulted in us getting a stern talking to from our parents and a ban from seeing each other. That there should have been a flag, but no, my stupid heart was in love.

JJ took me on an amazing date. We did dinner at a diner at the Pier and then we went to the movies. He was the perfect gentleman while in public, but we made plans to meet in the treehouse when everyone went to bed because neither of us wanted the evening to end, and that's what cemented it as the best date ever …

… After dinner and the movie, JJ walks me to the front door at nine fifty-nine. He kisses me on the cheek, like a gentleman, and then he heads home.

No sooner did the door close than Dad is on me. He grills me over the movie and when he's happy that I did in fact go to the movies, we all say good night and head to our respective bedrooms.

Heading to mine, I stop in my bathroom to freshen up. Then I climb out the window and make my way over to the treehouse to wait for JJ.

Before he arrives, I push the little table to the side and arrange the beanbags and blankets we keep up here into a comfy bed for two.

Thankfully, it's a full moon tonight, so we can see. The moon-light makes it kind of romantic, and then I start to wonder if tonight will be the night JJ and I sleep together. I know it's only our first date and we've only been officially dating for a week now, but I've known that JJ is the one I want to lose my V-card to from the moment he moved in next door. And if I'm being honest, he's the one I'm going to marry one day.

When you know, you know.

I may only be seventeen, but JJ is my first and last thought every day. He's the one I want to tell exciting news to and when I'm sad, he's the one I want to hold me and console me and tell me that it'll be all right.

Making more noise than a bull in a china shop, JJ finally arrives. When he climbs up the ladder, he finds me lying back in what I hope is a seductive pose and from the look in his moonlit eyes, I think I succeeded.

"Y-y-you are ... I-I-I have no words," he stammers.

"Come here," I command.

With a nod, he crawls into the treehouse and makes his way over to me. He lies down next to me and I snuggle into his side. We've lain like this many times before, but with my ear against his pec and the sound of his heart beating away, a feeling of being home washes over me.

"I had an amazing time tonight, JJ," I whisper.

"I always have an amazing time when I'm with you, Lex. You are a ray of sunshine on a cloudy day."

Lifting my head up, I roll onto my side and rest my head on my hand and stare across at my boyfriend. "Who knew you had a way with words?"

"There's a lot you don't know about me."

"Try me," I throw back at him.

He shuffles to his side and mimics my pose. He reaches over and tucks a tendril of hair behind my ear. "Well, for starters, did you know I have the sexiest girlfriend in the whole of Chicago?"

My cheeks darken at his comment and my heart flutters.

"You smell so good," he says, pulling my thoughts back to the present.

"Thank you," I tell him.

He sniffs me again and one would think that would be creepy and weird, but it's not. It's highly erotic. Then when he starts to nuzzle my neck and nip at my jaw, that sensation between my thighs intensifies.

Suddenly, I feel nervous and shy. How do you ask your boyfriend to pop your cherry? There's no rule book on that.

His lips reach mine and after a quick kiss, I just go for it. "JJ ... I want you to make love to me."

He doesn't say a word, just silently stares at me. The air in the treehouse becomes stifling and those nerves ramp up.

"Lex, babe, I ..." Ohh shit, he doesn't want to have sex with me. Me and my whorish ways have ruined us before we even had a chance.

"Forget it," I snap. "Just forget I asked, please?" Lowering my gaze, I feel, I don't know how I feel, but I would love to go back in time and never ask. Where's Doctor Who and his Tardis when you need him?

"Lexi," his says my name with force. Then he places his finger under my chin and raises my head up. Staring at him, I wait for him to shut me down. "I'm not saying no." My eyes widen and I smile. I haven't ruined this after all. "But I am."

"Ohh," I dejectedly mutter, feeling heartbroken.

"Just for now. I think we need to wait."

"Ohh," I utter again, but I don't feel any better.

"Lex, babe, we've only been together for a week, and losing our virginities is a big thing. Don't get me wrong, I want to. So, so much do I want to, but for starters, I don't have any protection and you aren't on the pill."

"You could pull out," I suggest. Oh My God, can I sound any more like a whore?

"I could, but that's not a reliable method, and if memory serves, your dad lost his shit over us just kissing. If he found out we slept together, he'd inject me with that shit and kill me before the high of having sex has even worn off."

"You know he's only joking about that, right?"

"I don't think he is, but I'm not going to do anything that would allow me to find out. Besides, you deserve to be wined and dined and treated like a queen the first time we have sex."

"You really are amazing, Jameson James."

"I know," he cockily replies, giving me his toothpaste ad

worthy smile. "You understand what I'm saying, right? Why I want to wait?"

"I do, yes, and I get it." Biting my lip, I sheepishly ask, "Well, can you at least kiss me?"

"That I can do and, for the record, you never have to ask me to kiss you."

Leaning forward, he presses his lips to mine. He slides his hand behind my head and holds me to him. I love kissing JJ and as our tongues slip and slide together, I know he's right. It's too soon for that, but one of these days, we will sleep together. I know it.

The two of us alternate between making out and chatting. We chat about everything and I learn things I didn't know. Like every year on his mom's birthday, he cooks her toast for breakfast, then he makes her a PB&J with the crusts cut off, and for dinner, they go to a diner, just the two of them. He also told me he no longer misses his dad and he feels his and his mom's lives are better off without him. He also hopes that one of these days, his mom meets someone and gets her HEA because she deserves to be treated like a queen. Apparently, she swoons over the way my dad treats my mom and if I'm honest, I do too. Preston Knight has set high expectations for me when it comes to the man I'm with, and I think JJ will give him a run for his money in the swoon stakes.

After making out one final time and saying we're going to call it a night, we lie back down for one last snuggle, just how our night started with my head resting on his chest. He wraps his arm around me and gently traces his fingers back and forth across my skin, causing goose bumps to appear.

Eventually, my eyes become heavy and with the thumping of his heart in my ear and his gentle touch on my arm, we both fall asleep wrapped in each other's arms.

The next morning, we are woken to the sound of my sister shouting, "Daaaaaad, Lexi and JJ are asleep in the treehouse."

"Shit," JJ hisses. "He's really going to kill me now."

I'm a shit girlfriend 'cause all I do is laugh, but my laugh dies in my throat when my dad's head pops into view. "Alexis Avery Knight and Jameson James, get your asses out here, right now."

Shit, he used my full AND middle name. He's really pissed.

Quickly, JJ and I exit the treehouse and when we get to the ground, we're met with an angry and fuming Dad. "Morning, Daddy," I sweetly say.

"Jameson, go home now," he growls. "Alexis, get inside. You and I need to talk."

JJ heads home and I follow my dad inside, where he grounds me until I'm forty and calls Lisa to arrange a 'chat' between the five of us.

I've never seen my dad so angry before and even though JJ and I are in deep trouble, I wouldn't change a thing. Last night was perfect in every way and whatever punishment comes our way will be worth it. JJ is worth any wrath that comes from my dad.

With that memory behind me, I make my way back to my dorm and repeat my mantra to myself. Fuck love and fuck *him*.

Would it be nice to have someone to talk to and to make love to and laugh with? Yes, it would, but I can't find that special someone because *he* is still fucking with me.

I'm pissed off that after all this time, he still has a hold on me and that I still think so fondly of that night. When will I ever get over Jameson James?

15

LEXI

...one year later

AFTER FOUR GRUELING YEARS AT USC, I'M FINISHED WITH MY studies. I made the decision not to do my master's and instead, I applied to be part of a developmental team run by Dr. Michael Michels. He's developing a rehabilitation program for elite athletes that will speed up their recovery by creating techniques to improve mobility. It will also aid in building up strength and stability needed when they return from their injury.

Apparently, Doc, as he likes to be called, has been watching me at USC and was impressed with my paper on hot and cold therapies, and my theory regarding the ideal time to switch from ice to heat treatment. Getting that precise moment can shorten recovery time and assist in the natural healing process and reduce additional swelling by increasing blood flow to the injured area. It's all very technical and I love it.

He was a guest lecturer in my second and third year. I was enthralled with him and his work. When I got the call to say I had been successful, I was over the moon. I'm so lucky, honored, and over the freakin' moon with excitement to be a part of this program. Last year, it became partly funded by the New York Crushers and now, together with their medical team, trainers, and us, we are going to revolutionize sports rehabilitation.

The best part about being partly funded by an NHL team is I also get to be a physical therapist, using the skills I gained in my degree on a daily basis.

Packing my bag for the morning, there's a knock on my apartment door. Making my way around the moving boxes, I open the door and I'm greeted with a delivery guy.

"Delivery for Lexi Knight," he says.

"That's me," I reply as I take the box from him.

Resting it on one of the boxes by the door, I tear into it and snort when I see what's inside. It's a basketful of lollipops and a card from my sister.

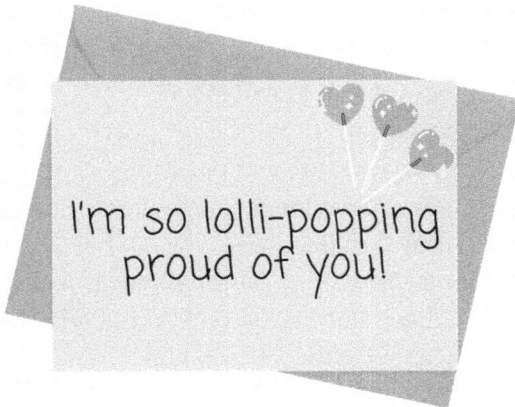

I'm so lolli-popping proud of you!

"That little bitch," I mumble with a shake of my head.

She and I are both traumatized over the times we've caught Mom and Dad in the kitchen together using the sweet treat for purposes other than a sugar hit. To this day, I haven't and will *never* put another lollipop into my mouth again. Walking in on your dad using a lollipop on your mom is traumatizing, but it did give Pepper and me something to bond and commiserate over.

Pulling my phone from my pocket, I shoot my sister a thank you text.

LEXI

Thanks for my gift … you bitch

No sooner do I hit send and my sister replies.

PEPPER

You are welcome … enjoy

No No and No. I will never suck a lollipop again

You should try it, I mean one.

My eyes widen and I immediately hit the FaceTime button, and then my sister's smiling face fills my screen. "What do you mean I should try it?"

"Ohhh, umm, well—"

"Pepper Knight, what are you not telling me?"

"Nothing," she replies, looking anywhere but at me.

"Pepper," I draw out her name.

"Okay, fine. I was telling Dallas about it, and well, one thing led to another, and well, I now know why Mom and Dad have a penchant for the lollipop kink."

"Oh My God, you hussy you. You're six-fucking-teen. Why are you even having sex?"

"I'm not having sex. I'm just … experimenting."

"With lollipops?" I question.

"Lollipops, plugs, beads, wands, vibrators, fingers, tongues, tongues AND fingers, ice cubes—" The more she talks, the wider my open mouth becomes.

"Stop, please stop. If thinking about Mom and Dad with lollipops gives me the heebie-jeebies, imagining my sister with everything being shoved inside her is going to traumatize me forever. I can see it now, my gravestone will read 'Here lies Lexi, traumatized to death by everything shoved in her sister's vagina.'"

"You are so over the top, but maybe you need to try something. It's been what, a gazillion years since you got laid?"

"I'm not answering that question."

"You answered with that, but I'm going to suggest you go out and have wild monkey sex before you start your new job tomorrow."

"Thank you for your advice, but I need to unpack and then I'm thinking a bath with a glass of red and a good book. Followed by Chinese."

"That does sound good, but please tell me there's an orgasm mixed in there with the red wine and good book? I can give you some really schmexy reads if you need some?"

"Pepper Knight, you're sixteen, how are you more … more adventurous than me?"

"Because I was raised by lollipop-loving parents and a sister who used to get down and dirty in our childhood treehouse."

"I thought I told you never to talk about *him* again?"

"I didn't specifically mention your childhood sweetheart, but while we are on the topic of him, I should—"

"Nope, we are not talking about him and I'm not talking to you anymore. I have shit to do."

"Fine, but good luck tomorrow and remember, I love you."

"Love you too, Pepper."

After hanging up from my sister, I do as I told her and unpack a couple of boxes, and then I fill the bath with my candy-scented bubble bath and pour myself a glass of wine.

Shucking off my clothes, I sink down into the tub and moan as I submerge myself in the steaming hot water. Leaning back, I close my eyes and sip on my wine. This is just what I needed to reset, refocus, and relax before my next adventure starts tomorrow.

"Welcome to the team, Lexi. We're excited to have you join us," Doc Michels greets me the next morning when I walk in.

"Thank you for having me, Dr. Michels. I won't let you down."

"I've told you before, it's Doc or Michael, and if you're anything like your father, I'm sure you won't." My face falls. Did I only get this job because of my doctor dad?

"You … you know my dad?" I hesitantly ask.

"Only by reputation." His words comfort me and then he adds, "Your father and I don't really run in the same circles, what with him treating children and me treating athletes. Even though, at times, some of my patients act like big babies."

A snort escapes me. "Yes, it's amazing how these big, burly athletes can run or skate or take on someone twice their size, but when they're injured they become a crybaby if we use too much pressure or tell them it will be X number of weeks for recovery."

"Exactly, and I must say, I'm impressed with your work ethic and tenacity. You remind me of a much younger me. I can already tell you're going to be an asset to this team and project."

"Thank you, Dr. Michels, I mean, Doc. I'm looking forward to being a part of your team."

He nods in that older man way and I feel comfortable in his presence. "I'll let you get settled in your room and then we can get started."

"I can't wait," I tell him.

With a nod, he walks out, leaving me to arrange things and set up my treatment room just how I like it. When I was at USC, I worked part-time at a clinic and I know how I like things to make it easier when working.

I'm unpacking the last of my things when I hear a laugh. A laugh I'd know anywhere. "It can't be," I mumble to myself, but there it is again.

Walking over to the doorway of my treatment room, I peer out in the main room and my eyes widen when I see *him*. He looks up and like the first time I laid eyes on him when I was sixteen, I'm transported back to *that* moment. Back to when he hadn't obliterated my heart. He waltzes over and stops before me. I'm assaulted with his scent, ice and leather, and as I stand here mutely staring at him, it hits me, we are going to be working together.

Puck my life.

16

JJ

"Lex? What the fuck are you doing here?" The question comes out harsher than I intended for it to, but I haven't seen her in over four years. Not since that fateful day when I walked away from her and moved to Colorado ... without her.

Colorado was tough on my own, but the gods showed some pity on me and, somehow, I ended up rooming with Kallen. Which was great because we shared most of the same classes and were teammates on the UC college team.

Once again, the gods were on our side and after we graduated, both Kal and I were drafted to the Crushers, but, like Bruno, we don't talk about him getting selected before me. Kal is one of the greatest goalies I have ever had the privilege of playing with.

We graduated before the summer and both moved to New York together last month. Before coming here, I went home to Chicago and stayed with Mom for a few weeks. That was a tense stay, especially around Dr. Knight. He's still angry with me for what I did to Lexi, but I still maintain what I did was the right thing to do.

Last I heard, she was smashing it in California and had just received an amazing job opportunity, which I'm now deducing is her being a part of Doc's rehab thingy-ma-giggy team.

"I'm, umm," she stutters. "You're a Crusher?"

"Yeah, I'm their new center. Kal and I both signed with them."

She nods but doesn't say anything. It's awkward and stilted with her, and I don't like it. Lexi and I always had an easy relationship, but I guess that's all in the past.

Squeezing the back of my neck, I take a moment to appreciate her. Lexi has always been sexy, but now, standing before me, she's beautiful, so fucking beautiful. Her sandy-brown locks are pulled up into a messy bun. She's wearing a black-and-white striped blouse that's tucked into black slacks and black ballet flats on her feet.

The words, "You look good," pass through my lips before my brain clicks in to tell me not to say that. We don't have that kind of relationship anymore. Actually, we don't have a relationship at all. I ruined that when I pushed her to go to California.

Pushing her away and breaking up with her was the hardest thing I've ever done in my life, but it all worked out for the best because she followed her dream and now she's here. Maybe this is my second chance to get the girl who still holds the key to my heart, but that thought crumbles when she sneers, "Don't. You don't get to pretend like nothing happened between us."

"I'm not, Lex. I—"

"No," she shouts, raising her voice. "You and I are going to pretend we don't know each other. We're going to go about our jobs and not let the past affect the future. You fucked my life up once, Jameson. I will not let you do it again."

Before I can reply, she steps back into the room she came out of. Our eyes connect and that magnetic pull is still there, until she snaps the connection by slamming the door in my face. The sound of the door lock clicking echoes through the locker room.

Lifting my hand, I place it on the handle because this isn't over, but when I hear a sniffle on the other side, I decide to leave her be … for now.

Turning around, I make my way back to my cubby and get my things to shower. Stepping under the spray, I hum along to "My Girl." I can't believe Lexi is here. What are the chances we'd be in the same place?

I haven't stopped thinking about her since we parted ways and as I soap up, I think back to a happier time. Back to when she and I were at our happiest …

… *"Fuck me, Lex," I mumble as she walks down the hallway toward me on the night of prom, "you look stunning."*

Our parents and her siblings are around us, but they all fade into the background. All I see is her.

My Lexi.

My everything.

She comes to a stop in front of me, readjusting my tie and allowing me to breathe her in. Subtly—I hope—I readjust my dick 'cause, fuck me sideways, she's a vision. That dress is stunning on her. Her makeup is understated and perfect. Her tits look phenom-enal—sue me, I'm an eighteen-year-old dude—and her smile would light up the sky on the darkest of nights.

Leaning forward, I press my lips to her cheek and feel a spark ignite between us when we touch. Her breath hitches and I know she feels what I feel, cementing that what we are going to do tonight is meant to be.

"And you look dashing, JJ," she says.

A sniffle from behind us garners my attention and when I look over, both our moms have tears in their eyes and Dr. Knight, as usual, I can't read him, but I do see the 'you hurt my daughter, I'll murder you' look he always has around me.

"Our babies are all grown-up," my mom sniffles. "It feels like just yesterday you were crawling around the place, shoving everything into your mouth."

"JJ was like that too?" Cress asks, wiping at her eye. "I couldn't take Lexi outside without her putting something into her mouth."

Leaning into Lex, I whisper, "I know something you can put in your mouth later." Her cheeks darken and I know she's remembering the other night in the treehouse. She subtly elbows me in the stomach. However, her cheeks are now pink and she's not wearing any of that stuff chicks put on their cheeks, but then she turns it back on me.

"I know somewhere else you can stick it, but I guess we can start with my mouth." She winks at me and taps my cheek before turning her attention back to our families.

Once again, I have to readjust my cock. It's going to be a hard —pun intended—night.

After a billion and one photos, Lexi and I climb into the limo our parents surprised us with, and we're whisked downtown to the Luxe Hotel where our prom is being held in the ballroom.

Earlier today, I dropped our things off and checked us into our room. I was surprised our parents approved this, especially Dr. Knight, but I think he finally understands the depth of our feelings for each other.

With the hottest chick in school on my arm, we walk into prom.

. . .

With that memory fading, I wonder if once again our relationship can change. Wrapping my towel around my waist, I walk back to my cubby and see Doc knocking on her door. She swings it open and smiles at her boss. She used to smile at me like that … before I fucked it all up.

Once again, our eyes connect and while she glares at me listening to whatever Doc is saying, I make a vow to change our relationship once again. I'm going to win back the girl who still owns my heart.

17

LEXI

Slamming the door in Jameson's face isn't as cathartic as I hoped it would be. *Maybe I should have punched him in the face and kneed him in the balls instead?*

Leaning back against it, a tear slides down my cheek and I bat at it as I choke back a sob. I refuse to shed any more tears over him, but seeing him just now is a kick in the vagina. He's just as good-looking as I remember, but then I remember his words, *I can't be with you anymore.* Those six words tore my whole world apart four years ago and four new ones, *I'm their new center,* just shattered my present.

I can't believe he's here. I'm going to have to quit and then I'm going to have to move to Bumfuck, Australia and live with the aboriginal people. They don't have ice, therefore there's no risk of *him* finding me.

Of all the teams in the league, he had to be drafted to the one Doc has partnered up with. I know technically he was here before me, but come on, universe, give a girl a break.

One thing I do know, I will never forgive or forget what Jameson James did to me.

A knock startles me and I jump. No doubt it's *him* wanting to send me away again, so I swing it open, ready to tell him to fuck off, but I'm shocked when I see it's Doc.

"Doc, what can I do for you?" I ask him.

Movement over his shoulder catches my attention and of course, it's *him*. Glaring at the asshole, I focus on what Doc is saying, but when *he* lifts his shirt over his head, all words and coherent thoughts in my brain evaporate. My eyes are glued to his chest. Now that he's a pro athlete, even his muscles have muscles.

Focus, Lexi, Focus.

Turning my attention back to my boss, I listen intently to what he says. Well, I try to listen while also trying my hardest to forget *he* exists, but JJ, I mean, Jameson—only friends use nicknames and we are *not* friends—has this aura about him that sucks you in. He can make the grayest of days seem bright and when you're down, he knows exactly how to turn your frown upside.

"Once you're all set, head on home and we can start fresh tomorrow," Doc says.

Nodding, I smile. "Sounds like a plan and thank you again for the opportunity. I won't let you down."

Doc nods and smiles, then he walks away from me, calling out to Coach Maxwell when he sees him pass the doorway. Turning back around, I head into my room and finish arranging it. Once I'm happy with the layout—for now—I start packing up for the day. I know what I'm like, and I'm sure I'll move things around for the next week or so until I'm one-hundred-percent happy with the layout and functionality of things.

Grabbing my bag, I flip off the light and head home.

Thankfully, the locker room is empty and I can make my escape without another encounter with *him*. Working with *him* is going to make things tough, but I'm tougher. I just need to block *him* out and focus on the task at hand. I'm not going to let Jameson James ruin this for me. I will just come in, do my job, and go home.

Easy.

Right?

Walking into Squires, the bar around the corner from my apartment, I find Bella waiting for me. And proving she's the bestest friend ever, she has a cosmo waiting for me and as I slide onto my stool, she informs me an order of Buffalo Mozzarella sticks is on the way.

Bella was my first New York friend and from the moment I bumped into her at the grocery store, I knew I'd found my new best friend. Bella Jamison is the COO—Chief Operating Officer—at the James Corporation. Her childhood best friend, Emerson James—no relation to he who shall not be named—owns the company. She inherited it after losing her family in a terrible tragedy a few years ago. Bella stepped in and looked after things while Emerson was grieving. Along the way, Emerson met her now husband. When Emerson decided to move to Nels Cove, Colorado, permanently, Bella was offered the position officially. She may be young to hold a position like that, but Bella Jamison is a ball buster and knows her shit. I wouldn't want to cross her in the boardroom.

"So, how was your first day? Get to rub any hotties?

Maybe accidentally grope a hockey stick?" She waggles her eyebrows at me and I can't help but laugh.

"No, no rubbing today."

"Ohhh, well, that sucks."

"But guess what?"

"What?" she excitedly asks, leaning forward, eager to hear what I have to say, but before I can regale my adventure from today, the server drops off our cheese sticks. And like always, she doesn't wait for them to cool. She bites into one of the fried cheese morsels and burns her mouth. She fans her tongue and chugs a glass of water to ease the burn. "So, what were you going to tell me?"

"Well, it turns out, my ex is on the team."

"No fucking way," Bella screeches, "I need all the deets now." She signals the waitress to bring a round of shots because apparently tequila is needed when you end up working with your ex.

Picking up my drink, I take a sip before I regale her with the full story of Jameson and me, ending with what happened in the treatment room.

"So what are you going to do?" she asks.

Before I answer, I drink what's left in my glass and then I signal for the waitress to bring another. "Well, as I was walking out, I decided I'm going to forget all about him. JJ is my past. Jameson James is the now. I'm going to focus on my job and be the best physical therapist the Crushers have ever had. Then once this thing with Dr. Michels is done and I have experience and this program under my belt, I'll move onto bigger and better things."

"Is it going to be that easy?"

"Yes, because JJ, I mean Jameson, is nothing to me." Even as I say that, I'm not sure I believe it. JJ was my everything, until he wasn't. It took me a long time to get over him, but he will always hold a place in my heart. I just hope the walls I built around my heart will stand up to him again.

"You've got this, babe." She raises her glass in a toast. "Watch out, world, Lexi Knight is coming for you."

"Exactly," I confirm and tap my glass against hers.

We finish our drinks and Bella tells me she's heading to Nels Cove in a few weeks to see Emerson and Chase before the baby comes, and we make plans to go baby shopping. Bella excuses herself to the restroom and I order another round of cocktails. I really shouldn't be drinking on a work night, but I need the distraction, and because the universe and Fate are bitches, Jameson and a few of the other guys on the team walk in.

"Fucking great," I mumble, slouching down to hide myself.

"What?" Bella asks, dropping back into her seat.

"Jameson and some of the guys from the team are here."

She spins around and I see when her eyes land on them. It's hard to miss them. It's like a prerequisite to be hot to play hockey or something because every man in that group is H O double T hot. It would be so much easier to forget *him* if he were ugly, but with his sandy-blond hair, chiseled jaw, green eyes, and body to die for, it's sometimes hard to forget what a jerkface he is.

Jameson is with Jett, Kallen, Anton, and the guy whose name I always forget. Thankfully, they don't see us as they head to the back to join the rest of the team.

"Do you want to get out of here?" Bella probes, but I shake my head.

"No, I'm not going to let him ruin our night. He ruined the last of my teenage years, I will not let him affect me anymore."

"That's my girl," Bella declares. Waiving down the waitress, she orders another round of drinks, but as I watch *him* with his teammates, I know I'm screwed.

18
JJ

"Isn't that Lex?" Kallen nods his head to the other side of Squires.

Like a heat-seeking missile, I look around the bar and my eyes immediately find her across the room. I take a moment to look at her, really look at her. She's just as gorgeous as I remember, but she now has a hardness to her that wasn't there before and I think that's because of me. Considering the anger she unleashed on me earlier today, I know I'm right, but I don't blame her. Teenage JJ was and is a dick. Not a day goes by that I don't regret what I did, but at the same time I don't because Lex and I are now both following our dreams.

"Yeah, it is," I tell him.

"She's fucking hot," Jett voices and my hackles rise.

"As if she'd go for you," I hiss.

"Wanna bet on that?"

"I'm not betting on a woman and if you need to take a

bet in order to get a date, you really need to reassess your-self. Regardless, Alexis Knight is off-limits."

"Alexis, hey?" he questions. "There history there?"

"A puckton," Kallen unhelpfully adds.

"Do tell," Jett says, settling in for story time.

"Nothing to tell, but she's off-limits. That's all you need to know. Plus, Jett, her dad would eat you alive."

"Who's off-limits?" Doucheman asks as he joins us. He has a shade of pink lipstick around his mouth and that 'I just got fucked' look on his face. We've been here for all of twenty minutes and already he's scored. "I'll need a special lady to take home after this, point me in her direction."

"Back off," I snarl at the douche. I've never hated a person before, but Stefan Däuchmen is the first person I have ever truly hated … and it's only been one day. Like seriously, if the guy was on fire, I wouldn't even piss on him to douse the flames.

Most of the team feel the same way about him too, but he's under contract, so we're stuck with him. Coach also hates him, for a whole other reason regarding his daughter, Chels, but he gets his revenge in training. Pushing Doucheman to his limits, hell, he even benched the douche in the final game last season due to what he did.

The Crushers would be a better team without him, and it seems everyone is counting down the days until his contract is up. Word on the street is he's going to be traded next season, but in this sport, you never take anything as gospel until the contract has been signed.

Standing up, I tap the table, commanding the attention of everyone. Once all eyes are on me, I look around at them and point my finger. "I'm going to say this once, and once only. Lexi Knight is off-limits. Anyone tries anything with her and they will deal with me."

Without uttering another word, I storm out of Squires to catch my breath.

Stepping out onto the busy street, I look to the heavens and take a deep breath.

How am I going to cope working alongside Lexi?

It's only been one day and I'm ready to kill anyone who looks at her … and she looks like she wants to kill me. Best thing I think I can do is steer clear of her, but Fate, the bitch, has other plans.

19
LEXI

...a few weeks into the season

I LOVE MY LIFE, WELL, MOST OF IT. THERE'S ONE PART, WELL, person, who can take a hike, but if I forget about *him*, life is grand. I'm in my element and working alongside Doc is amazing ... and that makes up for the *him* factor. Doc is a plethora of knowledge and I'm learning so much from him and the rest of the team.

Swinging my bag over my shoulder, I exit the subway and head toward the stadium. Just before I enter the staff entrance, a man steps in front of me, blocking my path. "Can I help you?"

He steps into my personal space and I back up, but before I can reply, Anton arrives, calling out my name.

The man freezes and then takes a step back, turns, and skuttles away without saying anything to me.

"Anton," his name rushes out in relief when he joins me.

"You good, Lex? Was that guy harassing you?"

Shaking my head, I smile. "Not harassing, but he did kinda freak me out, so thank you for appearing when you did."

Looking over my shoulder, I watch the man walk away. I have no idea who he is or what he wanted, and I hope I never see him again.

"You let me know if he comes back, all right?"

"Promise." I smile at the team captain. "We better get in there." I nod toward the door. Anton and I fall into step as we head into the stadium. He holds the locker room door open for me and I nod my thanks.

Of course, the first person I see is *him*. He's standing there shirtless and in a pair of gray sweatpants, every woman's kryptonite, and my eyes roam over his muscular chest. Biting my lip, I inwardly sigh because Jameson James is one fine specimen, even if he is a douchebag heartbreaking asshole. He catches me checking him out and smirks.

Rolling my eyes, I turn away from him and head into my treatment room to start my morning. I only have a half day at the stadium today. Doc is taking Brandon and me on a team-building exercise. He thinks the two of us need to get to know one another outside of work.

Doc tees off first and I'm impressed with his swing. For an older guy, he's pretty good.

"You look impressed, Lexi," he states, returning to the golf cart.

"You have a good swing. My dad would be envious."

"I don't know what it is about golf, but I love the sport. It's a good way to clear the mind."

Just as he says that, from the tee Brandon grumbles, "This fucking sucks." Those words transport me back in time …

· · ·

... JJ and I joined Uncle Flynn and Dad at the golf course, and I have never laughed so hard or so much in my life. To put it nicely, JJ sucks at golf. He's even suckier than me and that's saying something because sports and I go together like sardines and ice cream. Aka we don't.

"This game fucking sucks," JJ grumbles as he swings and misses. "Ugh," he groans after swinging and missing, again. Taking this holes miss tally to twelve, no thirteen.

Laughter echoes around the tee and it only pisses him off further. He repeatedly swings in quick succession and misses every time.

"Was that five?" Uncle Flynn asks with a chuckle.

"I think it was eleventy billion," Dad unhelpfully adds.

Golf is definitely not his sport, but luckily for him, he's an amazing hockey player and his lackluster golf skills, thankfully, don't affect him on the ice.

"Stop it," I scold the supposed parents of the group. Walking over to JJ, I put my hand on his shoulder. He lifts his gaze to mine and I smile at him. "Take a deep breath. Tune out everything around you and focus on the ball."

"Easy for you to say. You hit it every fu—flipping time."

"No, I don't. Remember the third hole? I think it took me seven shots to get it in."

He looks at me and smirks. "I know something I can get a hole in one with."

"JJ," I scold him. "My dad is right there." He shrugs and gives me what I like to call his sex look. "Seriously, I come over here to give you a pep talk and you take it to sex."

"What can I say, you unleashed my inner sex demon when you took advantage of me on prom night."

"Pfffft, whatever. I'll just leave you and your shitty swing alone then."

Sticking out my tongue at him, I walk over to join Dad and Uncle Flynn, and when my back is turned, JJ finally hits the ball.

Dad not so quietly under his breath sniggers, "Pretty sure CJ can hit it farther and he's ten. And built like a beanpole." Both Uncle Flynn and I are trying to hold back our laughs. But when JJ storms over and angrily shoves his club back into the bag on the back of his and Uncle Flynn's cart and hisses, "This game fucking sucks," Uncle Flynn and I can no longer hold our chuckles back, and the two of us laugh our heads off. JJ flips the bird at us and that causes us to laugh harder.

"You're up, Flynn," Dad says.

Uncle Flynn nods, grabs his club, and walks up to the tee for his turn. He hits his ball on the first swing and it lands on the green, next to Dad's, causing JJ to grumble again.

"How can an elite hockey player suck so much at golf?" Dad asks a still fuming JJ.

"Hockey is a precision sport," he snaps. "It takes skill to skate up and down a rink on a thin blade wielding a stick and hitting a puck."

He does have a point. With his skates and all his gear on, it limits his movements, yet JJ flies up and down the ice, wielding the puck like a pro.

Pushing off the cart, I walk over to him and slide my arms around his waist from behind. "It's okay, babe, we can't be good at all sports."

He spins around and glares at me. Lifting to my tippytoes, I give him a quick kiss, and then I huskily whisper, "Meet me in the treehouse later tonight and I'll make you forget all about how sucky you are at golf. You'll score a hole in one and an orgasm or two."

Waggling my eyebrows at him, he just glares at me.

"And now, I'm gonna be even suckier 'cause I'm sporting a semi thanks to you."

Shrugging nonchalantly at him, I walk back to my seat and chuckle when I see him rearranging himself before he climbs in next to Uncle Flynn.

The rest of the day goes by in a similar fashion and by the end of the game, JJ is fuming and the rest of us have stomachaches from laughing so hard.

Returning the carts, we drop our clubs off at the car, and then Dad and Uncle Flynn suggest lunch. They treat us to a gourmet meal in the clubhouse and before we leave, they run into a doctor colleague and excuse themselves to have a chat.

JJ and I wait in the foyer, but he keeps looking at me. He's not doing anything overtly sexy, but I need him and I need him now. Grabbing his hand, I tug and start dragging him down a hallway.

"Where are we going?" he asks, but I ignore him and keep walking toward my destination. Turning the corner, I come to a stop and open the door to my left. Quickly, I shove JJ in and then I follow, closing it behind me.

"We only have a few minutes," I voice as I drop to my knees and make quick work of his pants to free his cock.

"What are you doing?"

"I'm trying to blow my boyfriend," I tell him as I grip his shaft and begin to stroke.

He groans and pants, "But your da—" That word stops mid protest as I take him into my mouth and suck. Bobbing my head up and down in sync with my fist at his base, I suck and swallow his dick.

In the few weeks since I first blew him in the treehouse, I've learned a thing or two about blow jobs—thank you, Pornhub—and going by the sounds coming from JJ above, I'm a good student and a quick learner.

Relaxing my throat, I take him down as far as I can and repeat the process. Lifting my hand, I caress his balls and press on that magical spot between his balls and anus. He explodes in my mouth and I'm thankful he was no longer in my throat 'cause I'd be choking right about now.

Once he's finished, his cock pops from my mouth and I wipe at the side of my lip. "Best dessert I've ever had here at the club."

"You," he pants, "are the devil and I love it. Do we have time for me to return the favor?"

Shaking my head, I stand up. "Nope, but this wasn't about me. I just wanted to give you something to enjoy about today."

"Any day with you is amazing and any day you do that is fucking amazing."

"You can thank Pornhub. Now put your dick away. We need to go meet my dad and uncle."

JJ straightens up and no sooner do we step back into the hallway does Dad comes around the corner.

"Where did you two get to?"

"Just around," I nonchalantly tell my dad. He eyes us and nods, but I can tell he doesn't believe me. No doubt due to the pink on my cheeks and the fact that JJ looks like he's just been to heaven and back. "Shall we head home?"

"Sure," he replies and the three of us rejoin Uncle Flynn ... that afternoon is when I got the letter that changed everything for me.

"Lexi, you're up," Brandon grumbles.

Shaking off the day that is oddly similar to today—well, except for the BJ in a closet part because I'm not blowing Doc or Brandon—I grab my club and tee off.

Brandon once again huffs that I'm perfect and a princess. He basically thinks I suck and I'm pretty sure he hates me. I wouldn't go as far as to say I hate the guy, but if a sinkhole opened and swallowed him, I wouldn't be upset over that.

Doc and I discover he has a short fuse and golf is not his game.

Sitting at my desk with a cup of green tea with jasmine a few days later, I'm reading over the latest report on our program and I find myself smiling at the results. A knock on my door startles me and when I look up, I see Kallen Jones standing in the doorway.

My eyes widen when I realize he's just in a towel, but then I notice his jaw is clenched and sweat is dotting his forehead. In an instant, I go from admiring his abs and morph into PT mode. "What can I do for you, Jones?"

"Can you have a look at my back? I had a fall during practice."

"A fall," I hear Jameson snarl from the other side of the locker room. "More like you were plowed into by a raging asshole."

"I wouldn't say plowed," Kallen defends himself as Jameson walks over to the two of us. He's stripped down to his undershorts and it's really hard not to ogle him.

"Ohh, I'm sorry," he scoffs in response to Kallen. "How else do you describe Doucheman hitting you at full speed and Kronwalling you into the goal frame?"

"Well, yeah, technically, that's what happened—"

"Not technically, actually," Jameson spits at Kallen. His eyes roam over his friend, concern etched on his face. This is the version of him I know and remember. Always caring and worrying about others. "Doucheman is a real fucking douche for doing that." He points to the already forming bruise on Kallen's body. "This better not fuck up your season."

"I'm fine," Kallen growls at him through clenched teeth, but you can see the worry on both of their faces.

To put his mind at ease, I turn to Jameson. "You, out. I need to call Doc so he and I can assess Jones, and I can't do that with you being you, so out." Stepping over to the two of them in the doorway, I pull Kallen into the room and glare at Jameson. "Go on, scoot." I shoo him with my hand and surprising me, without arguing, he takes a step back.

Once he's out of the doorway, I slam the door in his face. That action causes my lips to lift a little, then I remember I'm at work and I need to focus on my patient. Looking at Kallen, I nod toward the table and he slowly makes his way over and carefully sits on the edge.

Pulling out my phone, I call Doc. "Doc, I need you in my room. Kallen Jones is here. He took a tumble on the ice and I'd like your opinion once I've assessed him, since this is my first time treating a player alone."

Doc tells me he's on his way and when I hang up from him, I place my phone on my desk and turn back to Jones. "Doc's on his way, but while we wait, talk to me, Jones, where does it hurt?"

"My back."

"Anywhere else?" I ask, but he shakes his head. "Can you lift your arms so I can have a look at your movements?"

Nodding, he lifts his left arm over his head, wincing the higher he raises it up. He does the same with the other arm, but the right side isn't as tight as the left.

Stepping behind him, I look at his back. "Holy shit," I whisper, gently running my fingertip over the bruise already forming on his back. Gently, I feel around, but no matter how careful I am, Jones hisses and flinches under my touch. A knock on the door startles me and I call out, "Come in."

I look up, just as Doc enters my room. "What have we got?" Doc asks when he joins me behind Jones. I fill him in on what Jameson and Kallen told me earlier. Doc nods and stares at Jones's back.

"Kallen, can you lie face down so I can have a feel around?"

"Sure," he replies. He shuffles onto his stomach, moaning and groaning with his movements.

Doc takes a step back. "Lexi, I want you to assess Jones and then tell me what you think the course of action will be."

Nodding, I step up to the table and run my hands over his back. Up close like this, I can see where he collided with the bar of the goal. Pressing on the spot of impact, Jones yelps and I feel bad.

"Nothing seems to be broken," I tell Doc. He nods and takes my spot. His touch isn't as gentle as mine and the sounds coming from Jones sound like a dying animal.

"I agree, nothing seems broken, but there could be a fracture. We'll get an X-ray to be sure." Doc looks at me with glee in his eyes, not at Jones being injured but at the fact that this is the perfect injury for our program. "I also want you to have an ice bath now. Do you have a hot tub at home?"

"Yep," Jones replies.

"Good," Doc states. Jones turns his head to face us. "Lexi will give you an action plan and I want you to follow it to a T. You need to take a few maintenance days, meaning no training. I want you to rest up. When you're back, come and see myself or Lexi each day. Once we're satisfied, we'll clear you to play again."

"But the charity thing is tomorrow," Kallen whines. *Typical player*, always thinking of the game.

"Do you want to be ready for the opener? Or do you want to attend a charity thing that's possibly going to set you back?"

"Both," he grumbles.

"Well, you can't do both," I snap at him. *Why are players so stubborn?* "After your ice bath, come back and see me. I'll rub you with arnica, using this new technique I read about to bring out any bruising. It should speed up the healing process and you'll be back on the ice before you know it."

"That's a great idea, Lexi," Doc says. "Make sure to document everything so we can refer back to it for future reference."

Nodding at Doc, I focus on Kallen. "Tomorrow we'll repeat what I do tonight an—"

"Won't that hurt?"

"Do you want to play the first game of the season?"

"Yes," he quickly replies.

"Then suck it up and let my hands work their magic." To reiterate my point, I wave my fingers at him and give him my 'let me do my job' look.

"Did anyone ever tell you, you're a sadist?"

An evil smile appears on my face. "Only you big, tough hockey boys when they have a boo-boo."

Doc laughs. "I'll leave you to it." He exits the treatment room.

After helping him up, we head to where the ice baths are located and I begin getting the ice bath ready for Jones.

Ten minutes later, it's all set and I help him climb into the tub. He groans at the chill as he submerges himself but lies back and closes his eyes. I see the moment he relaxes, and I know we are on the right treatment course.

"I'll be back in a few and then I'll give you your massage." He nods but doesn't open his eyes, so I leave him to it and head back to my treatment room.

Along the way, I run into JJ. "Is he going to be okay?" His voice is filled with concern.

"He will be. There doesn't seem to be any major damage. He's going to be sore, but if he follows our treatment plan, he'll be back on the ice in no time."

"Can you fix him?"

"Are you doubting my skills, James?"

"Never. If anyone can get Kal back on the ice, it's you." He stares at me and for a brief moment, I forget what he did to me until he adds, "Seems like you learned a lot at USC. I'm proud that you followed your dreams."

Pursing my lips, I take in a breath and process his words. At the mention of USC, it brings back all the hurt from him breaking up with me and pushing me away.

"I need to go." Before he can say anything else, I walk away from him. My heart once again hurts at the memory of what he did to me four years ago. Will that pain ever ease?

20

JJ

TOMORROW IS THE FIRST GAME OF THE SEASON AND TO SAY I'M nervous is an understatement. Mom flew in to watch and tonight I hung out with her, just the two of us. It was relaxing and exactly what I needed to prepare for the season ahead.

... *"I needed this. Thanks, Mom."*

"You're very welcome, JJ, but what's wrong? I know you're nervous about your first NHL game tomorrow, but there's something else. My mom instinct is strong right now."

"It's Lexi," I tell her.

"What about her?"

"She's working for the Crushers."

"Ohh," she draws that one word out. "And how's that working out for you?"

"She hates me," I dejectedly voice, then I add, "Like wouldn't pee on me if I were on fire hates me."

"JJ, you broke her heart," Mom unhelpfully states.

"That was years ago," I snap.

"And how's your heart all these years later?" She eyes me in that 'hmmm' kind of way moms do. "Now back to my question, how's that working out for you?"

"Mom, having Lex here and having her hate me is hard, really fucking hard." She eyes me for swearing. "Sorry. When I first realized she was here, I thought it was my second chance. My chance to win back the girl who still holds my heart, but the hatred she has for me is strong. I never realized how much I hurt her, but I don't regret doing it. Watching her work and seeing her do what she was born to do is worth her hate but ..."

"You miss her and want her back?"

"Yep," I reply, letting the 'p' pop. "How do I get her to forgive me?"

"Well, as I told you back then when you told me what you did, you're an idiot and you still are an idiot for not chasing after her back then."

"I can't change the past, Mom."

"Then you'll have to win her back the old-fashioned way."

"How's that?"

"Just be you. You need to show her that you love her. That you did what you did for her."

"Why is love so hard?"

"Because the best things in life are hard and worth fighting for."

Lying in bed, I stare at the ceiling, sleep eluding me. I keep playing Mom's words over and over, *the best things in life are hard and worth fighting for*, and she's right. Lexi is worth fighting for and I'm going to win her back, but first, I need to win the first game of the season.

The atmosphere in the locker room is electric. The cheers from the stadium are filtering in each time the door opens and it adds to the intensity in the air. We are all fired up and ready to get onto the ice. We're ready to show the world the Crushers mean business and the Cup is ours.

Glancing around the locker room, I take in my team-mates, and then I look over to Lexi's treatment room. Just as I look in that direction, she steps out. Our gaze catches and for a few brief seconds, it's perfect, but then in the blink of an eye—literally—her expression changes and that desire to kick me in the balls is there.

She walks toward me, but her eyes are on Kallen next to me. "You good to go, Jones?" she asks Kal, studying him intently. No doubt to make sure he isn't lying, but he nods, grinning like a loon because the regime Lex and Doc implemented worked. Kal bounced back quickly and I think he's fitter than ever.

"Of course I am," he tells her. "I have the best doc and massage slash physical therapist on speed dial."

She rolls her eyes at him. "Don't make me regret giving you my number."

Hearing that Kal has her new number and I don't raises my hackles. "How come you gave him your number but not me?"

"Because he needed my help," Lex snaps at me.

"What if I need your help?" I whine. I sound like a toddler whose favorite toy was just taken away from them, but Lexi is mine, not Kallen's.

"I'm sure Doc or Brandon will be on hand to help with anything you need," she growls at me and before I can say anything else, she turns on her heel and walks back to her room. Before she steps inside, she looks over her shoulder at Kal and me. "And, guys, good luck out there today."

Her gaze lingers on me for a few seconds, then she closes the door behind her, and that glance gives me hope I can win her back.

"What's going on between you two?" Kal asks me.

"Nothing," I snap, but a blind man could see something is going on between us. He raises his eyebrows in that 'do I look dumb' way and like always with Kal, I open up. "Dude, seriously, *nothing* is happening." I place emphasis on the word nothing, giving away the fact that something indeed has happened in the past. I don't know why I've never fully opened up to Kal about Lex. He knew I had a girlfriend in high school, but I never told him specifics. And once we became roommates and I ruined us, it was too painful to talk about her, so I pretended like she didn't exist … even though there was not a day that I didn't think about her.

"But you want there to be?"

"Dude, I've been in love with that girl since I was sixteen and Mom and I moved in next door."

"But?"

"I fucked it all up."

"What happened? What did you do to fuck it all up?"

"I was young and dumb."

"You are still young and dumb," Kal teases me, knocking me in the shoulder with his.

"Fuck off, asshole, at least I'm not lusting over the coach's daughter."

"Have you seen Chelsea Maxwell? Can you blame me?"

"You can have Chels. I have my eyes on someone else."

Looking across the room, I find Lexi again. She's rubbing Anton's calf and a wave of jealousy slams into me because I know what it's like to have those hands roaming over my body.

"Yeah," he scoffs, "a someone who hates your guts with a fiery passion." He tries again, "What did you do?"

"It's a long story, but CliffsNotes, I hurt her and all these years later, she still hates me."

"Yeah, she really does hate you," Kal states, dropping down to the bench next to me.

"Yep," I reply, letting the 'p' pop … which seems to be a thing of mine at the moment. "But I kinda deserve the hate."

"You never spoke about her when we were in college together."

"Because it hurt too much to think about her."

"She's your penguin, isn't she?"

"Yep," I reply again.

He looks over at where I'm looking, and that's the moment Lexi looks up and glares at me.

"Yeah, good luck with that," Kal teases.

Looking over at my best friend, I stare him in the eyes. "Lex fell in love with me once. I can get her to fall again."

"May the odds ever be in your favor, dude, 'cause from where I'm sitting, you have more luck at scoring eight goals in a single game and breaking McQueen's record than getting Lexi to fall in love with you again." He pauses. "Wanna make a bet on it?"

"Even though I know I'd win that bet, I'm not betting on this. Getting Lexi to love me again is all that's important."

"And winning the Cup," Kallen adds.

"Winning back the girl of my dreams and the Cup in my rookie year is going to be amazing." … I just hope I can do both.

21

LEXI

It's the weekend after Halloween. I've taken a few days off and headed home for the weekend. It's been a couple months since I've seen everyone. All this stuff with *him* is overwhelming and I need a mom hug and some advice. This weekend also happens to be our weekend to host the monthly barbecue. Meaning I can see all the extended family too.

For as long as I can remember, once a month, someone hosts a barbecue and the attendees are the Kelly, Knight, Cox, and Cruz families, plus Lisa and JJ on occasion. We're like this weird-ass *Brady Bunch* of sorts and I wouldn't change a thing … well, maybe I'd arrange a truce between my mom and Aunty Baylor. Those two are the definition of frenemies. No love is lost between them, but I have a feeling one day, those two will be just as close as Mom is with Aunty Avery. Who just so happens to be Aunty Bay's twin sister. See, weird-ass *Brady Bunch*.

At this precise moment, Mom is running around like a madwoman.

"Cress, babe, you need to calm down," Dad tells her as she nearly trips and face-plants while setting the table.

"Preston, don't tell me to calm down. I'm all in a fluster because I'm running late and you know I hate running late."

"It's a barbecue. It's not like the queen is coming."

"Bay's coming."

"Bay is not the queen."

"No, she's a bitch," Mom rumbles under her breath, but it's not as quiet as she thinks. You'd think after all these years, Mom and Aunty Baylor would be over being frenemies, but it's just as strong as ever.

Walking into the kitchen, I head over to Mom and Dad. "Mom, it will all be fine. Have a glass of wine and then when the others get here, you can all do it together … like you always usually do."

"When did you get to be so wise?"

"I've always been wise, Mom."

She taps my cheek, smiles, and then pulls me in for a hug. "It's so good to have you home, Lexi. I miss you."

"I miss you guys too, but now that I'm with the Crushers, we should be able to see each other more 'cause I'll be home when they play Chicago."

"I'd love that and as much as I want to catch up with you right now, I need to finish setting up."

Nodding, I just smile because Mom has been set up and ready for the last half an hour. All she's doing right now is rearranging things … before putting said things back to where they originally were.

"Well, as soon as you're happy with the setup, come and have a glass of wine with me. I could really use some mom advice."

"What about dad advice?" Dad asks, as I pop the top on his bottle of beer.

"You wanna talk about boys with me?"

"Umm, no … unless you need me to beat a boy up for you."

"Put the gloves away, Rocky Balboa, no one needs to get beaten up, but for what it's worth, I could totally take on any boy who wrongs me. I am a Knight after all."

"That's my girl," he proudly declares before grabbing the barbecue utensils off the counter and heading out to the grill.

Pouring myself a glass of wine, I head out back and spy my brother sitting by the firepit. I might be eight years older than him, but Clay, or CJ as he prefers now, and I have a great relationship. Same for our sister, Pepper.

"What's got you grinning like a carnival clown?" I ask as I take a seat next to him around the fire. There's a chill in the air already, so sitting by the fire is nice. Reminds me of all the times we did this when I was still living at home.

"Nothing," he says, schooling his expression, but my brother is the worst liar ever.

"I call bullshit on that, dear brother of mine."

"Seriously, it's nothing."

"Is it a girl?" I tease.

"No," he snappily refutes.

"Is it a boy?" I change pace and waggle my eyebrows at him. He's never given off any gay vibes before, but then again, what are gay vibes? And at the end of the day, as long as he's happy, I'm happy.

"It's not a guy and I'm not gay."

"Okay. Okay, so it's definitely a girl then?"

He sighs and rolls his eyes.

"Oh My God, it's totally about a girl. Is my wee lil'

I Pucking Hate That You Love Me

I Pucking Hate That You Love Me

brother in loooooove?" I add a million extra o's to the word love.

He laughs and shakes his head. "No," he snaps, but his eyes tell a completely different story.

"You're protesting too much, dude." He goes to interrupt me, but I raise my hand and stop him in his tracks. "Look, whoever she is, she better look after you."

"Isn't it generally the guy who gets the 'you better look after her' chat? Not the other way around."

Shrugging at him, I take a sip of my wine. "I'm not a parent, so I don't know the ins and outs, but as the big sister, I'm on your side."

"And I'm on yours, too. Speaking of, how's what's-his-face?" CJ has called *him* what's-his-face since he dumped me.

"Jameson is still an ass."

"Do I need to kick his ass?"

I'm just about to take another sip when I burst out laughing. "I'd pay to see you kick anyone's ass. You're the least ass-kicking person I know."

"You know nothing, Lexi Knight."

"Did you just Jon Snow me?"

"Yep, I sure did. You'd be surprised at what I can do."

"You constantly surprise me, CJ, and one day, you will meet Mrs. Clay and she'll be a lucky, lucky gal."

"Just like you'll meet Mr. Lexi and he, too, will be lucky."

Staring at my brother, I nod, but truthfully, I think I already have met, and lost, him. No one I've dated since *him* has lived up to the expectation of *him* because when we dated, he doted on me like Dad dotes on Mom. I loved him with everything I had and I think I always will, even with what he did. I think that's why I'm so confused right now. When we were together, I always thought one day, he'd play hockey and I'd be a team PT and we'd have the big, fancy wedding and live happily ever after. The first part has come true, but the rest will just be a dream, even if that spark is still there.

When I saw *him* that first day in the locker room, all the love I once had for him bubbled to the surface, but as soon as he said my name, all that hurt slammed into my heart. I don't think I'll ever get over what he did. That hurt is engrained into my soul. Fused over never to be released again. I cannot open my heart because what if he breaks it again? I wouldn't survive a second heartbreak.

22

JJ

THE LAST FEW WEEKS HAVE FLOWN BY AND THEY HAVE BEEN THE best weeks of my life.

The Crusher fans are amazing and the puck bunnies are crazier than I anticipated. I'd heard stories about how tenacious they can be and the stories do not live up to the hype.

There is one fan who keeps trying to get to me, but security is keeping him, yes, him, away. He even tried to get into the stadium while we were away in LA. Management has said if it keeps up, they will assign me personal security, but I told them it's not necessary. I can look after myself.

For now, I've won, but if this crazy guy keeps it up, who knows what will happen.

I'd always known I wanted to be a professional hockey player, but reality is so much better than my dreams. I just wish Doucheman wasn't on our team. Apart from him, it's perfect.

Then there's Lexi. She still hates me and I like to tell myself that her hate is thawing, but if anything, it's becoming stronger by the day. If I could go back in time, I'd do things differently. I'd still convince her to go to USC, but I would do it in a less dickheadish way. I'd do it in a way that allowed us to still be together and follow our dreams.

Coach is in a stellar mood this morning and he's putting us through our paces. He's pissed because we lost to LA last night. To put it plainly, we sucked. I'm pretty sure my peewee team could have played better than we did.

"Again," he shouts.

Sending us into our fifth bag skate punishment. I'd heard the rumors about Coach Maxwell and his bag skate punishments, and this is a hell I never want to be in again.

We fall into line and push off.

Skating down the ice, everything hurts and I feel like I could throw up, but I refuse to be *that* person on the team.

Reaching the end, I spin and push off to head back down the ice and something crunches in my groin. "Holy fucking shit," I hiss, dropping down and hitting the ice hard. I fall to my knees, drop onto my back, and roll into a ball. Tears well in my eyes and a pain like never before radiates from my groin and down into my thigh.

Pressing my hand into my groin, I groan, but I cry out in pain when I pull my hand away. I'd take a hit to the nuts over this any day.

"You good?" Kal asks me from above.

"If feeling like my groin is on fire and everything fucking hurts, then yeah, I'm fucking dandy."

"Pussy," Doucheman calls out, skating away, not stopping to see if I'm okay.

Coach Maxwell, our new assistant coach, and the team owner, Maverick 'Rick' McQueen, come over to where I'm lying on the ice.

My hero, Rick, and his wife, Rachelle McQueen,

purchased the team just before I was drafted to the Crushers. Rachelle and Rick McQueen are a powerhouse couple. They might be billionaires, but they don't let their money change who they are at heart. Rick made millions when he played and Rachelle comes from money, her daddy and grandfather and so on are in the oil business, but she's loved hockey since she was a little girl. Then she met Rick and it was game over for her. They are perfect for each other and now, they're taking over the hockey world together.

"You okay, James?" Coach asks.

Where I was snarky with Kal, I hold the snark back when I answer Coach. "Not sure—"

"What do you mean you're not sure? Either you are or you aren't."

"Well then, no, my groin is on fire and throbbing."

"You need to see Doc, get him to look you over."

"I'm fine," I hiss as I stand up. Well, I try to straighten up.

"If you're fine, then get back to it. You princesses need to pick up your act. Your performance last night, and just now, was embarrassing," Rick states. "My Cate can play better than you guys did last night, and she's three."

Finally standing up, I clench my teeth and when I push off to join the rest of the team, I cry out and fall back to the ice again.

"Off the ice and see Doc. Now," Coach growls.

Doc looks at my scan and nods. Turning to face me, I try to read his expression, but Doc Michels has the best poker face and doesn't give anything away. "There doesn't seem to be a tear, which is good. In my opinion, you've strained your adductor muscle—"

"My adda-whatta?" I interrupt Doc.

"Your groin muscle. Your groin is made up of the adductor longus, breves, magnus, gracilis, and obturator externus, aka your hip muscles."

"Okay, so what's the plan then?"

"Would you mind partaking in my trial? I'd be forever grateful."

"Will it get me back on the ice quicker?"

"That is the hope."

"Then sign me up, Doc. I'll play guinea pig if it means I'm back out there before we fly to Toronto this week."

"Not sure that will happen, James. These injuries can take up to three weeks to heal, but with my action plan, I'm hoping to get that back to two weeks."

"Two is better than three, Doc. So what does this entail? And when do we get started?"

"Excellent," when he says this, I imagine Monty Burns from *The Simpsons*. "We can start now. I want you to have an ice bath. The cold temperature will narrow your blood vessels and decrease blood flow to your muscles, which will help to reduce inflammation and swelling. I want you to follow that up with a massage to release the tension in the muscles, which will help with muscle spasms, thereby aiding the healing process. Then we'll get you into the sauna. For the next two days, we will repeat this process and then reassess."

"That's easy enough. Let's do it."

Doc goes about getting the ice bath ready for me and I hang in his room, waiting, when there's a knock on his door.

"Doc, you wanted to see me?" a sweet voice I'd know anywhere says. She's smiling as she enters Doc's office, but as soon as she sees me sitting on the bench, that smile falters.

"Hey, Lex," I say with a flick of my wrist in a wave.

"What are you doing in here?" she throws at me, all defensive.

"I had a fall and Doc is looking at me."

"Are you okay?" Her tone changes and I see concern etched on her face. "What happened? What treatment did Doc lay out? Do you want me to assess you too?"

"As much as I'd love to have your hands on me," I wink at her as I say this, earning myself an eye roll from her, "he's going with the ice, massage, sauna—"

"Great, Lexi, you're here," Doc says, joining us.

"I'm about to get Mr. James here into the ice bath, and then you'll massage him before we wrap things up with a session in the sauna …" While the two of them confer about my treatment, I sit here and watch Lexi. She's in heaven right now. Well, she is until she realizes *she* will be the one massaging me back to health.

"Can't Brandon do it?"

"I'd prefer you in this case. You have that magic touch when it comes to healing and don't tell anyone, but you're my favorite."

"Mine too," I add, earning myself a glare from Lex.

"Looks like the patient has spoken," Doc says. "James, let's get you into the ice bath. While I get you settled, Lexi, you can set up for the massage when he's done?"

Reluctantly, she nods. "Sure thing." She purses her lips so she doesn't say anything that will get her in trouble with her boss and then without another word, she leaves.

Doc helps me off the table and then the two of us head toward the ice bath. Once I'm in the tub, which by the way is colder than I thought. I'm positive my balls have pushed themselves inside my body, making my already sore groin sorer.

"So how many massages will I need as part of this?" I ask, trying to take my mind off the cold.

"Every day to start and then we can reassess from there." Nodding, I make a face and Doc must take it for concern because he reaches out and squeezes my shoulder in that reassuring kind of way. "Don't worry, James, you're in good hands with Lexi. She's an amazing young woman, and I can see her going far in this industry."

"Yeah, she is," I tell him. He looks at me inquisitively. "Lexi and I went to high school together," I tell him. He nods, but the sound of his phone ringing prevents any further conversation. He answers and then tells the person to hang on. "I'll be back in fifteen minutes to help you out."

Nodding, I watch him walk away. Taking a deep breath, I lean my head back and close my eyes. I can't believe I'm going to be out for a few weeks. This is not a good start to my season, but I guess the silver lining of my accident is that Lexi and I will be spending time together. Maybe, just maybe, this is my chance to win her over.

23
LEXI

Since joining the Crushers and being part of Doc's program, I've learned so much and I have to say, I've missed hockey. Watching the guys fly up and down the ice is thrilling.

Ever since *he* dumped me, I avoided hockey like the plague. When Doc Michels asked me to join him, I was almost going to turn it down because it was for a hockey team, but my dad convinced me to do it. He said, "What are the chances of Jameson being on that team?" We both laughed, but I guess the laugh is on me because he *is* on the team.

"Doc's asking for you," Brandon says as I walk back from the lunchroom.

"Thanks," I tell him with a nod. I really don't like him. Actually, not many people here do. He's a pompous asshole, who thinks that a woman, aka me, should not be in this position. Personally, I think he's dirty because, not to toot my own horn, but I'm a better PT than him, and the guys generally come to me before him when it comes to massage or injury relief.

"Doc, you wanted to see me?" I say, walking into his room since the door is open, but I come to a sudden stop when I see Jameson sitting on the edge of Doc's treatment table.

"Hey, Lex," Jameson says and the way my name sounds passing through his lips reminds me of when we were in school … before he crushed my heart.

"What are you doing in here?" I hiss at him.

"I had a fall and Doc is looking at me."

He had an accident. Shit, that's not good. "Are you okay? What happened? What treatment did Doc lay out? Do you want me to assess you too?" I rapid fire the questions at him. PT Lexi is front and center now, that is until he opens his stupid, beautiful mouth.

"As much as I'd love to have your hands on me, he's going with the ice, massage, sauna—"

"Great, Lexi, you're here," Doc says, joining us. Facing him, I await his direction and hope with everything I have that Doc didn't see Jameson's wink just now.

This is my job. I can't be seen flirting with the players, not that I'm flirting. "I'm about to get Mr. James here into the ice bath, and then we'll get him to massage and wrap it up with a session in the sauna. He's pulled his adductor muscle and I want to use the ice/massage/heat treatment plan you've been working on and see if we can have him back on the ice quicker than usual. I'll oversee the ice bath and then you can massage—"

"Can't Brandon do it?"

"I'd prefer you in this case. You have the magic touch when it comes to massage and don't tell anyone, but you're my favorite."

I can't help but feel all warm and fuzzy at hearing Doc say that. To have praise like that come from your mentor and boss is an honor, but that feeling dissipates when JJ agrees, saying, "Mine too."

Throwing a glare at him, I'm about to protest again when Doc speaks in *his* favor. "Looks like the patient has spoken," Doc says. "Let's get you into the ice bath and while I get you settled, Lexi, you go set up for the massage."

"Sure thing," I reluctantly say. Before I say something I shouldn't, I head to my treatment room next door and get the table set up for what's going to be the massage from hell.

A knock at my door startles me and when I look up, I see Doc in the doorway. "JJ can hop out of the ice bath now. Do you mind assisting him? I have a meeting that I forgot about, and I need to get across town or I'm going to be late."

"Sure thing, Doc," I tell him with a smile, but inside I'm chanting, *no, no, fucking no.* The less time I spend with him the better.

"You're a gem," he says and then he's gone.

Taking a breath, I exit my treatment room but before I get far, Brandon verbally attacks me. "You're such a suck-ass." He snickers at me.

"Excuse me?"

"Sure thing, Doc," he repeats my words in a condescending tone. "You and I both know you only got this 'cause you have tits and your dad is a doctor."

"What do my tits and my dad, who by the way is a pediatric doctor, have to do with this? I got this position because

I work hard and I graduated top of my class. I'm the first one here every morning and I'm usually the last one to leave. I work just as hard as anyone here, well, except for you. Brandon, no one here likes you because you're a conceited, arrogant jerk. Put the work in and then maybe, just maybe, you will get treated with respect."

"I bet you've fucked half the guys on the team or at least sucked their dicks. That's why they all rave about how good you are. It's not because you're a great PT, it's because you're a whore." Before I can stop myself, my hand flies out and I slap Brandon across the face.

"Fuck you, asshole. I'm no whore. I work hard, that's why I'm the best. Now, if you excuse me, I have a patient to get out of the ice bath."

Pulling open the door to where the ice bath is with a force I didn't mean to, it slams into the wall, causing Jameson to flinch. His eyes open suddenly and he winces from the sudden movement.

"Shit, Lex, I thought you were supposed to be healing me, not scaring me and making me flinch."

"Sorry, I'm just …" But I don't finish that. *He* doesn't need to know about what just happened with Brandon.

"Just what?" He leans forward, wincing a little as he sits up. Silently, we stare at one another. "You used to talk to me about everything."

"So did you, until one day you decided I couldn't make decisions for myself," I snap at him as memories of that day filter into my brain. Pain once again slams into me.

Closing my eyes, I breathe in deeply. This is not the time or the place to think about that. Inhaling deeply once more, I calm my inner beast and when I open my eyes, heartbroken Lexi is gone and PT Lexi is in place. "Okay, let's get you out of there and into my treatment room."

He nods at me. "Can you, umm, help me up, please?"

Nodding, I walk over to the tub and help him stand and climb out. He's stiff and sore and I can tell he's in a lot of pain. "You good?"

"Mmmhmpf," he replies through clenched teeth.

Handing him a towel, he dries himself off. "Come on," I urge him and together we silently head to my treatment room.

"I just need the bathroom," he tells me and without waiting for my reply, he heads to the bathrooms.

Turning on my heel, I make my way to my room and I grab the cream I'll use when I massage him. Resting my palms on the shelf, I close my eyes and psych myself up to do this. I'm going to be massaging Jameson in a very private area. In an area that I can no longer touch as I please. This is going to be the hardest massage of my life … and I will be massaging him for the next week or so while I treat his injury. "Fuck my life," I mumble under my breath just as he returns.

The door clicks closed and suddenly the room feels smaller with just the two of us in it. Turning around, I lean against the shelf and watch him walk in. There's a definite limp on his right side and seeing that, any awkwardness I just felt dissipates and PT Lexi is front and center. I intently watch him and his movement, assessing him as he climbs onto the bed. He lies on his back and shuffles around until he gets comfortable.

"Ready?" I ask and he nods.

Picking up the cream, I walk over and smile down at him. Lifting the hem of the towel, I raise it up and my eyes widen when I realize he's naked. "Umm, where are your clothes?"

"I took them off. I thought this would be easier … plus,

it's not like you haven't seen my dick before." He waggles his eyebrows at me.

"I'm here as your PT, Jameson. Quit fucking around."

"Someone's testy," he throws back at me. Lifting his arms, he slides them behind his head and I see every gorgeous muscle he has. My eyes roam over his arms and chest. He clears his throat and I lift my gaze to his. "Like what you see?" My eyes widen when I realize I was just ogling him. "You can touch me if you like. I really won't mind."

Giving him a sweet smile, I push the towel to the side and I press my thumb into his groin, causing him to hiss. "Was that too hard?"

"No," he groans, "you know I love it when you're rough with me."

"Jameson," I plead.

"Lex," he replies, but neither of us says anything else. When the silence becomes too much, I start the massage. The quicker I do this, the quicker I can get away from him.

Focusing on his groin, I begin to rub. Taking note of when he winces and which spots to focus on.

"I've missed having your hands on me."

"You do not and please, be quiet. I'm trying to focus."

"I love you focusing on that area. Feel free to focus a little to the left. Maybe give my dick a lil' rub. I seem to remember you love rubbing my dick." At the mention of his dick, my eyes drift there and the asshole chuckles. "I'd also be happy for you to use your mouth. I've heard that blow jobs are great for groin injuries."

Lifting my gaze to his, I glare at him. "I will never touch or suck your dick again, Jameson."

"My friends call me JJ."

"I'm not your friend," I snap, "because friends don't

break friend's hearts and throw away their love." I hate that I'm showing my emotions, so I focus back on his groin and the massage.

"I know, we are so much more than that. Always have been and always will be."

"That's where you're wrong. I hate everything about you, Jameson," I hiss, pressing my thumb harder into his groin than is necessary, but Jameson with his suave "you still want me" aura is pissing me off. He groans and lifts his leg, trying to ease the pain I just inflicted. This is so unprofessional but then again, him turning up naked and wanting a blowie is also unprofessional, so fair's fair.

"No, you love everything about me, Lex." He throws back at me, a cocky smirk on his face. On the face I both want to punch and kiss.

"If by love, you mean love the thought of jamming a rusty fork up your ass sideways, then yes, I love you." And that thought is very, very appealing right now.

"Love is love," he nonchalantly replies with a shrug. "You and I never tried it rough when we were together, but maybe it's time we explore new options."

"Hell will freeze over before that ever happens. Now, please bend your leg so your legs make a P of sorts."

He does as I ask and he winces as he moves into position. Dipping my fingers into the ointment, I begin to massage him again and due to the location, my fingers keep brushing the base of his dick.

"A little more to the left," he says again and like before, I ignore the comment.

Ten painstakingly long minutes later, I'm finished with the massage. "You can hop up now," I tell him as I step back from the table and put the ointment away.

Turning around, I watch as he sits up and swings his legs

over the edge. "How does it feel now?" I ask as he shuffles off the table and stands up.

He winces but tries to school it. "It's all good," he lies.

Shaking my head, I'm disappointed he lied to me just now. He forgets I know how to read him. Walking over to him, I come to a stop in front of him. I'm close enough that I get a whiff of him and he smells just like I remember—ice and leather. "Don't lie to me, Jameson. How is it really?"

"Fine," he lies again, but before I can tell him not to lie to me, his lips are on mine. His tongue pushes into my mouth and muscle memory takes over and I kiss him. My tongue slips and slides with his, in and out of each other's mouths. He walks me backward toward the wall and my back hits it with a thud. He slides his leg between mine and he rubs me. His thigh grazes my clit and my nether region begins to tingle and my blood begins to simmer.

With every movement, every nerve ending in my body lights up like fireworks on the Fourth. As much as I hate the asshole, he knows my body. He knows how to bring me to orgasm, even without sex. He always has and all these years later, he still knows how to drive me wild.

I hate him, but he's right. I also pucking love him ... and I think I always will.

I'm so pucking screwed when it comes to Jameson James.

24

JJ

KISSING LEXI JUST NOW WASN'T PLANNED, BUT WHEN SHE GETS angry like that, it turns me on and right now, I'd let her hate fuck me if I didn't think she'd snap my dick off.

I'm not letting this second chance go.

I fucked up once with Lexi Knight. I will not do it again.

She pushes on my chest, shoving me away from her. Her cheeks are flushed and her lips are swollen from the kiss. She raises her hand and slaps me. My cheek stings from the connection, but as I stare at the woman who still owns my heart, I see desire in her eyes and I know, deep down, she still loves me too.

"You can't do that again," she breathlessly pants.

"I can and I will because, Lex, you and I will be together again."

"No, we won't. Just go and find someone else to lavish attention on."

"Not gonna happen, Lex. If I don't have your attention, I don't want anyone's attention."

"Bullshit," she hisses at me. "You've hooked up with plenty of puck bunnies. I've read the tabloids. I've seen the pics. I'm—"

"Photos don't always portray the truth and on my nanna's grave, I swear to you, I haven't slept with anyone since you came back into my life."

She blinks at me in shock, her eyes wide as she processes my words. "Bull—"

"Do not fucking say bullshit again. It's the truth, Lex. When have I ever lied to you?"

"Ohh, I don't know. How about the time you told me you couldn't be with me anymore because you had to focus on your career?"

"I had to tell you that. I couldn't let you pass up that opportunity in California. Lex, you would have regretted not going, and look where you are now. You're here, doing what you love because you went to California. I had to break up with you. I had to lie about how I really felt."

"Do I not get a say in us? We could have done the long-distance thing. We could have made us work. I loved you so, so much, Jameson. And you threw our love away without thinking about me. Us. Our future. You broke my heart and I will never forgive you, and I certainly won't ever love you again, Jameson."

Jameson, I hate her calling me that. Makes me feel like I'm in trouble.

"I never stopped loving you, Lex, and I don't regret what I did." Running my hands through my hair, I look at her. "As I stand here before you, I'm going to win you back, Lexi Knight."

"I pucking hate that you love me, Jameson James. I wish I could forget I ever knew you, but you're wedged so deep in my soul that a lifetime of hating you will never remove you from that spot, but I don't have to listen to my heart. You broke it before and I fixed it. I won't let you break it again."

"Lex—"

"No, Jameson, no." There's my full name again.

Her eyes are filled with tears and I hate that I'm the cause of them, so I do the one thing I know makes her happy. Well, it used to. Taking a step, I slip one hand around her waist and pull her into me. I slide my hand up into her hair and lower my lips to hers. I kiss her softly, just how I know she likes to be kissed. She begins to kiss me back, but then she puts her hands on my chest and pushes me away from her again. "Don't ever kiss me again without my permission."

"Next time, I'll remember to ask."

"There won't be a next time, Jameson. Just forget me. You do your job and I'll do mine."

Before I have a chance to reply, she reaches for the door handle and races out of the room, leaving me alone. Stepping into the doorway, I watch her race through the locker room and with each step she takes away from me, I realize how much I hurt her when we were eighteen.

I was truthful when I told her I haven't hooked up with as many women as the tabloids think I have because, deep down, I only want her. A love like we have doesn't ever extinguish, and I'm going to fan those embers and make our love burn once again.

I'm going to do whatever it takes to win her back. To get her not to hate me because Lexi Knight is just as amazing now as she was back then. She's still it for me … now I just need to find a way to make her realize we belong together.

25
LEXI

Time is flying by. In the almost six months I've been here, I've learned so much from Doc and working on this program is great. The guys on the team are willing to help and dare I say it, Jameson's accident the other month was a game changer for our research.

I'm sitting in the family suite in the back corner. This is my place to think and focus on paperwork. Normally, it's just me in here during the week, but today the guys will be filming videos and interviews for Chels to load on the socials leading into the back end of the season and the playoffs, and this is ground zero.

The Crushers are currently sitting at the top of the Eastern Conference leaderboard and are the favorites to win the Cup this year.

"What's up with you and JJ?" Chelsea asks, dropping into the seat next to me.

Her question surprises me because, well, Chelsea and I

don't chat often, and I thought Jameson and I were hiding our non-relationship from everyone.

"Nothing, why?"

"It seems like you two are trying to avoid one another when really you both want to puck each other's brains out."

"I assure you, I don't want to puck him. Punch him? Maybe, but definitely not puck." That's one thing I've noticed about Chelsea, she uses the word puck in lieu of fuck. She's the nicest chick I have ever met. She also happens to be Coach Maxwell's daughter and she's currently dating Kallen, the goalie. Talk about forbidden taboo romance.

"I think you do. Maybe you just need to puck each other so you can move on, or maybe it will spark something."

"Been there. Pucked that. Got the brokenhearted T-shirt and I don't want to open myself up to that again."

"You already pucked?" she shouts, garnering the attention of Jett and Anton, who are the only two here. Those two are always the first to arrive. I don't think I've ever seen them running late … it's a shame others on the team can't be like them. "Spill, lady, and don't leave anything out."

Looks like I won't be finishing up this report, so I close my iPad and turn to face her. "Jameson and I know each other from back in Chicago …" I proceed to fill her in on our life, relationship, and the demise of said relationship.

"Puck me," she murmurs when I finish.

"Yeah, puck me," I repeat with an eye roll.

"Well, for what it's worth and an outsider's perspective, that boy has it bad for you still. Yes, he did a bonehead thing when you guys were eighteen, but he did kind of do it for a sweet reason. He just went about it the wrong way, but, Lexi, it's been nearly five years and he still clearly loves you. And I think if you push the hate aside, deep down, you love him too."

Before I can reply, the rest of the guys arrive and Chelsea has to get to work.

Sitting here, I think over her words and watch as Chelsea corrals the guys into doing what she wants. It's amazing to see them fall into line for her. For a meek thing, she knows how to command a group of big, burly hockey players.

"Great, first up, I'll have Anton." He jumps up and walks toward her. "You're on your own since you're the team captain. Hope that's okay?"

"All good, Chels."

"Sweet. Head on down to the rink and I'll be there in five." She looks back at the rest of the guys here. "Kal and JJ, you'll be next and then Stefan, Jett, and Cliff, you three will finish up the day today. Then tomorrow morning will be everyone else, and we'll finish off the day with the group thing. Then I just have to work my magic and voila, all done."

"Why is marketing crap always fun with you but when marketing, marketing arranges it, it's like watching paint dry?" Jett asks.

Everyone nods in agreement and even I find myself nodding. Chelsea did a piece on us the other week and it was fun and out there. Not your typical boring dot point interview that marketing usually demands.

"'cause I'm awesome," she says, a smile gracing her face.

"Yeah, you are," Kallen sings out before blowing her a kiss across the room. She pretends to catch it and tuck it into her jeans pocket. Jameson groans and rolls his eyes, just like I did. Jameson then repeats the kiss to Jett and he mimics Chelsea's reaction with a flourish. A laugh slips out and Jameson turns his attention to me and for a brief moment, something passes between us, but it's broken when Chelsea chastises them for mucking around on her watch. "All right, you two, cut it out. When Anton comes back, JJ, Kal, you two come on down."

"*The Price is Right,*" Jameson singsongs out, while I sing it in my head. Once again proving that we're in sync on so many levels.

"Don't make me wait, guys. I want this done and dusted before four. I have something I need to do," Kallen states, giving Chels a look that could quite easily get her pregnant with how smoldering it is. He walks over to her and places a quick kiss on her lips before she heads out to the ice to oversee her project.

"And now they're giving each other fuck-me eyes," Jameson groans.

"You're just jealous that my girlfriend is hotter than your girlfri—ohh that's right, you don't have one."

"I'm trying," he snaps, but their interaction is halted when Däuchmen saunters into the room. In an instant, the entire atmosphere changes and in seconds, he and Kallen get into it.

Däuchmen goads him and Kallen retaliates by agreeing with all that Däuchmen said, just as Chelsea walks into the room, only getting the tail of the rant. The look of hurt on her face even hurts me, but before Kallen can defend himself, she races out of the room.

Däuchmen doesn't know how to keep his mouth shut and he makes the situation worse, causing Kallen to snap. He lays into Däuchmen, repeatedly punching him, only stopping when Coach Maxwell shouts for him to stop.

A broken and hurt Chelsea is hiding behind her dad and when Kallen looks up, she turns and runs off.

The room is silent. No one moves or breathes, until Kallen leaps into action and chases after Chels.

Hopping up, I tend to a beaten and bruised Däuchmen.

"You really are a douche," I inform him as I wipe at his face when we get back to the locker room.

"Tell me something I don't know," he snaps. "I don't need a lecture from you. I just need this trade to happen so I can get the fuck out of here."

"Stefan, you have the biggest opportunity of your life before you and you're pissing it away. You need to pull your head out of your ass, or you're going to lose everything you've worked so hard for."

"Fuck you, Lexi. I don't need a lecture from a physical therapist. I make ten times what you do. I can get any woman I want. Why would I listen to you?"

"Don't speak to her like that," Jameson comes to my defense, joining us in the locker room.

"Fuck off, James."

"No, Doucheman, you fuck off. You're a joke, an absolute joke. Lex is right, you're pissing your career away because you think you're better than everyone. Well, let me tell you something, you're not. You might be an amazing defenseman on the ice, but off, you're a deplorable human being. I used to look up to you when I was in college and I was excited to play on the same team as you, but you've really showed your true colors. You're an ass, and like you, we all can't wait for this trade either. The team will be better off without you."

"Whatever," he hisses. Däuchmen stands up and storms out of the locker room, shoving me into the locker on his way past.

"Hey," Jameson shouts. He grabs Doucheman by the collar and slams him into the wall. "Apologize," he growls.

Stefan looks at me and I see remorse on his face, but Stefan being Stefan, he pushes JJ off of him and storms out. JJ shakes his head and then turns his attention to me. "You okay?"

Nodding, I smile. "I'm fine. He didn't hurt me."

"Are you sure? Do I need to call Doc?"

"Jameson, I'm fine," I tell him. Reaching out, I squeeze his forearm to reassure him.

"I hate that you call me Jameson. I always feel like I'm in trouble."

"I … I can't call you JJ because JJ hurt me. When I call you Jameson, it's easier, but at the same time it's not, because it's still you."

"I'm sorry, Lex. I really am. I … I want to fix us."

"I don't think we can be fixed. That broken part is irreparable. We need to find a new norm, but I'm not ready for that. I'm sorry, Jameson, I just … I just can't right now."

Smiling sadly at him, I walk out of the locker room. Before I step into the corridor, I look back at him and see hurt etched on his face. I didn't mean to hurt him just now, but I meant what I said. Our relationship is over and I don't think we will ever get back to Lexi and JJ.

26
LEXI

AFTER THE BLOWUP THE OTHER DAY, SHIT HIT THE FAN AND A terrible accident involving a bus, Kallen, and Chelsea occurred. All thanks to Stefan and the shitstorm he caused. He was already hated on the team and after this, that hate level increased.

I'm feeling out of sorts, so I ask Doc for a few days off so I can head home and visit my family. I need to be around them right now, and I'm hoping my parents can impart some words of wisdom on me. I'm so confused when it comes to Jameson. I keep replaying our kiss over and over, and on a few occasions now, I've woken in the middle of the night with my hands in my panties and *his* name on my lips as I bring myself to climax.

Hell, I've even had to bust out my PowerBullet Essential 'cause my fingers weren't enough and thoughts of *him* were still playing on my mind.

"Morning, Princess," Dad says when I shuffle out of my room on Sunday morning. I have bed hair and my mouth feels like the bottom of a dirty ashtray. I'm so glad my flight doesn't leave till later tonight because right now, I don't think I'd survive the two-hour flight home.

Mom and I may have indulged in a few too many cocktails last night. Dad and I had to carry her to bed, but just as we reached their room, she vomited all over herself. I hightailed it out of there because if I smell puke, I want to be sick as well.

"Morning, Dad. Where's Mom?" I ask as I take the coffee he hands me.

"Still in bed. She didn't stop throwing up until the sun was just coming over the horizon."

"She okay?"

"She will be, but how are you?"

"I'm fine. Why do you ask?" Furrowing my brows, I look at my dad in confusion.

"You had loose lips last night and you told us about JJ and the kiss."

"Ohhh, that," I say, bringing my mug to my lips and breathing in the java goodness.

"Wanna talk about it now that you're sober?"

"No," I huff before I quickly add, "Yes. I don't know."

"Let's head out back and chat," he suggests and I nod.

Sitting on the back steps with my dad has been our thing for as long as I can remember. This was where I told him I was in love with JJ, to which he replied "Der, I have eyes." It was where I broke down in his arms after that fateful day when my heart was shattered by the boy who stole it. And now, it will be the place where I can hopefully get clarity regarding the boy who stole my heart.

"Dad, I'm so confused right now. When they say there's a thin line between love and hate, they're right. On one hand, I hate him for hurting me, but on the other, he's JJ, the boy who stole my heart … and then broke it. I pucking hate him."

"Pucking?" Dad questions.

"My friend, Chels, she says puck instead of fuck and it's rubbing off on me, but as I was saying, whenever I think about him, I just get angry and the hurt he caused slams into me again."

"Don't look back in anger, Lex. Life's too short to hold grudges," my dad states matter-of-factly as we head outside and sit on the steps together.

"Dad, did you just Oasis lyric me?"

"Guess I did … and you just made your dad proud knowing a nineties song."

"Well, I did grow up listening to that music."

"The nineties produced some of the greatest tunes around."

"Now you're just sounding old."

"Tell me about it, kiddo. The songs that used to play in the clubs are now played when I do the groceries."

"Should I start calling you old man?"

"Dad is fine, and music aside, you need to forgive JJ. You need to leave what he did in the past and open your heart to this new version. Let him in, let him prove himself to you." He pauses and then turns to face me. He has that 'I mean business' look in his eyes, and knowing my dad, he's about to impart some words of wisdom … and I really need to hear them. I've been so confused since Jameson kissed me the other week. It's like that kiss was the acid needed to break through the iron locked around my heart. "Lex, I bet, deep in your heart, you still love him and I think you always will. Just like he always will."

"My love and heart aren't the problem, Dad. It's my

head. What he did hurt and I can't just forget or even forgive."

"Don't get me wrong, I still want to kick his ass for what he did, but, Lex, he did it so you'd follow your dreams. I've never told you this, but he came to me and asked me what he should do."

"You told him to—"

"God, no," he interrupts, shaking his head vehemently. "I told him to talk to you and together the two of you could make a decision, but he did the opposite and made the decision himself."

"Yeah, he obliterated my heart and my trust in men."

"I hope not all men?"

"Not you, Dad, you will always be my number one." He's not my bio dad, who died in prison. That fact alone shows I'm better off without him.

Preston Knight is my hero. He saved my mom and he treats me like a princess. Even when Pepper and CJ came along, he didn't treat me any differently, even though he and I aren't biologically related. The day he officially adopted me was one of the best days of my life. I am who I am today because of him and I will forever be grateful that my mom fell for Dr. Knight.

"Lex, sweetheart, I suggest when you get back to New York, you talk to him. Tell him your fears. Yell at him for breaking your heart when you were eighteen. Make him see you're struggling with what to do, but from where I'm sitting, I think you already know what you want. And we both know he still loves you just as much as you still love him."

"How do you do that?" I ask.

"Do what?"

"Know that I already know what I want to do."

"It's what I do, Princess."

"Thanks, Dad." Leaning over, I give him a hug and he hugs me back.

"Anytime, Princess. Anytime."

Mom rises just after noon and the five of us head out for a late lunch/early dinner before they drop me at the airport.

As I sit at the airport waiting for my flight, I shoot off a text to Jameson and hope when I get back, I can fix this mess once and for all.

27

JJ

TRAINING TODAY WAS BRUTAL.

Our coaches must both have their periods or something because they really put us through our paces. I get they're nervous since we're no longer on the top of the leaderboard. The Florida Fireflies are ahead of us now, all because the last time we played them, Kal let the puck through in a sudden death shoot-out. He really beat himself up, but really, we should have gotten that last goal, sealing our win. And it's a team sport. *We* as a team lost the game.

When we go up against them next, it's game-fucking-on.

We all shuffle off the ice after practice. The mood in the locker room is somber. All of us are aching and exhausted. Stepping into the shower, I turn the water on and wanting to loosen up the atmosphere, I start singing "Wonderwall." Soon after, the rest of the guys are singing too.

A good sing-along is just what we need right now. We may sound like a bunch of dying cats, but it definitely lifts spirits in the locker room.

With my towel around my waist, I head back to my locker to get changed when my phone vibrates. Picking it up, my eyes widen at the sender. It's Lex. Swiping open the message, I stare at the screen and I don't know how I feel.

LEXI

We need to talk when I get back to New York

Dropping down to the bench in front of my locker, I stare at the message and read it again, hoping to maybe read between the lines because when someone says 'we need to talk' it's never a good thing. Life has taught me that. I still remember the day I got home from school when I was five and Mom was sitting on the steps of our apartment in Port Ewen. She patted the top step next to her and said, "Jameson, baby, we need to talk."

That was my first 'we need to talk' moment. That was the moment Mom informed me Dad was gone.

The next 'we need to talk' moment was when she got the job in Chicago and she was telling me we were packing up and moving eight hundred miles away. That 'we need to talk' moment turned out to be pretty okay because I met Lex when we moved.

"You good?" Kal says, dropping to the bench next to me.

"Not really." I show him the message. "We need to talk is never good."

"Not always," he says.

"Name one time when 'we need to talk' is good?"

His mouth opens and closes.

"Exactly," I snap when he has nothing to say. "This is fucked."

"What's pucked?" Chelsea asks, walking over to us. She

drapes her arms over Kal's shoulders and presses a kiss to his cheek.

"Lexi wants to talk when she gets back from Chicago," Kallen tells her before I can speak. "He thinks it's ominous because we need to talk…" He air quotes those four words. "…is never a good thing."

"It's not always bad," Chels repeats, like Kal just did.

"That's what he said." I poke Kal in the arm.

"Two against one, we win," Chels states. "Wanna head to Squires? Margot is gonna meet me there."

"Sure," Kal and I say at the same time.

We finish changing and then the three of us hail a taxi and head to Squires. Kal and I order water since we're in training mode for the playoffs, but we do cheat and order some wings. Chicken is protein, so it's okay. Well, that's what we tell ourselves.

"Why do you look down, Jones?" Margot asks me when she arrives.

"I'm fine."

"You know when someone says they are fine, they are anything but, right?"

"Seriously, I'm fine."

"He's pining over Lexi," Chelsea says and then her eyes widen. "JJ, think quick, do you love her?"

Without missing a beat, I nod. "Yes."

"Then go to the airport," she says. "Be waiting for her when the plane lands. Lay your heart on the line and tell her you can't live another day without her by your side. That she's it, she's *the* one."

"Oh My God! Yes!" Margot screeches, clapping excitedly. "That's like the ultimate romantic gesture."

Sitting across from the beaming girls, I process their words. "That's all well and good, but I don't know what flight she's on, and there's like a billion flights from Chicago."

"A billion flights could not possibly depart Chicago in one day," Margot states, causing Chels and Kallen to laugh.

"Why don't you call her dad and ask him for the details," Kallen suggests.

"He's a scary dude and I'm kinda scared he'll say no. I mean, he still gives me dirty looks over the fence for what I did when I was eighteen."

"JJ, we all make mistakes when we're eighteen. But a gesture like this, it shows you're a changed man and you still love his daughter."

"And it's not like he can kill you. He's in Chicago and you're in New York," Margot adds.

"He might be in Chicago, but I wouldn't put it past this man to know how to get to me here. He loves his daughter fiercely."

"And that's why this romantic gesture will win him over."

Nodding again, I pull my phone out and figure, what the hell. If he says no, I'm not meant to win her back.

"Jameson," he says by way of greeting when he answers.

"Dr. Knight, I need a favor."

"You want a favor? From me?"

"I need to know what flight Lexi is on."

"Why?"

Taking a deep breath, I close my eyes, and then I let it all out. "Because, sir, I am still ass over tit in love with your daughter, and I need to be there so I can win her back."

"What if she doesn't want you back? You really hurt my princess and you're lucky I didn't hurt you for hurting her."

"Sir, I was eighteen and dumb back then. But now, I'm twenty-four. I'm still dumb, to an extent, but I still love your daughter just as much as I did back then." I'm met with silence. Pulling my phone from my ear, I look at the screen and it's still connected. "Sir?" I say into the line.

"She's on a Southwest flight getting in at ten fifty."

"Thank you, sir."

"Jameson," he says my name forcefully.

"Yes?"

"You hurt her again and I will—"

"Inject me with something that will kill me and it won't show up on an autopsy, allowing you to get away with murdering your daughter's boyfriend. I know the drill. I was lucky to escape your wrath once, but I won't hurt her again. Last time, I was young and stupid, but now I'm older and wiser. If she gives me another chance, I won't puck it up."

"Don't make me regret giving you her flight details."

"I won't, sir, I promise."

Hanging up from Dr. Knight, I look at the clock and realize I need to leave now if I want to be at the airport to meet Lex. Standing up, I pull my wallet out and throw some bills onto the table. Looking at my friends, I smile like a carnival clown. "I'm going to win back Lexi."

28

LEXI

Ugh, that was the longest flight in the history of flights. Well, it feels like it was, but in fact, the flight was on time and I got upgraded. Collecting my things, I exit the plane. Walking up the jetway, I sigh, ready for bed, but when I step into the terminal, I stumble because standing before me is Jameson with a bunch of yellow roses, my favorites.

Walking over, I stop before him and stare into his green eyes, processing the fact he's here. He hands me the flowers and I bring them to my nose. Closing my eyes, I breathe in the sweet smell. "Thank you," I mumble. And when I open them, he's the one staring now. "What are you doing here, Jameson?" I ask.

"You said you wanted to talk, so here I am."

"I did, but I didn't mean tonight." Silence falls between us. "How, how did you know what flight I was on?"

"I called your dad."

"You called my dad?"

He nods and nervously bites his lip.

"And he just gave you my flight details?"

"Well, I had to beg him and then when I got here, I had to buy a ticket to Ponce so I could get through security."

"You really bought a ticket to Ponce?"

"Yep, I hear it's nice there this time of year."

"I'll have to trust you because I have no fucking clue where Ponce is."

"Me neither," he confirms with a shrug and the two of us laugh … just like we used to. "I love your laugh," he says and when I stare at him, I feel all warm and fuzzy, but mixed with that is hesitation and hurt.

"Why are you here?" I ask him again.

"You wanted to talk and I …" He drifts off, shoving his hands into his pockets and looking unsure, all of a sudden.

"You what?"

"I want you, Lex. I've made it clear I want you back. I know I hurt you when we were eighteen, but I was dumb and scared and dumb."

"Being dumb is no excuse for obliterating my heart and that's what you did, Jameson."

"My name is JJ," he hisses.

"You haven't earned me calling you JJ. You broke me, Jameson. It took me a long time to accept you were gone. You know, I don't even remember my first year at USC because I was in this fog. I existed in body only because my spirit and soul had been crushed, but then one day, I realized I needed to move on. You had and if I continued living how I was, I'd end up resenting life. So I put all my memories of you into a box and I locked them away in the back of my mind. I pretended you didn't exist and got on with my life. I threw myself into my studies and became the person I am today. I guess I should thank you because I am living my dream, but I always envisioned living my dream with you by my side."

"And you can. I'm here now. Lex, baby, you're my first and last thought each and every day. I'm going to do whatever it takes to make you mine again, but make no mistake, Alexis Avery Knight, you will be mine again."

Staring at him, I process his words. I want to believe him, but that hurt from before is still there. "But what happens when the next opportunity is thrown at you? Will you just cast me aside again? Will I be a second thought? Again?"

"You are never a second thought, Lexi—"

"I want to believe you, I do, but I … I think I need to think of me. I wouldn't survive heartbreak like that again, so the best thing for my heart, and for me, is for me to walk away. And that's what I'm going to do. This time, I'm the one walking away."

Stepping into him, I kiss him on the cheek. "Goodbye, Jameson."

Without waiting for a reply, I move around him and head toward the exit.

He doesn't follow me and I don't know how I feel about that.

Resting my head against the back of the seat in the taxi, I close my eyes and wonder if I made a mistake just now. I meant what I said, I would not survive a heartbreak like that again … but what if he *doesn't* break my heart again?

"Gah," I groan, slamming my fist into the seat.

The taxi drops me off and I make my way up to my apartment. Dropping my things in the entryway, I text my mom and dad, letting them know I got home safely, and then I walk into the kitchen.

Pouring myself a glass of wine, I take a calming sip. Then I chug it back and pour another. Bending down, I grab a vase and pop my flowers into it. Bringing them to my nose, I breathe in the scent again. No one since him has bought me flowers, and I smile sadly at the thought.

With a sigh, I drop down onto my sofa. I'm just as confused now as I was before I went home. I know my dad says I need to forgive Jameson, but forgiving and giving a second chance are two very different things. Maybe, for now, I start with forgiving.

And because I'm a chicken, I text him.

LEXI

Hi, Jameson, it's me, Lexi.

I forgive you for what you did when we were eighteen and if you're open to it, I'd like to be friends. That's all I can offer right now.

I'm sorry it's not what you want, but you need to crawl before you can walk.

Throwing my phone onto the coffee table, I head into the bathroom to take a shower and rinse off all the plane germs and get ready for bed.

It's already after midnight and I need to be at the stadium bright and early in the morning.

Just as I'm about to climb into the shower, my phone pings with a text and I know if it's Mom or Dad and I don't reply, they'll send the police to do a welfare check … and I'm not joking. They did that. Once. When I was in California and in my Jameson fog.

Since I live alone, I walk into the living room naked and pick up my phone, but it's not from either of my parents. It's from Jameson.

Dropping down onto my sofa, I read his message.

JAMESON

I'll take friends for now, but, Lexi, I'm not
giving up on us. You and me, we will
happen. I lost you once and now that I
kinda sorta have you back, I'm never letting
you go again.

I reread his message, again and again. My fingers hover
over the screen as I contemplate what to reply with, but
when I still don't know what to write five minutes later, I
plop my phone down and finally take my shower.

Bringing my wine with me—classy, I know. I climb into
the stall with my wine and lean against the wall. The water
hits my chest and cascades down my body as I drink my
wine and think over the events from when I landed. Jameson
being there was totally romantic. I mean, he bought a ticket
to Ponce, for God's sake.

Finishing my wine, I lean out and pop the empty glass on
the vanity and then I wash myself. Once I'm clean, I hop out,
dry off, and pull my pajamas on. Then I climb into bed, but
sleep eludes me. I lie here and stare up at the ceiling. My
mind is racing right now, playing out all different scenarios
regarding Jameson and me.

Eventually, I drift off to sleep and I have a restless night,
dreaming, well, reliving that fateful day when my world was
turned upside down.

My alarm goes off the next morning and when I wake, I
don't feel refreshed at all. I was hoping my trip home would
reinvigorate me. Instead, it's left me more confused than
before I left.

Climbing out of bed, I go through the motions and get
ready for work. With a to-go coffee in hand, I pick up my
phone and see another text has come in from Jameson.
Swiping it open, I read.

JAMESON

FYI, Ponce is in Puerto Rico and one day,
we're going to go there … I hear it's nice

A laugh breaks free as I read his message. I know I walked away and left him at the airport last night. That was the most romantic thing anyone has ever done for me, but can I trust he won't hurt me again? One airport declaration, a ticket to Puerto Rico, and a bunch of flowers doesn't erase the past, but maybe it's the start of clearing the path for the future.

Our future.

Locking my door, I lean my head against the cool wood and sigh. I'm so pucking confused right now.

29

JJ

WELL, LAST NIGHT DIDN'T GO AS I PLANNED. HOWEVER, getting that message from her just as I was climbing into bed ignites hope in my chest that I can, in fact, win Lexi back. I've reread it a million times already this morning and each time a new plan formulates, but none of them feel like 'the one.' And because Lexi is *the one*, I need to come up with 'the' plan.

But what will win her over?

Lexi isn't a flowers and chocolates kind of girl. I need something big, but what?

"Dude, where's your head at this morning?" Kallen asks, shoving me in the shoulder.

"I'm here," I defend myself, but from the look Kal is giving me, he knows I'm full of shit. Hell, I know I'm full of shit. "Fine, it's Lexi."

"Well, no shit, I guessed that. What happened after your grand gesture last night?"

"Nothing happened. I bought a ticket to Ponce and—"

"Where the puck is Ponce?"

"Puerto Rico, but that's not the point."

He eyes me.

"To get through security, I needed a ticket, so I bought a ticket to Ponce and then I made my way to her gate."

"And she ignored you?"

"No, we spoke but—"

"She shot you down and now you're all brokenhearted and playing like shit."

"I'm not playing like shit," I scoff.

"But you are brokenhearted," Kal throws back at me. There's a smug look on his face and if I had the puck right now, I'd flick it at his smug face.

"I wouldn't say broken, but my ego did take a hit. I really thought showing up with flowers would win her back."

"Sorry to break it to you, but you need more than flowers and a ticket to Pontiac—"

"Ponce, it was to Ponce."

"Not the point." He furrows his brows. "We need rein-forcements and I think I know who can help."

"Who?"

"Chelsea. She's a girl. She'll be able to give insight into the female mind and give you the most perfect idea on how to win Lexi over."

"You think she'll want to help?" I ask, wondering if he's trying to help or just be a jackass.

"She will … and if she resists, I have a tongue and I know how to wield it."

"Gross, dude." I scrunch my face up at the thought. "I seriously do NOT want or need to picture that, but I would love the help. I need to pull out all the stops to win Lex back."

"That's the spirit. Now, let's get back to practice and after Coach kills us, we can work on winning your girl back."

With a new plan in place, I can focus once again and the rest of training flies by … then the hard work begins.

30
LEXI

Watching the guys on the ice is thrilling. They work together like a fine-tuned machine, and that includes Doucheman. When he's not being a douche, at least. At times, he's actually a great guy—but don't tell anyone I said that—and when he's in the zone, he's a phenomenal player.

"See you tomorrow," I call out to Doc as I walk past him in the corridor.

"Night, Lexi," he says, lifting his hand in a wave.

Stepping out of the stadium, the humidity of summer slams into me and I crash into a hard body. When I look up, I see a man. He looks familiar, but I can't place where I've seen him before.

"Can I help you?" I ask.

"I need to speak with Jay," he says. His eyes dart around the parking lot.

"I'm sorry, who?"

"Jay!" he shouts. "I need to speak to Jay."

"I don't know a Jay. Are you sure he works here?"

"Of course I'm sure. I'm not an idiot," he snarls and from the anger radiating off of him, panic starts to build.

"I'm sorry." I try again, "I don't know anyone by that name."

"I need to speak to Jay," he yells again, spittle forming at the side of his mouth. "I need to speak to Jay," he repeats.

Instinctively, I take a step back, but this angers the man and he steps closer and reaches for me. I take another step back, but I hit the door I just exited. The man grips my upper arm and squeezes. "I need to speak to Jay," he hisses again. "I need to speak to Jay."

"I don't know a Jay," I repeat. Tears begin to well in my eyes. I know I need to get away from this guy, but I'm frozen with fear right now. Closing my eyes, I take a deep breath and know what I need to do.

Opening them again, I strike.

Lifting my leg, I slam my heel onto his foot. He lets go of my arms and with everything I have, I shove the asshole and he falls to the pavement.

Turning around, I swing my bag over the door key card swipe and hope like hell it scans. Thankfully, it does.

Swinging the door open, I step back into the stadium and pull it shut behind me. Leaning back against the door, I'm breathing heavily. The tears that were welling in my eyes begin to flow down my cheeks as I slide to the ground.

My breathing is hurried and I know I need to calm down, but I can't control my breaths or the rapid beating of my heart.

Someone calls out my name, but it's all muffled. My focus is blurry and I can't see straight due to the avalanche of tears falling down my face. My chest is tight and breathing is becoming difficult.

"Lexi, baby, look at me," a deep voice says from above. I

try to lift my head to look toward where the voice is coming from, but my body has shut down. I'm once again frozen. "Lexi," they shout again.

Placing their hands on my cheeks, they ground me. Their touch is somewhat familiar and I lean into it, but my focus is still skewed. They repeat my name and add, "You're safe."

And I do feel safe.

On reflex, my arms wrap around them and I hold on for dear life. They embrace me in a comforting hug and again, a sense of déjà vu and familiarity washes over me as the fog I'm in begins to lift.

"I've got you," they repeat, rubbing my back soothingly.

Closing my eyes, I lean into the soft and warm chest, and I listen to them repeat, "I've got you. You're safe," over and over.

My heart rate is back to a steady thump and my breathing has returned to normal. That all-encompassing fear has passed and, finally, I feel safe and like me again.

Breathing in, my eyes fly open when the scent registers in my mind. I know who has me cocooned against them. Gently pushing on his chest, he loosens his grip and I lift my head. I stare up into the concerned eyes of Jameson James and behind him are Anton, Kallen, and Jett.

Being in his arms used to be my safe place and it seems, even though I despise him, his embrace is still a safe place to be. "Thank you," I whisper as I wiggle around and pull away from him.

"No need to thank me, but, Lex, what happened?"

Rapidly blinking at him, I process his question as memories of the man come crashing back into me. "There was a man. He … he was asking for someone who worked here, but I didn't recognize the name and then, then he grabbed me …" My eyes well with tears again as I recount what happened.

"He can't hurt you," Jameson says. Reaching over, he takes my hand and squeezes it before lacing his fingers with mine. He sits with me by the exit door while I break down again.

Mitch, the head of security at the stadium, comes over and I recount what went down. He assures me they will look into it. Rick, the owner of the Crushers and our assistant coach, offers me a driver to take me home.

"I'll do it," Jameson says.

"James, you have a practice bright and early tomorrow and you have the next game to focus on," Rick reminds him. He nods, but he looks at me to make sure I'm going to be okay.

"I'm fine, Jameson," I tell him. He winces when I use his full name and, to be honest, it felt weird calling him Jameson just now. "I'm going to go straight home, have a glass of wine and a bath, then I'm going to crawl into bed. I'm going to get a good night's sleep, and I'll be back here in the morning refreshed and ready to tackle whatever comes my way."

"Are you sure?" he asks me again.

Pulling my hand free from his, I reach up and cup his cheek. "Really, I'm fine now."

He nods and covers my hand on his cheek with his. "Message me when you get home."

"Yes, Dad," I deadpan and his lip lifts in that sexy way, and I find myself not wanting to leave.

"Your car is here," Rick's assistant says, interrupting us.

Rick steps in front of me while Jameson, Anton, Kallen, and Jett flank me on all sides.

We make our way over to the car and Rick opens the

door for me. "I'm glad you're safe, Lexi. Please use this service tomorrow as well. Can't have anything happen to our best PT in the lead up to the playoffs."

"Thank you, sir, but I'll be fine."

"No car, no work," he states matter-of-factly, reminding me of my dad when he's in protective mode.

With him not giving me much of a choice, I nod and smile. "Thank you, sir, I appreciate it." Then I look at the others. "And thank you all for the escort." Smiling at them, I climb into the car and before the driver pulls away, the rear door on the other side opens and Jameson climbs in.

"I'm just making sure you get home safely."

Nodding, I smile over at him and the driver pulls away and out into the afternoon traffic. New York traffic is crazy this afternoon and it takes nearly an hour to get to my apartment. Jameson and I don't utter a word the entire trip and, surprisingly, it's not awkward.

The driver comes to a stop outside my building. I thank him and then I look at Jameson. "Thank you for this afternoon." Before he can reply, I climb out and slam the door.

"Lexi," he calls out my name and I turn to look at him through the lowered window. "I'd do anything for you, Lex, anything, and I meant what I said the other week. You will be mine again. I'll bide my time until that happens, but make no mistake, Alexis Knight, you will be mine again."

He puts the window back up and the car pulls away.

Standing on the sidewalk, I watch it drive down the street and think over his words. Then I think about what my dad said and I begin to wonder if, maybe, I should open my heart to Jameson and the possibility of love again.

31

JJ

LEXI USED THE CAR SERVICE THAT RICK ARRANGED FOR HER TO get to the stadium this morning and when I heard she did, it made me happy. Security has been ramped up around the stadium and it's all everyone is talking about. Everyone is wondering who this Jay person is. It makes me think of my dad. He used to call me Jay, but it couldn't be him, could it?

The last I heard, he was working up in Alaska on the rigs there with some tramp named Delilah.

Seeing Lexi so frightened yesterday after the incident with that guy made my heart ache. Cementing just how much I really do love and care for her.

Coach pushed us hard again today, but it was a great session. Doucheman was even in a good mood. Word around the locker room is that a trade deal is in the works, so I'm guessing it's going well since he's being nice, well, Doucheman nice.

While I was in the shower, I dropped the soap and when I bent down to pick it up, I felt a twinge in my groin. Not wanting to aggravate it so close to the playoffs, I decide to see Lexi. Which is no hard feat, to be honest. Walking over to her treatment room, I knock on the door.

She spins around and her eyes light up when she sees me. "Hey, what's up?" she says with a smile, and I inwardly smile because I wasn't met with my usual scowl.

"My groin feels a lil' tweaky," I tell her.

"What were you doing when you noticed it?"

"Would you believe me if I told you nothing in particular?"

She eyes me.

"Seriously. It's been fine, the occasional twinge, but just now in the shower, I dropped the soap—"

"Hey, what you do in the shower is your business. I don't need the specifics," she teases and I laugh.

"Ha, you're so not funny. Anyway, as I was saying, I dropped the soap and when I bent down, it pulled, so I came here."

"Jump up on the table and I'll have a look."

Nodding, I walk into the room and climb up onto the table, wincing as I lift myself up. When I'm in position, I see Lexi looking at me, concern etched in her face. She walks over and closes the door. The click of the lock engaging echoes around the treatment room. She turns to face me and leans back against the door. I'm accosted with memories of pressing her into said door and kissing her the other week. And from the expression on her face, she's remembering too.

Shaking her head, she takes in a deep breath. "Okay, Jameson, I need you to explain the sensation when it happened and point to exactly where the pain occurred.

Spreading my legs wider, I shuffle forward and to the side to show her where, and I notice her gaze flicks to my dick. Holding back my smirk, I point to the spot where it hurts.

She walks over to the table and me, and when she places her hand on my thigh, a spark ignites. I will my cock not to react. I do not need to be sporting a woody while my ex-girl-friend turned physical therapist is assessing me. She moves her hand to my groin and when she presses down, I nearly leap off the table … any hardness of my dick dissipates and it's replaced with pain.

"I'm guessing that's the spot?"

"Mmmhmpf," I reply through clenched teeth, but then she does something and like she's a magician, all the pain is gone. "What the fuck? You … it's … I'm …"

"Yep," she replies with a smile.

"You're a miracle worker. Th—"

"Before you get all gushy, lie down. I want to try a few other things."

Nodding, I do as she asks. She bends me this way, pushes here, and finishes off with a massage that has me moaning and groaning, but when I stand up after she's finished, I don't feel a thing. "I reiterate, you're a freakin' miracle worker, Lex. I don't have any pain right now."

"Just doing my job," she nonchalantly replies, but it doesn't come across as cocky. She walks over to the sink in the corner and washes her hands.

"A job that you were made for," I honestly tell her.

She turns to face me, wiping her hands on a towel, and then she applies a raspberry and vanilla moisturizer. The scent is Lexi to a T—sweet and addictive.

Silence befalls us and as we stare at one another across the room, and something passes between us. It's like the hate she has for me is starting to evaporate. Breaking the silence, I say, "Thanks again, Lexi, I really appreciate it."

"Happy to help, Jameson."

She walks toward me and, surprising me, she pulls me in for a hug. Wrapping my arms around her, I hold on to her tightly. Apart from touching me while she's treating me or clinging to me in fear yesterday, this is the first time she's willingly touched me.

Breathing her in, a sense of belonging washes over me. She pulls back and smiles at me. Not wanting to jinx our perfect moment, I step around her and make my way to the door. Looking over my shoulder, I take her in and smile. Without another word, I exit her treatment room and close the door behind me.

Leaning against it, I drop my head back and take a deep breath.

"You good, James?" Brandon, the dickhead, asks me. I really despise this guy, as do most of us.

"Yeah, I am now. Lexi is a miracle worker," I tell him, rubbing salt into the wound. "She's done an amazing job with my groin and it's better than ever."

"Saint fucking Lexi." He sniggers. "She's probably blowing you all. That's why you fuckers all gush over her."

"What did you say?" I growl, pushing off the door and walking over to him.

"You heard me. That bitch thinks she's the fucking queen."

"That bitch, as you referred to her, is just doing her job. A job she was born to do. Maybe if you pulled your head out of your ass, you'd learn a thing or two from her."

"Like I'd want to learn from a chick who got a job because her dad is a doctor. She's probably fucking Michels—"

"That's enough," Doc Michels bellows from behind him. "Brandon, I've put up with your arrogance for months now, but that comment there crossed the line. Pack your things and get out. You're fired. You are no longer part of my team."

"But—"

"No, no buts, Brandon. I was hoping you'd change, but a leopard never changes its spots, and it's a shame because you have skill, but it's your attitude that brings you down."

Brandon stares at Doc in shock, then he shakes his head. "Fuck this," he snarls, throwing his hands in the air. He pulls off his ID badge and throws it to the floor before storming off, kicking a trash can on his way past.

"What's going on?" Lexi asks, stepping into the locker room.

"Brandon is no longer with us," Doc informs her. "It's going to be me and you until I can find a replacement."

"Ooookay," she draws the word out. "Just let me know what you need and I'll do it."

"Thanks, Lexi, I appreciate it." Doc turns and walks away, mumbling to himself about not needing this right now.

"What happened?" Lexi asks when Doc is gone.

"Just Brandon being his usual dick self and it finally caught up with him."

"I really hate that guy," she says.

"You and me both, but, to be honest, I'm glad he's gone." I catch sight of the clock on the wall. "Shit," I hiss. "I'm gonna be late." Looking at Lexi, I smile. "Thanks again for the rub. I'll see you tomorrow." Before she can say anything, I grab my things and hightail it out of there and hope like hell I make it in time to meet up with Kallen and Chelsea.

This morning, he told me he and I have a coffee date this afternoon with Chels at his place. Apparently, she's going to help me come up with a plan to win Lexi back. As each day passes and she isn't mine, that ache in my chest intensifies.

I need her like I need my next breath.

"Sooo, you want my help to win back the girl you screwed over when you were eighteen 'cause you were a puckhead?" Chelsea states. She has one hand on her hip and said hip is cocked to the side. She's staring intently at me and it reminds me of Coach, her dad, when he's in the zone … minus the hip cock because David Maxwell *does not* cock his hip. For someone so quiet, I'm quaking in my boots right now.

"I'm open to suggestions," I tell her.

"Do you promise to do as I say and name your firstborn after me?"

"Chels," Kallen growls, "he's naming his firstborn after me. You can't take that from me."

"Well, he and Lexi will just have to have boy and girl twins and they can be named after us."

"How about I get the girl first, then we can talk about it … but for the record, Lexi and I will be naming our kids Ashley and Porter. We decided that when we were seventeen." My mind drifts back to that night …

… It's the monthly barbecue. Lexi and I are sitting on the sofa in the family room while Juno plays in the background. A thunderstorm came out of nowhere and it was a mad dash inside. The

adults are all in the kitchen and dining room, laughing and drinking, and us kids are in here watching a movie.

"That's not a newborn," Lexi voices, pointing at the screen.

"And how do you know what a newborn looks like?"

"I have two younger siblings," she throws back at me.

"And you were there when they were handed to your mom? Still covered in the baby jelly goo?"

"Well, no, but when I did go and visit, they did NOT look like that." She wiggles her finger at the screen again.

"Guess we will find out for sure when I knock you up."

"Not for many years yet. You need to shine in the NHL and I want to pave my way as a physical therapist."

"Why can't we do both?" I ask her.

"Well, I guess we could, but Ashley and Porter *will not be raised by nannies."*

"Ashley and Porter, *huh?"*

"Yep, why, don't you like our kids' names?"

"I love them, just like I love you."

"Love you too, JJ." She leans over and kisses me.

"Daaaaaaad," Pepper shouts, "they're kissing again."

"What are you laughing at?"

"Just remembering the day Lexi and I agreed on our kids' names." With that memory fresh in my mind, I turn my attention to Chelsea. "Okay, Chels, hit me up with this plan."

She explains her idea and the more she talks, the more excited I get. It's time to win my girl back.

32

LEXI

...mid-February

WITH BRANDON NO LONGER ON THE TEAM, MY DAYS ARE BUSIER than ever and I love every minute of it. I'm cleaning up my room when there's a knock on my door. Looking over my shoulder, I see Chelsea standing there. "Hey, girl, what's up?"

"You're needed down on the ice," she tells me.

"Yep, sure, is everything okay?"

"Perfect," she sings, smiling brightly.

Walking over to her, she links her arm with mine and rather than heading the usual way to the ice, she leads me out of the dressing room and we enter through the gates the spectators use.

"What's going on?" I ask her because the lights in the stadium are low and Katy Perry's "The One That Got Away" is playing over the speakers. Chels covers my eyes. "What are you doing?"

"Just go with it," she states, not giving me a chance to refute.

Blindly—literally—I follow her and then we come to a stop. "I'm going to uncover your eyes, Lexi, but you need to keep them closed. You'll know when to open them."

"Okay," I tell her.

She removes her hands and like I promised, I keep my eyes closed. She squeezes my hand and whispers something that sounds like "He's a keeper," and then I feel her walk away.

Impatiently, I wait with my eyes closed.

The chill from the ice causes goose bumps to prickle my skin. My heart is racing and the longer I stand here with my eyes closed, the more nervous I become. Then I hear a voice murmur, "Open your eyes."

Opening my eyes, they widen as I take in the scene before me. There in the middle of the ice rink is Jameson. He's standing next to a scene straight out of a movie. There's a blanket on the ice decked out with beanbags and pillows, reminding me of the treehouse back home. Behind him are Anton, Kallen, Jett, and a few of the other guys. They start clicking their fingers and then a cappella style, they start singing "Back for Good" by Take That.

From his position on the ice, Jameson outstretches his hand and silently beckons me forward. Without even thinking about it, I place one foot in front of the other and make my way down the rest of the grandstand and out onto the ice.

Carefully, I shuffle over to Jameson and come to a stop in front of him. "Hi," I nervously whisper.

"Hi, yourself," he replies, tucking a strand of loose hair behind my ear.

"What's all this?" I wave my hand over the setup behind him.

"I wanted to recreate our first moment in the treehouse, but it's hard to find a treehouse in New York, so I went with the next best option, my second happy place."

"And where's your first happy place?"

"Wherever you are."

"Jame—"

"No, Lexi. No more Jameson, it's JJ. I've always been JJ and you've always been Lex. I know I fucked it all up when we were eighteen, but I promise you, not a day has gone by that I have not thought about you. Do I regret what I did? Yes and no. No because it allowed you to follow your dreams and seeing you now, living your dream, it's made all the hurt worth it." He pauses and takes a deep breath. "Please know, pushing you away was the hardest thing I ever had to do, but I did it for you. I love you, Alexis Knight. I. Love. You and I want you back. For good. Lex, I—"

I press my finger to his lips, shushing him. "I...I." I start to shake my head, but then Dad's words suddenly play in my mind, *Don't look back in anger, Lex. Life's too short to hold grudges.* Even when I hated him, I also loved him and I realize in this moment that I always will. Jameson James is my endgame. "Fuck it," I mumble. "I love you too, JJ. I always have and I always will." Gripping his cheeks in my palms, I lean forward and press my lips to his. I kiss him with everything I have because he is my everything. He slides his arms around my waist, pulling me into him and deepening the kiss.

Breaking apart, he rests his forehead against mine. "Lex, you've been my heart since I was sixteen, and I promise I will never hurt you again."

"JJ, that's the past. It happened and, yes, it sucked big,

hairy donkey dicks, but it got us to this moment, so let's focus on the now and our future."

"I like the sound of that." He covers my mouth with his. He taps my ass and I jump up, wrapping my legs around his waist. As we stand here kissing, with the guys wrapping up their song, everything in the world feels right again and now that I have him back, I'm never letting him go.

33

JJ

KISSING LEXI IS JUST AS AMAZING AS I REMEMBER. "I MISSED kissing you," I utter against her lips.

"Mmmhmpf," she mumbles, not pulling away from the kiss.

The guys finish singing and I can hear them shuffling away. I owe them big for doing that for me, but it helped me win Lexi, so any payment they request will be worth it.

When I know we're alone, I lower Lexi down to the makeshift bed and cover her body with mine. Cocooning her underneath me, I continue to kiss her. My tongue plunges in and out of her mouth. It reminds me of our first kiss in her treehouse when we were sixteen.

Breaking the kiss, I stare down at Lex. Her cheeks are flushed. Her lips swollen from our kiss. She stares up at me. "This reminds me of our first kiss," she whispers.

"It's as if you're in my mind. I was just thinking that."

"Except this time, we don't have my sister to snitch on us to my dad."

"No, this time, it's your coach telling you to get your ass off the ice and take it elsewhere."

Both our eyes widen and when I look up, I see Coach Maxwell and Rick standing over by the bench. Both have their arms crossed, but both are sporting smiles.

"Seems you owe me fifty dollar bucks," Rick gloats to Coach, bumping his shoulder before he holds out his hand for his winnings.

"What the hell is a dollar buck?" Coach asks, confusion written all over his face, but he grabs his wallet and hands over a fifty.

"The currency in *Bluey*," Rick and I say at the same time.

"You watch *Bluey*?" Lexi asks me just as Coach growls, "What the puck is *Bluey*?"

How he doesn't know what *Bluey* is is an atrocity, but before I can tell Coach about the wonders of *Bluey*, Rick beats me to it. "Dave, it's an amazing cartoon out of Australia. Some episodes are heartwarming, and some are sad, but they always end with a message that leaves the viewer feeling good and with a positive outlook."

"Couldn't have summed it up better myself, Rick," I tell him.

"Why don't you and Ness come over this weekend? The ladies can catch up and the kids and I can fill you in on the wonders of *Bluey*."

"Can't believe I'm agreeing to come over to your place to watch a cartoon, but sure, we'll be there." We all chuckle at his answer. "Come on, let's get out of here. I need a beer." Rick nods and then looks back at Lex and me. "And you two." He points toward us and flicks his finger back and forth. "Glad you finally got your shit together."

The two of them walk away and Rick begins explaining the wonder that is *Bluey*.

"Guess we should take this elsewhere?" Lexi says.

"Yep," I reply, once again letting the 'p' pop. "Your place or mine?" I ask her.

"What did you have planned for after this?"

"I, umm, shit, I didn't think past that."

"Take her back to your place," a feminine voice calls out from the tunnel.

"Chels, get back here," Kallen hisses. "Leave them alone."

"I will. Now they know where to go." She pokes her head out, covering her eyes. "And for the record, I'm so pucking happy you two are together. We will double date soon. K. Bye," she calls out and then she's gone. "Kallen," she squeals and then there's the sound of a hand landing on an ass. "Put me down," she growls and then she moans, causing Lexi and me to laugh.

"Those two are disgustingly in love," Lexi says.

"Maybe we need to give them a run for their money."

"Please," she scoffs, "we'd win hands down. We were prom king and queen, after all."

"Yes, we were," I agree. "What do you say we pack this up and head back to my place?"

"I'd like that, but first …"

"First what?"

"You need to kiss me again. We have almost five years' worth of kisses to catch up on."

"Your kiss is my command."

She chuckles at my corny joke, but I muffle her laugh when I cover her mouth with mine. The kiss heats up pretty quickly, our hands roaming each other's bodies. She palms my dick and I nearly come in my pants there and then. Hey, sue me, it's been a while and Lexi knows how to play my body. No one brings me pleasure like Lexi Knight does.

Breaking the kiss, I stare down at her. "Lex, as much as I want to take that next step here and now, I don't want it to be on the ice where anyone could walk in. We need to put the brakes on, pack this shit up, and get to my place. Ohhh, and just so you know, once we're inside, you won't be leaving for the next twenty-four hours, and when you do, you won't be able to walk properly."

"Game on," she throws back at me.

With one more hot and heavy make-out session, we reluctantly break apart and pack up. Grabbing our things, I lace my fingers with hers and we exit the stadium and make our way to my apartment.

The atmosphere in the taxi is heated and as soon as the door to my place clicks closed, it's just like Lexi said, it's game on.

34
LEXI

As soon as the door to JJ's place closes, things become frantic.

It's as if now that we are hidden away, all our inner desires and wants have bubbled to the surface and there's no stopping us.

JJ does that sexy move where he grabs his shirt at the base of his neck and pulls it off, leaving him in just his jeans. He lifts his hand to his button and I find myself standing here ogling him. Biting my lips, my gaze roams over his upper torso. Ridge after ridge forms his abs and don't get me started on his V muscle that makes women—hello, I'm women—go gaga.

It's toned.

It's defined.

And it leads to what I remember is a beautiful dick. Well, as beautiful as a dick can be, 'cause let's be honest, they are not the most attractive of appendages.

"Like what you see?" he asks, his tone cheeky, which matches the sexy smirk on his face.

"Very much so. It's been a long time since I've seen you naked."

"I'm not naked yet," he throws back at me and I can't help but laugh.

"Well, get to it then."

With a nod, he pops the button open and lowers his fly. With his eyes locked on mine, he hooks his fingers into his waistband and in one fell swoop removes both his jeans and his boxer briefs. But in his haste, he forgot he's still wearing his shoes and he struggles to remove them completely.

Dropping to my knees before him, I untie the laces on each boot and, one by one, I tug them off.

JJ kicks off his underwear and jeans, leaving him gloriously naked before me. From this position, it leaves me at dick height. The tip glistens with precum and I lick my lips. Then like a moth to a flame, I lean forward and swipe my tongue over the tip. Circling around, his arousal coats my tongue.

"Lex," he groans my name from above and it turns into a moan when I suck his shaft into my mouth.

Up and down I bob my head, sucking him in deeper each time. The tip hits the back of my throat and I gag a little. Relaxing my throat, I take him all the way in, earning myself another guttural moan. He slides his hands into my hair, the strands slipping between his fingers.

Gripping my head, he guides me up and down. Each time I pull out, I circle my tongue over the tip before sucking him back in.

"Lex, babe," he hisses, "you keep that up and I'm gonna come."

With my eyes locked on his, I waggle my eyebrows and

increase the pressure of my suction, but before he gets to his release, he pulls out. "The first time I come with you after almost five years will not be down your throat." He cups my cheek in his palm and runs the pad of his thumb over my lower lip. "You deserve to be worshipped, Lexi Knight, and that's exactly what I'm going to do."

He scoops me up into his arms and carries me through his apartment and into his bedroom. Placing me on my feet at the end of his bed, his gaze roams over me. My skin sizzles from the intensity of his stare. Quickly, I kick off my sneakers, not bothering with undoing the laces. My breathing is shallow and my heart is erratically beating. With his eyes locked on mine, he grips the hem of my Crushers shirt and lifts it over my head. He makes quick work of removing my bra and when my tits spring free, he lowers his head and sucks on my nipple.

My head drops back and I give myself over to the sensation of his lips on me. When he stops, I cry out at the loss, but when he drops to his knees before me and begins to trail kisses down my abdomen, I don't mind the loss so much now. He circles his tongue in and around my belly button. No one has done that to me before and I moan like a wanton hussy at the sensation. He kisses down to the band of my leggings before he hooks his fingers in the top and tugs them down my legs.

Discarding them to the side, he leans forward and kisses my pussy through my panties. The material is soaked from my arousal.

JJ breathes in. "I missed your smell," he says before kissing my mound again.

"JJ, please," I pant.

"Please what?"

"Just please," I reply.

My brain isn't braining right now. I can't form the words needed to tell him what I want, but as if he's in my brain, he does exactly what I want. He pushes the material of my panties to the side and slides his tongue between my folds.

"Yes," I mewl. It turns into a porn-worthy moan when he circles his tongue over my clit and presses a finger into me. "Yes," I pant.

Lifting my hands, I massage my boobs as he fingers and sucks me.

I'm close to the edge.

So close to my release when it all stops.

He removes his fingers and face, and when I look down at him, his chin is glistening from my arousal and he's never looked more beautiful.

"Why did you stop?"

"As I said, the first time we come, it won't be with our mouths. Now, Lex, get on the bed and let me fuck you."

35

JJ

Lexi stands up, but before she climbs onto the bed like I asked, she grips my cheeks in her palms and kisses me. It's hurried and frenzied but also perfect in every way. Her tongue slips into my mouth. Mine slips into hers. Sliding my hands around her waist, I pull her into me, her breasts smashing against my chest as we make out.

She pulls back and with her puffy lips and flushed complexion, I'm in awe over her beauty. She steps back and climbs onto the bed. She crawls up the mattress, giving me a view of her delectable ass. In a sexy move, she rolls to her back and lies on my pillows. She spreads her legs and with her eyes locked on mine, she trails her fingertip down her sternum and over her abdomen. Lower and lower her finger goes, and I intently watch as she slips it between her folds and presses it into her. She wantonly moans and as I watch her finger herself, I grip my shaft and begin to stroke. My dick is rock-hard and I cannot wait to sink myself balls deep inside of her.

With her free hand, she beckons me forward with her forefinger. Resting one knee on the mattress, I lower myself down and crawl up her body. Gripping her ankle, I kiss the inside of her foot and begin to pepper kisses up her legs. Alternating between kissing and licking, I bypass her pussy and keep kissing upward. When I reach her breasts, I take a few moments to lave the girls with the attention they deserve.

Once Lex is writhing in pleasure beneath me, I continue my path upward.

Licking up the column of her neck, I nip and suck her jawline before I finally reach her lips. Covering her mouth with mine, I kiss her deeply. I kiss her like it's our last kiss and when she moans into my mouth, I know it's time.

Severing the connection, I stare down at the woman who owns me, heart and soul.

"Please, JJ," she whispers.

Nodding, I push myself upright and grip my shaft. Giving it a few strokes, I line it up at her entrance and with my eyes locked on her pussy, I press inside.

It feels like coming home.

"Unnugggh," I groan as I push deeper into her and when I'm fully seated, I lift my gaze to hers. Her eyes are full of lust. Her cheeks and chest are that shade of arousal pink and her chest heaves.

"Please, JJ," she breathlessly asks. She doesn't say anything else, but I know what she's asking. Moving back and forth, I slide in and out of her wet channel. Her pussy clenches my dick and if she keeps that up, I won't last long, but I refuse to come before her. Slipping my hand between us, I find her clit and press down on her sensitive bundle of nerves.

"Yes. Yes. Yes," she chants, throwing her head back as the

pleasure builds. "I'm close," she pants and I internally scream for joy because I'm close to the edge.

Pressing down on her clit again, I pinch it and she screams my name, drawing out the last J for several seconds as her climax detonates. Seeing her come undone beneath me is pure bliss, and it's what I need. My body stiffens and falls down on top of her as I come. I come harder than I ever have before, releasing my seed inside of her.

Nuzzling into her neck, I ride out my release and then I sit up abruptly. "Shit," I hiss. "We didn't use protection."

"I'm clean and on the pill," she quickly replies.

"Me too," I tell her.

"You're on the pill too?" she questions with a playful grin on her face.

Digging my fingers into her side, I shake my head. "Hardy har har. You know what I mean."

"I do and I trust you, but we will just have to remember to be more careful in the future."

"Future," I repeat. "I like that word and, Lexi, now that I have you back, any and all decisions regarding our future will be made together."

"Together," she repeats. "I like that we're together again. *Together*, we will make any decisions regarding *our* future."

Leaning down, I cover her mouth for another kiss. I will never tire of kissing this woman. With a strength I didn't know she possessed, she flips us over so she's straddling me. Resting her palms on my chest, I notice her gaze is once again heated. "I know we just talked about protection, but, Lex, I umm, I don't have any."

"Really?" she questions.

"Really. I told you I haven't slept with anyone since you came back and it's not like I had a stockpile of them. I'm not Doucheman."

She snorts. "Well, let's take this to the shower and get cleaned up. Then we can head out for a bite to eat and on the way back here, we can get a stockpile happening."

"Sounds like a plan to me, but when we get back, I'd like us to start in this position. Because like this I can see your glorious tits bounce as you ride me and I can lie here and watch you fall apart on my dick."

"So you want me to do all the work while you lie back and stare at these." She cups her breasts and I steadfastly watch as she pushes them together. "Is that what you're saying?"

"For the next time, yes, but then, once you've come riding me, we will swap positions and I will fuck you hard and fast. And the time after that, I'm going to press you against the window so all of downtown can see me fucking you. Then I'll bend you over the edge of the bed and fuck you from behind."

"That's a lot of fucking. We better buy a bulk pack then."

"Babe, I will buy the entire fucking condom section because I have almost five years of fucking to catch up on.'

"Well then, I guess we better get started." She presses her finger to my lips when I go to state that we don't have any protection. "And before you say anything about protection, you're going to pull out and paint me with your cum."

A smile appears on my face and I just nod. Sliding my hands behind my head, I waggle my eyebrows at her. "Well, have at it."

36

LEXI

"Well, have at it," he states ... and have at it I do.

Lifting myself up, I line his cock up with my entrance, then I slide down his shaft until I'm fully seated. With my eyes locked on his, I begin to ride him. Cupping my breasts, I stare at him as I pinch my nipples between my fingertips. He lifts his hands and pushes mine aside. His large palms cup my tits, and he begins to massage and fondle them. Rolling my nipples between his fingers, my head drops back and I moan. Hoisting himself up, he takes one of my stiff peaks into his mouth, gently biting the nub before sucking and kissing the pain away.

"Yes," I mewl as he repeats the action over and over.

Massage.

Bite.

Kiss.

Repeat.

The feeling of his hands on my breasts is exquisite and the sounds coming from my lips are carnal. Anyone listening will know exactly what we're up to and I don't care. A zombie attack could break out and I wouldn't even notice. Never have I felt pleasure like this with another man. Jameson James knows how to play my body just as well as he can wield a stick and puck on the ice. He's drawing out every ounce of pleasure from deep within my soul.

After he laves the girls with attention, he slides his arms around my waist and I wrap mine around his shoulders. Within our embrace, we begin to rock back and forth, his cock slamming in and out of me.

In this position, I stare into his green eyes and I can see deep into his soul. I see nothing but love reflecting back at me.

That tingly feeling begins to develop low in my belly.

Leaning forward, he covers my mouth with his. Our tongues slip and slide in and out of each other's mouths in sync with his dick and my vagina. The rhythm is methodical, hitting *that* spot with each thrust of our hips.

My body begins to tighten and out of nowhere, my insides begin to quiver and I explode. The most intense orgasm unleashes and I turn feral. Throwing my head back, I cry out, "Fuuuuuuuuuuuuuuuuuuuck," as the orgasm that won't end continues to hold me in its grip.

My pussy strangles his cock and it causes him to come. At the last second, he quickly pulls out and sprays my abdomen with his release.

"We really need to get condoms because that would have been so much better if I finished inside of you," he breathlessly pants.

"Mmmhmpf," is all I can manage. I entered a subspace with my climax and I don't know what's up and what's down right now.

JJ falls to the mattress and since I'm straddling him, I fall with him. His release squishes between us, but I'm too exhausted to care. Lying on top of him, a smile graces my face. "I missed this," I whisper into his neck.

"I missed everything about you, Lex, and now that I have you back in my arms and bed, I'm never letting you go. Never again will I make a bonehead decision on my own. Where you go, I go."

Raising my head, I stare down at him and nod. "Where you go, I go."

"And right now, I say we go to the shower and get cleaned up. Then I'll order us some dinner and once I've fed you, we'll take a walk and get some condoms. Then once I've had my fill of you, we'll drift off to sleep in each other's arms and when we wake up, we can do it all again."

"I like that plan."

After fucking in the shower and a blow job while we waited for our food to arrive, we are finally eating our Chinese take-out. Rather than sitting in his kitchen, we're sitting crossed-legged on the living room floor, eating off the coffee table.

"Do you remember that time your dad caught us on the side of your house during one of the family barbecues?" JJ asks as I shove another eggroll into my mouth.

"Yes," I say with a laugh after swallowing, "I thought he was going to kill you."

"I did too. Your dad is a scary guy, but you saved my imminent death by saying lollipop."

"Ahhh, yes, lollipop."

"What's up with that?" he asks me and all I can do is laugh.

All these years later and I have never told that story to anyone. Well, except for Pepper. I mean, who wants to admit they've seen their parents getting down and dirty in the kitchen with a "Cress-flavored" lollipop? Exactly, no one, but like any good daughter, I will use it to my advantage if and when I need to get out of trouble.

"Are you ever going to tell me the specifics?"

"You really want to know?"

He nods.

"Are you sure? Because once I tell you, there's no going back."

"It can't be that bad," he states. "Just tell me."

"Okay, but just remember, you asked." So I recount the kitchen scene with the details I left out, and now, he too is traumatized.

"Oh My God," he barks. "I've eaten off that island. Hell, we made gnocchi on that countertop."

"How do you think I feel? I've had to look at that countertop and them AAAAAND the lollipop jar ever since, but it is the best 'get out of jail free' card."

"You know, you just ruined lollipops for me forever now."

"Hey," I refute, "I warned you, but for what it's worth, now we can suffer in silence together."

"There's that word again."

"What word?" I furrow my brows in confusion as I steal some of his sweet and sour pork.

"Together. It's my new favorite word."

"Is that so?" I ask him.

"Yep," he states matter-of-factly.

"For what it's worth, it's my new favorite word too, but you know what else I love?"

"Lollipops," he cheekily states.

"Hardy har har, no, I was referring to sleep. Copious rounds of sex and a blow job followed by Chinese makes me sleepy, so I better get going."

"Orrrrrr you can stay the night," he suggests. "To sleep," he quickly tacks on.

"I'd like that," I tell him.

We pack up the leftovers and flick off the lights. Walking into his room, he hands me a shirt of his, and I change out of my clothes and pull the tee over my head. Lifting the material to my nose, I close my eyes and breathe in.

"Did you just sniff my shirt?"

"Mmmhmpf," I reply with a nod. "I missed your scent."

"I missed everything about you," he states before pulling me into his chest and hugging me.

Placing his fingers under my chin, he lifts my head up and places a kiss on my lips. It starts out soft and gentle, but it quickly turns heated. "Lex," he murmurs against my lips. "I never stopped loving you."

Pulling my head back, I smile. "Deep down, I don't think I ever stopped loving you either." And I follow it up with a yawn.

"Come on." He tugs on my hand and guides me to the bed. Pulling the duvet back, I climb in and he covers me up. Bending down, he kisses me on the forehead and walks around to his side. He does that sexy one-handed shirt removal thing again and I moan at the sight.

"You right there objectifying me?"

"Yep," I state, letting the 'p' pop. "It's not my fault I find it sexy when you do that."

"Taking my shirt off is sexy?"

"Yes, for two reasons. One, I get to stare at your wash-board abs. And two, I get to watch your arms flex as you pull your shirt over your head, showing me said abs from point one."

He lifts up the blanket on his side and climbs in. We both roll to our sides, facing one another. Lifting my hand, I run my fingers through his hair. "Is this a dream?"

"It's real, Lex, as real as can be."

"I'm scared when I wake up in the morning, this will have all been a dream and we aren't really back together."

"I assure you, it's real and now that I have you back, I'm never letting you go. I love you, Lex."

"I love you too, JJ."

He pulls me into him and places a kiss on my head. Lying here in bed with him is the happiest I've been in a very long time and nothing can tear me down.

37

JJ

"AGAIN," COACH SHOUTS, AS WE START ON OUR NEXT deceleration suicide. Once that's completed, Coach calls time on the session and we all shuffle off the ice and into the locker room.

Sitting in front of my stall, I rest my elbows on my knees and drink some water. That was a tough session and I was a little sluggish today due to the events of the last few days, but I wouldn't change a thing. Having Lexi back in my life is all that matters … and maybe winning the Cup later this year. Winning that, as well as the girl, would make this the best year ever.

"Great session today, everyone," Coach says when he rejoins us. "Rest up and I'll see you back here bright and early tomorrow for the game against the Fireflies. We may be back at the top of the leaderboard, but that doesn't mean we can afford to slack off."

"Yes, Coach," we all repeat.

He leaves and we all begin to chat. The guys probe me on what happened the other night, but I'm tight-lipped on the specifics. These guys are bigger gossips than the WAGs, aka the wives and girlfriends. And our captain, Anton, is the biggest gossip of them all.

Stripping off, I wrap my towel around my waist and head toward the showers. Stepping under the spray, I start singing "Wonderwall" by Oasis and soon all of us are singing away. When we finish, a single slow clap echoes around the showers.

"Thank fuck I won't have to put up with this shit next season," Doucheman states. No sooner has he finished his rant and Anton starts to sing "I'm Gonna Be (500 Miles)" by The Proclaimers, and soon the rest of us join in too.

Doucheman growls, "Assholes," and then storms out of the showers.

For the next ten minutes, we rotate through different karaoke songs and when I walk back to my locker in nothing but my towel, I see Lexi enter the dressing room.

"Hey, hey, pretty lady," I call out, garnering her attention.

"Hey," she replies with a smile and walks over to me. "Let me guess, you started that just now."

"What can I say, I'm a great singer."

"You keep telling yourself that, James. You keep telling yourself that." She looks around quickly and when she sees it's just us, she leans in and kisses me. I have this fantasy of the two of us in here. We fuck against the side of the lockers and then we take a shower together and, well, you can guess what I want to happen while we are wet and naked. "How's the groin today? You had, umm, quite the workout over the last few days."

"Yeah, I did." I waggle my eyebrows at her as memories of fucking her against the windows of my apartment play back in my mind. "But it's good. I have an amazing PT and a hotter than hot girlfriend looking after me."

"Hotter than hot, hey? Am I going to have to take out the competition?" She pretends to push her imaginary sleeves up and raise her fists into a fighting pose, holding her hands completely wrong.

"You fight like that and you'll hurt yourself more than your opponent. You need to hold your fist like this." Lifting my hands up, I show her how to hold her hands, tucking the thumbs in to keep them safe. "You hit like you had your hands and you'll break something."

"How do you know how to fight? You in some kind of club?"

"First rule of fight club—"

"We don't talk about fight club," we both say in unison.

Back when we first started dating, we watched it on repeat and if you ask me, that twist at the end, is one of the best twists in cinematic history.

"We should watch that movie tonight," I tell her as I drop my towel and pull on my boxer briefs. I don't miss the fact that like my towel, Lex drops her gaze too.

"Will there be popcorn?"

"Of course. It's not a movie without popcorn."

"What movie are we watching?" Anton asks, slinging his arm around my neck. Looking over my shoulder, I see that the rest of the guys are here now. I hadn't even realized they'd returned from the shower.

"*Fight Club*—"

"I love that movie," Kallen states. "Best twist ever."

"Right?" Anton nods in agreement. "I did not see that one coming, but then again, I generally miss most twists. Hell, I missed Hans being the bad guy in *Frozen*."

"How did you miss that?" Lexi asks him.

"Probably the same way I missed the signs that Mel wanted a divorce."

Silence falls over the room. We all knew something was going on, but this? I don't think any of us expected that.

"Shit, man," I say, "that's rough."

"It is what it is," he nonchalantly says, but you can tell he's bummed.

"My place at seven," I tell everyone.

Anton smiles, an Anton this-is-why-I-got-a-toothpaste-commercial smile, and I know I made the right choice inviting everyone over. As much as I would love to spend tonight alone with Lex, our teammate needs us right now.

I finish getting changed and then I swing by Lexi's treatment room. "You coming to movie night?"

"Yep." She nods. "Chelsea and I are going to head over when we finish here. She roped me into doing a spotlight on myself."

"And you'll be the sexiest spotlight so far."

"You need your eyes tested, James."

"My eyesight is fine, as are you."

"That was totally corny."

"Yeah, it was, wasn't it?"

"Lucky for you, I like corn … and you."

"Yeah, you do. What's not to love?"

She shakes her head at me. We say our goodbyes and I head out. On my way home, I stop by the grocery store to grabs snacks and popcorn for an impromptu team movie night … and hopefully another sleepover with my girlfriend.

Practice today was brutal due to the late night after our impromptu team movie night. I'm getting too old to stay up late watching movies and binge eating popcorn and peanut butter cups—Shhhh, don't tell our coaches or nutritionist about that.

Today also happens to be my twenty-fifth birthday. Since I was born on a leap year, and today is the twenty-ninth of February, I get to celebrate my day of birth on the actual day. And because it doesn't happen often, Lex has gone over and above for me. The celebrations all started with me waking up with Lexi's lips wrapped around my cock and I have to say, birthday blow jobs are fucking awesome.

When I got to the stadium, my stall had been decorated with balloons and streamers. When I walked into the locker room—late, thanks to my birthday BJ—the guys all sang me "Happy Birthday." Then Coach came over and gave me the team birthday cape to wear during practice. It's ugly as all hell, but it does give you a free pass since it's your birthday.

After our morning skate, we head into the gym for a cardio session. After pumping iron for a few hours, as a team, we all head to a restaurant of my choosing for lunch. I'm in the mood for sushi, so we head to Sushi Samurai before heading back to the stadium for a weights session, but when we get back to the stadium, instead of a weights session, we attend my surprise birthday party.

Lexi and Chelsea put together a surprise party and there's a surprise guest, my mom. "Mom!" I shout when I see her. Racing over to her, I wrap my arms around her and swing her around. "What are you doing here?"

"It's my baby boy's birthday. Where else would I be? I haven't missed one yet and I wasn't going to start now. Happy Birthday, JJ." She hugs me again and I see Lexi over her shoulder, smiling brightly at me.

"Thanks, Mom, I'm so glad you're here."

A massive cake in the shape of a hockey puck arrives with twenty-five candles on it. Everyone sings me "Happy Birthday," and then Anton calculates how *old* I actually am since I, technically, only get a birthday every four years. FYI, I'm officially six, according to Anton, and he has now coined me the nickname, Lil' Chirp ... Thankfully, it's only him calling me Lil' Chirp, so I think it will be a fleeting nickname.

The party is winding down and there are only a few people left. Lexi comes over and slides her arm around my waist and sidles up to me. "You have a good birthday?"

"The best. Thank you ... thank you and for getting my mom here too. How will I ever repay you?" I waggle my eyebrows at her.

"With your mom in the next room, I don't think that will happen. Plus, I'm going to stay at my place tonight. Give you and Lisa a few nights together. I know she misses you."

"But I'll miss you." I pout like a baby.

"You'll be fine. I'm sure your mom is going to spoil you and, no doubt, she'll cook all your favorite meals, and then stock your freezer up with said meals too."

"Yeah, she will," I boast. "My mom loves me."

"And I love you too, JJ, if that counts."

"Ohhh, it definitely does. Lex, as I've said before, I've loved you since I was sixteen years old and saw your head pop up in your treehouse, and I will continue loving you until I take my last breath."

"You can dial back the swoon. You've already got me."

"I will never dial it back. I've lived without you knowing what I really feel and I never want to feel that again." I mean that, all those years without Lexi were hard. Not a day went by that I didn't think about her and now that she's back, I will love and cherish her forever. It's the least I can do for being a puckhead.

38

LEXI

… a few weeks later

TODAY, ACTUALLY THE WHOLE WEEK, HAS BEEN LONG AND taxing. Thankfully, the guys have a rare three days off, meaning I also get a few days off, so tonight I'm catching up with my girl, Bella.

I'm meeting her for dinner and drinks at a little bistro she found on Central Park West that, in her words, is 'ah-freakin-may-zing' and we have to go there. It's kind of out of the way, but it's been ages since I've seen her, and she's been talking up their cocktails for weeks now, so tonight is the night.

Chelsea was going to join us but decided last minute to take a rain check. Personally, I think it was code for 'spend the night with Kallen and fuck his brains out.' Those two can't keep their hands off one another … or his dick out of her vagina. I don't know how many times I've caught them in a compromising position in the locker room. They're game if you ask me. What if I was her dad?

"Night, Doc," I call out as I walk past his room.

"Night, Lex, see you in a few days' time and try to rest. I know what you're like."

Nodding, I laugh and with a wave goodbye, I make my way through the locker room toward the exit. It's so quiet in here when the guys aren't here joking around and JJ isn't singing something off-key. Like golf, he sucks at singing, but he still gives it his all. That's one of the things I love about him. He doesn't let the fact he sucks at something get him down. He keeps pushing on and along the way, manages to give everyone else a laugh.

Pushing open the door, I step out into the parking lot. It's just after six and the sky is starting to turn bright orange as the sun sets. This time of night is magical, especially this time of year. Standing here, I take a few moments to appreciate the view before me.

Hailing a taxi, I give him the address and due to an accident, we get stuck near Columbus Circle. Huffing in frustration, I look out the window and see the entrance to the park and since it's a nice night, I tell him to drop me here and I'll walk the rest of the way. It's been too long since I took a stroll through Central Park, so I take the opportunity while I can.

Climbing out, I cut through the standstill traffic and enter the park. Pulling my phone out, I shoot off a text to Bella 'cause I'll now be a little late since I'm walking.

LEXI

Accident on Columbus. I'm walking now.
I've just entered the park, be there soon

Bella replies straightaway because her phone is always glued to her hand.

BELLA

Why can't people just drive normally? I'll order a margarita while I wait

Order one for me in 7 minutes

7 minutes, hey? Someone is optimistic

If I'm not there in 10 minutes, dinner is on me

Deal

Walk slow

A laugh escapes me and while I have my phone in my hand, I start to shoot off a text to JJ when someone shoves me from behind, causing me to drop my phone. Turning around, I'm ready to yell at whoever just did that, but when I see who it is, my eyes widen.

"It's all your fault, you know?" he growls at me.

"What did I do?"

"You have everyone wrapped around your little finger. Doc. JJ. Every-fucking-one. Everything was perfect and then Princess-fucking-Lexi arrives and it all turns to shit." He steps into my personal space and I scrunch my nose up. He smells like a brewery. His eyes are glassy, his clothes are wrinkled and unkept, his hair looks oily and like it hasn't been washed in weeks. "You cost me my job, my apartment, and my boyfriend left me."

"None of that is on me, Brandon. You—"

"Don't you fucking dare say it's all me because I didn't do anything wrong." He steps into my personal space and pokes me in the chest. "I. Didn't. Do. Anything," he sneers through clenched teeth.

"Exactly, Brandon, you didn't do anything. You're lazy. You expected everyone else to do the work and you would only step in at the last minute to claim ownership or praise." Shaking my head, I take a step back, but he follows. Taking another step, I look around for an escape or for someone to realize I'm in trouble, but no one seems to be around. How in a city of eight million people can no one be around when I need assistance?

Reaching out, he grips my upper arms, squeezing. I can feel his heated breath on my face and my heart begins to race. Pain increases in my arm as he squeezes tighter and tighter.

"You're hurting me," I cry.

"Ohh, please, this is nothing. Bitches like you like it rough."

"Brandon, please," I beg, but he doesn't give up. I can see a few people around now, but not one person stops. It's clear the man with me is intimidating me, but those around me just pass on by like nothing is amiss. "I … let me talk to Doc, see if I can get you your job back."

"Like I want to come back when you're there. You'll just find another way to fuck me over. Bitches like you always walk over the lil' man."

"No," I plead, shaking my head. "I wouldn't do that. I … I just want—"

"STOP!" he bellows. "Just stop fucking lying." He squeezes my arms tighter, his nails digging into my flesh. There will definitely be bruises after this. "Stop talking and let me fucking thi—"

Before he finishes his sentence, a fist flies through the air, narrowly missing my face. It slams into Brandon's and from the sudden attack, he stumbles and falls. With his vise-like grip on me, I fall with him, landing on his chest. Before I have time to move, I'm shoved to the side and the puncher straddles Brandon and begins to rain punch after punch into his face.

NOW people stop, but still, no one intervenes. They just stand there and watch this man attack Brandon. A few moments and a spell of luck later, the park patrolmen on horseback arrive. They pull the puncher off and I see it's the man who accosted me at the stadium a few weeks back.

Shock at seeing him again has me shuffling away in fear. My hearing becomes muffled, but I can't take my eyes off the man from the other week. One of the officers comes over to me and when he squats down in front of me, he blocks my attacker from view.

"Are you okay, miss?"

"He … he aaaaattacked mmmme," I stammer.

"You're safe now," he says. Reaching out, I flinch when he goes to touch me and he quickly pulls his hand back. "Do you know that man?"

"Bbbbrandon used to work with me. He was mad and yelling and then, hhhhhe attacked him," I splutter. The first tear falls down my cheek and sitting on the ground in the middle of Central Park, I break down.

People are milling about around us, but I can't focus on anything. The sound of my phone ringing snaps me out of the trance I was in and I look around for it. "That's my phone," I utter. I see it behind the officer and point to it. "I … I need my phone."

The officer leans over, picks it up, and hands it to me. The screen is cracked, but I see a distorted image of Bella on the screen.

Swiping to answer, it connects the call. "B-b-b-bella," I manage to stammer.

"Lex, babe, where are you? What's wrong?" she shouts into the phone.

"I … I'm, he … he grabbed and then he hit … I—"

"Where are you?" she repeats.

"The, the park. I'm still in the park," I tell her.

"I'm on my way," she rushes out and the line goes dead.

Sitting here, I hold the phone to my ear, even though the call has finished, and I stare at the man who attacked me and Brandon.

"Miss," a voice calls from above and when I look up, I see the officer standing there with a paramedic. "Do you mind if Jayde has a look at you?"

Blinking rapidly, I stare up at them, my gaze flickering back and forth. I see their lips moving, but nothing really registers in my mind. I hear the words shock and hospital, but none of what they're saying makes any sense. Then in amongst the fog, I hear my name being called out.

Turning my head toward where the voice is coming from, I see a panicked Bella racing toward me. She drops to her knees in front of me and takes my hands in hers. "Lexi, what happened? Are you okay?" Blinking rapidly, my mouth opens and closes, but nothing comes out. "Lex. Babe, talk to me."

Nodding, I stare at her. "He … he grabbed me and then he hit him and then …"

"Who grabbed you?"

"Brandon, and—"

"Brandon hit you?"

Shaking my head, I open my mouth, but again nothing comes out. From the corner of my eye, I see the man from the other week in handcuffs. My head swivels in his direction and I focus on him. The more I stare at him, the more familiar he becomes to me, but apart from the other week, I can't recall where I've seen him before.

Bella squeezes my hand again and I turn my attention to her. As much as I'm grateful she's here, I don't want her.

"I need JJ," I mumble. Looking intently at her, I say it again. "I want JJ."

Bella nods and takes my phone from my lap. She brings up JJ's contact and calls him for me. He picks up and I can hear her talking. She gets very vocal and then she tells him where we are. Then she's hanging up. "He's on his way," she tells me.

Nodding, I smile. "Thanks, Bells."

Jayde, the paramedic, comes over again. "Can I take a look at you now?"

Once again, I nod. "Can I have some water?"

Bella, the ever-prepared Boy Scout she is, pulls a bottle from her handbag and passes it to me. Uncapping it, I take a sip. And then another. After my drink, I let Jayde do her thing and I recount to her what happened. The officer comes back and listens in too.

"So the man who attacked you a few weeks ago, attacked the man who attacked you today?"

"Yeah," I say on a laugh and shake my head. "It sounds like something from *Days of Our Lives.*"

"And you have no clue who the other man is?"

"No, prior to the other week, I'd never seen him before."

"Lexi," a deep voice calls out. Looking up, I see the people standing around part and then JJ is there.

"JJ," I call out and push myself up. We race toward one another and then I'm in his arms. As soon as I feel his embrace, I break down again. "You're here," I blubber into his chest.

"Shhhh, I've got you," he whispers, rubbing his hand up and down my back. "I'm here now," he reassures me. Just being in his arms is soothing and I immediately start to feel better. Closing my eyes, I relax, but then I hear a deep voice call out, "Jay?"

We both stiffen at the sound of the voice. Lifting my head from his chest, we both turn toward the voice and JJ stiffens further. Then he shocks me and utters, "Dad?"

39

JJ

"Dad?" that one word comes out like a question.

"Dad," Lexi repeats, her head snapping toward me. "He … he's your dad?"

Nodding, I keep my eyes focused on the man I haven't seen since I was five.

"What are you doing here?"

"I've been trying to see you for weeks, but no one would let me get to you, Jay."

"So you assault my girlfriend in hopes of seeing me?" I snap at the man who abandoned my mom and me. I'd always dreamed of the day I'd see him again, but I never expected this scenario. I never expected him to assault my girlfriend.

"I didn't assault anyone," he sneers, eyeing Lex. I don't like the look in his gaze, but when he lifts his back to mine, that look vanishes. "I just wanted to see my son."

"You don't get to call me son," I snap at him. "Especially not after what you did to Lexi." Shaking my head, I scoff,

"Dad, you attacked Lexi the other week and it seems that today, you beat this guy too. Ergo the definition of assault."

"I saved her. You should be thanking me."

"Fine, thanks. Now you can go."

"Please, Jay," he begs. "I just want to see my son."

Shaking my head again, I step away from Lex and go over to my dad. "Why now, huh? You haven't been in my life for twenty-fucking years? You left Mom and me to fend for ourselves. What makes you think I want anything to do with you?"

"Jay, please." He steps toward me, but I take a step back and hold my hand up.

"No, Dad. Just no."

Looking at my dad, I don't feel anything. Nothing. Turning my back on him, I walk back over to Lexi and I lead her away.

"Are you okay?" she asks, sliding her hand into mine.

"I'm fine, just … confused, but don't worry about me and my family issues. Are you okay?"

"I am now that you're here. I just want to go home. I want to forget this day ever happened."

"Let's get you out of here, then."

Pulling her into my side, we begin to leave, but one of the patrolmen stops us. "Sorry to bother you, but we need you to come down to the station and make a formal statement."

"Tonight?" I question. "Lex has been through a lot. I just want to get her home."

The officer's gaze flicks from Lexi to me, but then he reluctantly agrees, "Fine, but tomorrow I need you to come down and make a statement."

We both nod. "We'll be there before lunch." He hands us a card and lets us leave.

Pulling Lexi back into my side, we exit the park, with

Bella hot on our heels.

Hailing a taxi, the three of us climb into the back with Lexi squished between us. She's quiet and just stares ahead at nothing.

"Where to?" the driver asks.

Leaning forward, I give him my address, but Lex mumbles, "No," and shakes her head. "Can we go to my place?" Her voice is soft and hesitant. She turns her head toward me and adds a somber, "Please?"

"Sure." I give the driver the new address and I feel Lexi sigh in relief beside me. The driver pulls out into the evening traffic and I pull Lexi into my side. She slides her arm over my waist and snuggles in. Her body is still tense at first, but eventually she relaxes into me.

Leaning my head back against the seat, I begin processing the events of the evening. You'd think I was living in a soap opera, what with Lexi getting attacked by Brandon. My dad stepping in to protect her in his own messed-up way by beating Brandon to a pulp. But the real kicker, discovering it was my dad who accosted her the other week at the stadium.

Why is he back?

Why now?

What does he want?

The taxi pulls up at Lexi's apartment. Bella pays before I get a chance, but it works out well because Lexi is asleep. Climbing out, I shuffle her around and lift her into my arms. Bella takes her bag and the three of us head inside.

Once in her apartment, I take her straight to her bedroom and gently lower her onto her bed. Pulling the covers over her, I step back and stare down at her. She looks so peaceful right now.

Exiting her room, I meet Bella in Lexi's kitchen. She has

two coffee mugs out, but I see she also has a bottle of Jack Daniel's in her hand.

"Figured we need this over coffee."

Nodding, I walk over to her and grab my mug, frowning when I see it's empty.

"Give me a sec." She shakes her head. "I can only work so fast."

Unscrewing the cap, she grabs the mug from my hands and pours some amber liquid into it and slides it back over to me. She pours some into hers and as she lifts it up, she raises it and murmurs, "Bottom's up."

Tipping my mug in her direction, I bring it to my lips and take a sip. The liquor burns a fiery path down my throat, but at the same time warms me from the inside out. Bella does the same, but she scrunches her face up. "Not a fan of JD?"

"Not really, but it's all I could find." She bites her lip. "What are you going to do about your dad?"

"That's the million-dollar question," I tell her. I haven't been able to stop thinking about him since I realized everything.

"How long has it been since you've seen him?"

"I was five when he left. Mom and I haven't seen or heard from him since. I didn't even know he knew I was in New York."

"Considering you're a starting player for the Crushers and your face, well, body, is all over Times Square thanks to your deal with Monty's Lingerie, it wouldn't be hard. By the way, your billboard is a chef's kiss and I can speak from experience, Peyton Montpellier is an amazing designer."

That's information I did not need to know about Lexi's BFF, but I just nod and smile at Bella's praise. I was hesitant to take the Monty's deal because prior to this line, she'd specialized in women's lingerie—sexy lingerie—but she recently wanted to branch out. Her husband, Cole, is a Crushers fan and I was his first choice as face of the line when she ran the idea past him. She reached out through my agent, Jaxon, at All Too Sports and together we collaborated. And as they say, the rest is history. My mom was over the moon when I told her about the deal and thinking of my mom causes me to hiss, "Shit."

"Shit what?" Bella asks.

"I'm gonna have to tell my mom about this."

"How will she take it?"

Shrugging at her, I watch as she takes another sip and then she leans over and pours the rest of her Jack into my mug. Then she rinses hers in the sink, walks over to the fridge, and grabs a bottle of wine. Opening the bottle, she fills the mug with wine and pops the bottle back in the fridge. Taking a sip, she lets out a little contented sigh just as a shrill scream comes from Lexi's room.

Slamming my mug down on the counter, I race into her room. Lexi is thrashing about in her bed, shaking her head from side to side. Dropping to the edge of the bed, I run my fingertips over her forehead, pushing away the hair that's fallen over her eyes. "Lex, baby, open your eyes," I whisper. "It's just a dream. You're safe."

Blinking open her eyes, she looks around and her eyes connect with mine. Fear radiates from them, but when she sees me, it slowly begins to ebb away.

"JJ," she mumbles, tears welling in her eyes.

"I'm here," I whisper. Climbing onto the bed, I pull her into my arms and she snuggles into my side and breaks down.

"You're here," she repeats.

"I'm here," I say again, pressing a kiss to her temple.

"JJ?" she asks a few moments later.

"Yeah?"

"Thank you."

"For what?"

"Being here."

"There's nowhere else I want to be."

Lifting her gaze, she stares at me for a few beats. "Make love to me. Make me feel good."

"And on that note, I'm gonna get out of here," Bella utters from the doorway to Lexi's room.

Lex freezes in my arms and I can't help but chuckle. My chuckle earns me a smack in the stomach and I let out a little *oomph*.

Lexi sits up and crosses her legs and she looks over at Bella. "Sorry I missed dinner."

"It's fine, but are you okay?" Bella asks, walking into the room. She climbs onto the bed and mimics Lexi's pose. She takes her friend's hands in hers and brings them to her lap and holds on tight.

The two of them are close. Their relationship reminds me of Kal's and mine.

Lexi nods, but we both know, right now she's anything but okay. "You scared the shit out of me, Lex. I have never heard you sound so scared before … and we've watched *IT* and I know how you feel about those C-word things." This causes me to chuckle again because Lexi has an irrational fear of clowns. Bella then adds, "Ohh, and by the way, you owe me dinner 'cause you were late."

Lexi snorts and smiles at her friend. For some reason, seeing that smile and hearing her snort is comforting.

The two of them start gossiping and seeing Lex come back to life as she chats with her friend eases my worry, and I know that she's going to be okay, but I'm not sure I will be.

My dad is back and I'm not sure what to make of that.

40
LEXI

I'm walking down a path. It's almost dusk, the trees above shroud the way in darkness. Businessmen are walking home. Kids are running from their parents. Couples are out for an evening stroll, holding hands. People in running gear dart around those walking slowly in front of them.

Someone stops in front of me. Their face is covered in darkness. "It's all your fault," they spit at me.

Poking me in the chest, I step backward, but they keep poking me and shouting, "It's all your fault!" over and over.

No one stops.

Everyone keeps going about their business, not paying me any attention.

"It's all your fucking fault," he bellows and this time, he pushes me to the ground. He hovers over me, but in the blink of an eye, his face morphs into someone else's. "It's all your fault Jay hates me," he hisses. He lifts his fist and it comes flying toward my face.

I scream out …

. . .

"Lex, babe, wake up. It's just a dream."

My eyes fly open and I see a figure hovering above me. I try to shuffle away, but I hit the headboard. I'm trapped. My breathing is labored. I'm confused and disoriented.

Fear has wrapped its talons around me and I'm frozen where I lie.

"Lex, it's me," a familiar voice says, but I'm imprisoned in that space between awake and asleep. Everything is fuzzy and groggy. Blinking rapidly, the face before me comes into focus and I see it's JJ. Concern is etched on his face.

"It's just a dream," he repeats. "You're safe."

Nodding, I stare up at him as he continues to whisper sweet nothings. He reaches out and cups my cheek in his palm. Leaning into it, I close my eyes and the fear dissipates. I start to relax. My breathing returns and when I open my eyes again, I smile up at him.

Lifting my hand, I cover his with mine and I stare up at him. He gazes back at me, and all the fear from my nightmare disappears.

JJ is my safe place.

My home.

With him by my side, I know I'm going to be okay. "Make love to me, JJ. Make me feel safe and loved and cherished." This time Bella isn't here to vaginablock me, and the longer he just sits there and stares has me thinking he's going to turn me down. For the longest time, he doesn't say anything, but then he smiles and leans down and covers my mouth with his. His lips press to mine in a soft and sensual kiss. Draping my arms over his shoulders, I hold on to him as he kisses me back to life. His tongue slips into my mouth, and mine slides into his. With each lash of his tongue, the last remnants of the nightmare fade into oblivion.

Now all I can focus on is JJ and the pleasure building within.

He slides his hand down my body and grips the hem of my shirt. Lifting it over my head, his fingertips softly graze over my skin, leaving goose bumps in its wake. Tossing my shirt aside, JJ stares down at me. "You're fucking gorgeous, Lexi Knight."

"As are you, Jameso—" He leans down and presses his finger to my lips, cutting off my reply.

"It's JJ. I hate it when you called me Jameson. I absolutely hate it."

"JJ," I purr, "you have too many clothes on."

Reaching behind his neck, he does that sexy one-handed pull his shirt off move and a moan escapes me. I bite my bottom lip as my gaze roams over his muscular chest.

"You can see my chest," he croons, dropping his shirt to the floor, "but yours is currently obstructed."

With my eyes locked on his, I reach behind my back and unclasp my bra. Wiggling my arms free, I throw it aside and lie back on the mattress. Lifting my arms over my head, I lie bare before him. "Better?"

"Much … but the pants need to go now too."

Nodding, I watch intently as he makes quick work of my leggings and panties. In one fell swoop, he drags them both down my legs and off. He quickly pulls off his own and he kneels between my spread thighs.

"Play with yourself," he demands. "Get yourself wet for me, baby."

Slipping my hand out from behind my head, I trace my fingers down between my breasts, over my belly, and down to my clit. Spreading my legs wider, I circle my finger over my clit. The sensation sends waves of pleasure through my body. Wiggling my hips, I slip my finger into my folds and press the digit inside. The warmth of my pussy and my arousal coats my finger. A moan escapes as my finger slides in and out of my hot, wet channel.

JJ grips his thick cock and begins to stroke himself. His eyes are locked on my hand between my thighs and mine is locked on his hand moving back and forth on this cock. His tip glistens with arousal and he smears it over his shaft.

Licking my lips, I throw my head back in delight as I rock my hips and ride my hand. My finger plunges in and out, bringing me closer to release.

I'm right there, ready to come apart when JJ reaches forward. He grabs my wrist and pulls my fingers from my pussy. He brings my arousal covered fingers to his lips and he licks them, sucking them clean.

Reaching over me, he grabs a condom from the side table drawer and sheaths his cock. With his eyes locked on mine, he slides into me.

"Yes," I mewl. Covering my breasts with my hands, I massage my mounds and tug on my nipples as JJ fucks me. His movements are slow and deep, hitting that magical spot deep within each time. That feeling low in my belly begins to simmer and I know I'm going to explode any second now.

"I'm close," I whisper.

JJ reaches out and presses on my clit, pinching it. That's the detonation I need and I explode. Crying out, I ride the wave as pure ecstasy washes over me. My pussy clenches down on JJ and he joins me. His body stiffens as he comes, filling the condom.

Pulling out of me, he removes the condom and ties it off. Dropping it to the carpet, he collapses onto the mattress next to me. Both of us lie here breathlessly panting. Turning my

head toward him, I find him staring at me. "Thank you," I
tell him.

"What are you thanking me for?"

"Being here. Making me forget. Replacing his touch with
yours."

"You don't need to thank me for looking after you, Lexi. I
take care of what's mine and you are mine. Now that I have
you back, I'm never letting you go."

Rolling to my side, I snuggle into JJ and rest my head on
his chest. The beating of his heart lulls me back to sleep.

I'm pleasantly woken early the next morning with JJ's head
between my legs. He rubs his cheek against my thigh and he
nuzzles my clit with his nose. He inhales deeply and lets out
a guttural sound. "Fuck, babe, you smell amazing."

Before I have a chance to reply, he sticks his tongue out
and licks between my folds. Up and down his tongue slides
before he thrusts it deep into my hole. Pulling his tongue
out, he licks back up to my clit and gently sucks. He alter-
nates between gently biting and sucking my clit while he
inserts two fingers into me. I'm so wet that they effortlessly
slide in and out.

"JJ," I pant. "More."

He pulls his fingers from me and slips them farther
down. Circling my puckered hole, he spreads my arousal
around before slipping his finger into my ass. I only
recently discovered I love having him in my ass. We
haven't tried anal-anal yet, but I think I want it. "Please,"
I beg.

"Please what?" he asks, pressing his finger deeper into my ass.

"Fuck my ass, JJ. Please."

"What my girl wants, my girl gets," he tells me. "Reach into the top drawer and hand me the lube. I want to make this as pleasurable for you as I can."

"Mmmhmpf," I moan. It already feels amazing, but if he can make this feel even better then sign me up.

Reaching over, I grab the lube and hand it to him. He flicks the cap open and squeezes some onto me. It's cool when it hits my crack and I hiss at the shock. Gently, he massages it into my ass, then he rubs up his dick and shuffles between my legs. Pushing my legs toward my chest, he grabs his shaft and guides it to my hole. With his eyes locked on mine, he presses in. It's painful at first, reminding me of our first time at prom, but that pain turns to pleasure the deeper he pushes in.

Just like our first time, he makes sure I'm okay every step of the way.

Pulling all the way out, then he pushes back in. Over and over, he fucks my ass and never have I felt pleasure like this before. It's nothing like his finger … it's that and so much more. So fucking much more.

"Fuck, babe, it's tight. I'm not gonna last long."

"JJ," I moan, "fuck, this is …" I drift off, unable to finish my thought.

I'm teetering on the edge, but I can't quite get there. Lifting my hand, I slide it down to my clit. Circling the sensitive bud, I press down and from the pressure on my clit and JJ's cock in my ass, I come.

Crying out, my body continues to spasm and I ride out my release. My release sets him off and he comes in my ass. Filling me up as he empties himself.

Pulling out, he collapses onto the mattress beside me. "Fuck, babe, that was everything I thought it would be and more."

"Mmmhmpf," is all I can manage as a reply.

My eyes droop closed and I fall back to sleep just as the sun is cresting the horizon … all memories of my dream and attack forgotten.

41

JJ

WHEN LEXI AND I WAKE FOR THE SECOND TIME, WE CLIMB INTO the shower. Lexi has her back to me and I watch as she steps under the spray. The water cascades down her body. My eyes follow the liquid's path and that's when I notice the fingerprints on the back of her upper arms.

Lifting my hand, I trace over the marks marring her beautiful skin. Leaning down, I gently kiss the bruises. "I hate that he marked you."

"I'm fine," she whispers. Turning around to face me, my eyes widen when I see the bruises from the front.

"Lex," I hiss her name. "Do they hurt?"

She shakes her head.

"Are you sure?"

This time she nods. "Really, JJ, I'm fine."

Grabbing her loofa, I squeeze some of her jasmine-and-lime-scented bodywash onto it and gently I wash her body. Dropping the loofa, I use my hands and slide them over her soapy wet skin, giving her breasts extra attention.

A smile forms on her face. "I think they're clean," she huskily murmurs.

"Can never be too sure," I reply.

Shaking her head, she squeezes some of her bodywash into her hands and begins to wash me. Her hands trace over my pecs and one slides lower and lower. She wraps her hand around my dick and like always when I'm naked and Lexi has her hands on me, it hardens in her grip.

Lexi gazes at me with a heated look in her eyes. She flips us around so I'm in the spray and the soapy bubbles wash away. Then she drops to her knees and before I can tell her this isn't necessary, she opens her mouth and sucks my cock deep into her throat. My dick slides in and out between her lips and, sooner than I would like to admit, I come down her throat. I'd like to say it's because Lexi is a master cocksucker, and she is, but when a wet and naked Lexi takes my dick into her mouth, it's game over.

Helping her to her feet, I cover her mouth with mine. I slide my hand down her body, ready to return the favor, but the water turns cold and we both let out a yelp.

"Ugh," Lex complains, "I hate my hot water system. It's so freakin' tiny."

"It's probably for the best," I tell her. "Because if I got started doing what I really want to do, we wouldn't be leaving this shower for a long time and we have places to be."

Turning off the water, we climb out. Wrapping a towel around my waist, I hand Lexi her towel. Standing here, I watch as she dries herself off. The fluffy cotton sliding over her skin, soaking up the water droplets.

"What?" she asks when she notices me staring.

"Nothing, just admiring you."

"Feel free to return the favor," she says, wiggling her eyebrows at me.

Untucking my towel, it falls away, baring me to her. "Nice." She licks her bottom lip and bites it.

"Don't," I warn.

"Don't what?" she sweetly asks, but from the gleam in her eye, we both know what she's doing.

"You know what, and I'm going to walk away before I can't control myself."

Spinning on my heel, I walk into her room and start to pull on my clothes from yesterday. Lexi walks into her room stark naked and makes exaggerated movements as she gets dressed for the day.

Groaning, I shake my head and walk out to get started on breakfast. Lexi, the minx, chuckles. I can't find it in me to be mad because last night was taxing for her and it's nice to see her be herself again. She seems okay, but I'm waiting for everything to catch up with her.

After a quick breakfast, we head down to the station to meet up with the officer and for Lexi to give her statement.

The officer sees us straightaway and escorts us into a room. Taking a seat next to Lexi, I listen as she recounts the events of the evening. Hearing them again makes my blood boil. I'm angry at Brandon for taking his incompetence out on Lexi, and I'm furious at my dad for scaring Lexi the other week. At the same time, I'm thankful he was there to save her from Brandon, but the way he saved her was uncalled for. Yes, Brandon is a dick, but he didn't deserve to be beaten to a pulp like that. Apparently, he's in the hospital with a broken nose, jaw, and a mild concussion.

"Ms. Knight, did you want to press charges against him?"

"I don't want to press charges." Lexi's words shock me and my eyes widen.

"What the hell, Lex? He assaulted you." My voice is raised, but I can't believe what I'm hearing right now.

"He didn't assault me. He, he just, umm, he just frightened me."

"Then explain the bruises on your arms?" I snarl. "Did they just appear suddenly overnight?"

"JJ," she pleads and for some reason the tone of her voice has me stopping in my tracks. "I just want this nightmare to be over. I'm not hurt." I roll my eyes at that. "Okay, fine, I'm not not hurt. I'm just a little bruised. Mentally, I'm good, thanks to you. I just want to move on and forget."

"But he hurt you," I argue again. I know it's a fruitless endeavor because when Lexi Knight has made up her mind, there's no changing it … hence, why I broke her heart all those years ago. "Lexi, I can't believe I'm saying this and defending *him,* but what if my dad hadn't intervened? What would have happened then?"

"The patrolmen who arrived on horseback would have come and saved me."

"You don't know that." My frustration builds the longer we talk about this. Running my hands through my hair, I stand up and push the chair back. "I can't be here." Before Lexi can say anything, I storm out of the room they escorted us into and march outside. My anger rises with each step I take.

Stepping out onto the busy New York street, I want to scream and shout. I feel like a toddler on the verge of a temper tantrum.

Dropping to my ass, I sit on the steps, rest my elbows on my knees, and cradle my head in my hands. I'm not surprised that she doesn't want to press charges and I get where she's coming from, but it doesn't make the events of last night any easier to accept.

"JJ," a soft voice says sometime later.

Looking over my shoulder, I look up at the woman who holds my heart. Staring back at me is a strong woman. My woman. Even in jeans and a casual tee, she looks strong and sexy, and my dick agrees with what we see. "Are you okay?" she asks, dropping down next to me.

"Yes. No. I don't know." I sigh. "I'm—"

"Worried about me and the next game and your mom. Confused over your dad."

"Yeah." I chortle. "All of that." I pause. "How did you know?"

"Because I know you, Jameson James. You worry about everything and everyone. You want everyone to be safe and when you can't control a situation, you hate it."

"You really do know me."

"Yes, yes, I do … now, I have a suggestion on what we can do to take your mind off all of this, and I will even have you back in time for practice this evening."

"Coach gave me the day off," I remind her.

"I know he did, but skating is everything to you and you need to be on the ice, but right now, you need to let off a little steam."

"You are the best, Lexi Knight."

"I know," she cheekily gloats. Leaning over, she presses a quick kiss to my lips and that one action calms me and I know everything is going to be okay.

"So modest," I tease. "Now, what's this idea you have?"

"Golf," she states with a super big Lexi grin.

"Golf," I repeat, my tone giving way to how I really feel about this sport, not that it should be called a sport because it's stupid and real sports aren't stupid. "You want to play golf?" She nods. "Really?" She nods again. "Fine," I relent, "but you better make it up to me when we get home."

"Babe, when we get home, you will get your hole in one, but first, it's time to get our golf on." I didn't make it back for practice, but I did get a cardio workout in … and finally, a hole in one when we got back to my place after golf.

"You know, I think you somehow got worse at golf," Lexi says as we walk hand in hand toward Squires to meet up with the team. Tonight will be our last hurrah before we head into our training regime in the lead up to the playoffs. I can taste the victory on the tip of my tongue. If we keep playing like we have been, that Cup will be ours.

Lexi decimated me on the course over in Jersey City. Golf and I do not get along, but, for my girl, I suck it up and play with her since she loves it so much. Personally, I hate the game, but Lexi has played since she was a teenager. Dr. Knight introduced her to the game and it became a thing the two of them would do with her uncle Flynn.

"Ohh, shut up," I huff, "we can't all be sexily perfect at everything like you are."

"Sexily perfect, hey?"

"Yep," I tell her. Stopping in the middle of the street, I pull her into my arms and cover her mouth with mine. "I think you wore this …" I slide my hand down her body, squeezing her ass that's encased in the sexiest pair of pants. Adding to her sexiness is the navy polo tucked into her pants. Her shirt is tight across her tits and the V at the front gives the tiniest hint of her cleavage. "… just to distract me. You know, I'm positive that's why I suck at golf."

"Babe, even if I wore a burlap sack, you'd suck. Golf just isn't your game and that's okay. We can't be good at everything."

"You are," I defensively reply.

"Pfffft, I'm not good at everything," she argues.

"Yeah, you are, and you know what you're the best at?"

"What?"

"Taking my cock in that sweet, sweet pussy of yours and making me com—Dad?" I stop mid sexy rant when I see him standing on the street out front of Squires. "What are you doing here?"

"Hey, Jay," he nervously greets me, shoving his hands into the pockets of his jeans. "I was hoping we could talk?"

42

LEXI

JJ's body tightens as he stares at his dad. In all the chaos of yesterday, we haven't been able to discuss his return. I'm still shocked it was his dad who saved me last night and that he was the man from the other week too.

Now as we stand before the man, I'm kicking myself because I don't know what JJ wants to do about him. In all the years I've known about him, Chet James has been a nonentity to JJ and Lisa. After the first time he told me the story of him leaving, that was it. It was like his dad didn't exist and I guess, in a way, he didn't … until now.

"You want to talk? Now?" JJ's voice is laced with something I've never heard before. Sliding my hand into his, I give it a little squeeze and I feel him relax, but his body is still tight.

"Yeah, Son, I do."

"Don't call me Son," JJ snaps. "You lost that right when you walked away and left Mom and me. I have nothing to say to you." He turns his back to his dad and storms off.

Because my hand is in his, I stumble from the sudden movement, but I quickly gain my footing and follow JJ into Squires.

He heads straight to the bar and orders himself a beer, me a margarita, and two shots.

Slade, the owner of Squires, senses JJ is on edge and before he gets the other drinks, he places the two shot glasses on the bar top. No sooner has Slade filled the glasses and JJ slams the shots back, one after the other in quick succession. He hisses at the burn, then leans his hands onto the edge of the bar and drops his head.

Slade pops the top on JJ's beer and slides it over to him before he starts on my margarita.

Stepping closer to JJ, I rest my hand on his back and gently rub. "You okay?" He shrugs in response. "JJ, talk to me." He lifts his head and turns it toward me. I offer him a timid smile before I ask again. "You okay?"

He sighs dejectedly. "Yes. No. I don't know."

"Wanna talk about it?" I offer, smiling at Slade when he drops off my margarita.

"Yes. No. I don't know," he answers, smiling to himself after repeating his previous answer. Picking up his beer, he takes a sip and sighs, this time in contentment.

"Better?"

He smirks at me and opens his mouth, but I press my finger to his lips.

"And you better not answer yes, no, I don't know. You've used your quota of those tonight."

"But yes, no, I don't know sums everything up perfectly right now."

"Yeah, nah, it doesn't," I tell him, shaking my head. "Maybe you need to speak to your mom."

"We both need to speak to our parents. You need to let

yours know about last night, and I need to tell my mom about the reappearance of you know who."

"Yeah, nah, that can wait. My dad is going to go all protective and I don't want to deal with him telling me to come home 'cause New York isn't safe blah, blah, blah."

"And then he's gonna call me and demand to know why I didn't protect his princess blah, blah, blah."

"Yeah, we're both screwed," I joke. "How about we take tonight to get drunk with our friends and then tomorrow we can FaceTime the 'rents together."

"Safety in numbers," he says. "I like it." He reaches over and cups my cheek. "Thank you, Lex."

Furrowing my eyebrows in confusion, I ask, "What are you thanking me for?"

"For being you. For being here, but most of all, for giving me a second chance."

"I pucking hated that you still loved me, but at the same time, I didn't because I still pucking loved you too. I always have and I always will, JJ."

At the same time, we lean together and when our lips connect, everything in the world feels right again. Well, not really, 'cause it's still a shitshow when it comes to Brandon and JJ's dad, but with JJ by my side, we can face anything.

43

JJ

"Jameson, why did you not protect my daughter? I knew her living in New York, something would happen and look, I was right. I'm coming out there. Clearly you need your father because Jameson certainly isn't looking after you. You should have—" Dr. Knight berates me through the screen.

"Daaaad," Lexi interrupts her dad. "This is not on JJ. Brandon is the one who is to be held accountable. No one could predict he would do something like this."

"She's right, Preston. Brandon is at fault, not JJ." Cress comes to my defense and I smile thankfully at her through the screen.

"I guess," he relents. "What did they charge him with?" her dad asks.

"Nothing," Lexi answers.

"What do you mean nothing? The police force there is clearly inept at their jobs."

"Dad, I didn't pursue it."

"What?" he growls at his daughter. "Why not?"

"Because he didn't hurt me. He was just upset and, Dad, before you yell at JJ again for not making me press charges, he tried. Like you, he wasn't happy with my decision, but I don't want to. At the end of the day, I'm fine and I'm a grown woman. I can decide if I want to press charges against someone."

"She has a point, Preston," Cress defends her daughter and then her mom and dad start bickering back and forth. While they're having their argument, I lean into Lex and whisper, "Maybe you need to play the lollipop card."

"What did you say?" Dr. Knight hisses.

My eyes widen and Lexi just giggles from next to me. "Dad, we have to go," Lexi says, saving me from answering. "But I promise you I'm fine. He didn't hurt me. I was just frightened. I'm tougher than I look."

"While I don't agree with you not pressing charges, you and your mother are right. You're a grown woman and you've never made a bad decision in your life ... but I'm still coming for a visit. It's been too long since I've seen you."

"Dad, I was home a few weeks ago."

"That's forever in dad time." Lexi and I both chuckle at that. "I'll text you my flight details as soon as I know them."

We say our goodbyes and hang up, then Lex looks at me. "Time to call your mom." Nodding, I stare at the phone in my hand.

"Why is this so hard?"

"Because she's your mom and you love her, and this new development and news may upset her."

"I fucking hate him," I hiss, throwing my phone down onto the coffee table in anger. It skitters across the tabletop and lands on the floor.

"And throwing your phone won't change anything ... but it might cost you a thousand bucks to get a new iPhone."

"I know," I reply on a sigh. Hopping up, I grab my phone off the rug and thankfully it's not broken. No sooner do I pick it up and it rings. My mom's smiling face fills the screen. It's like she knows I need her.

Swiping the screen, I answer, "Hey, Mom."

"Hey, JJ, how are you?"

"Gooooood," I draw the word out, dropping back to the sofa to sit next to Lexi. She reaches over and takes my hand, lacing our fingers together. She gives it a little squeeze, offering me silent support, and it's just what I need.

"Wanna try that again, JJ? You forget, I know you. When you answer with gooooood, drawing the word out, I know you're anything but good." She pauses. "Did something happen with Lexi? Were you a bonehead again?"

"Thanks for the vote of confidence, Mom, but everything between Lexi and me is fine. Actually, we're better than fine, we're—"

"Did you propose?" Mom squeals into the phone, interrupting me. "Are you two engaged?"

"No, Mom, I did not propose." *Yet*, I silently add. We may have only just gotten back together, but as I said on my birthday, she's my endgame and I'm never letting her go. "But, I … umm, I do have something to tell you." I pause. "Are you sitting down?"

"I am now," she tells me. "What's going on? You aren't dying, are you?"

"No, Mom, I'm not dying, but, umm, Dad's back." I'm met with silence. Pulling the phone from my ear, I check to make sure we're still connected. "You there, Mom?"

"Yeah, I'm here," she murmurs. "You … you saw Chet?"

"Mmmhmpf," I reply with a nod and then I fill her in on what's happened with Dad in the last few days and Lexi's encounter with him the other week.

"Is Lexi okay?" Mom asks.

Looking over at her, I smile and nod. "She's perfectly perfect, Mom."

"I'm glad. She's good for you and I'm glad she gave you a second chance."

"Me too, Mom, me too. And now that I have it, I will do everything I can to not puck it up."

"Good, 'cause I don't want to have to disown my son."

"You wouldn't," I reply in exasperation.

"Well, I guess we'll never know because one day, you will propose and I will get the daughter I always wanted."

"What do I do about Dad?" I ask her.

"What do you want to do about him?"

"I don't know. He's been gone for so long I sometimes forget I even have a dad, but now that he's back, he's all I can think about. On one hand, I hate him, but on the other, he saved Lex and I'm thankful for that but …"

"You don't want to open yourself up to hurt again?"

"Exactly. What do I do?"

"I can't tell you what to do, JJ, but at the end of the day, he's your dad. If you want a relationship with him, I won't stand in your way."

"But what about you?" I ask her. It's all well and good for her to say she's okay, but this is the man who up and left his son and the woman he supposedly loved. I know firsthand how much it hurt and I was only a kid, but Mom, she was a grown woman. He was the man she'd vowed to spend the rest of her life with, till death do them part, but in this case, the part was because he took off.

"JJ, what I feel for your father shouldn't be an issue for you. What happened between him and me is exactly that, between him and me."

"Will you ever forgive him for walking out?"

"I don't know, JJ. I haven't thought about him or the possibility of him coming back in so long now, but a boy needs his dad—"

"Mom," I interrupt, but she interrupts me right back.

"Let me finish," she snaps at me. It's not often Mom does that, so I know she means business right now.

"Okay," I tell her.

"A boy needs his dad and he was never there through the years when you needed him the most. I did the best I could, but, JJ, there was always a part of me that wished Chet was there to help you in a way I couldn't. Maybe this is the chance for him to be the dad I know he could have been."

"Mom, you're the best mom I could have ever asked for. Did it suck not having a dad? Yeah, at times it did, but I am who I am now because of you. I … I don't want to hurt you if I decide to pursue a relationship with him."

"JJ, you won't hurt me if you want to see him. I made my peace when it comes to Chet James a long time ago. I'll support you, whatever you decide, because that's what a mother does. She supports her child."

"I think if he reaches out again, I'll give him a chance. Give him the opportunity to explain and then I can decide what I want to do."

"I think that's the right choice, JJ." She pauses. "I'm so proud of you."

"Why?" I ask her, genuinely confused about her statement.

"You've grown into a fine young man and you make me proud each and every day. You're following your dreams. You give your all to everything you do. You own up to your mistakes, but most of all, you care about other people. I mean, look what you did for Lexi all those years ago? You sacrificed your happiness for her to follow her dream. Not many young men would do that, but Fate gave you a second chance and now you're living your dream with the woman of your dreams. Maybe the same thing will happen with your father too."

"Thanks, Mom. I love you."

"I love you too, JJ."

We chat for a few more minutes and then we hang up. "You good?" Lexi asks me when I drop my phone into my lap.

"I think so. Mom thinks I should give Dad a second chance."

"For what it's worth, I think you should too, or at least you should hear him out."

Nodding, I look over at her. "If he reaches out again, I'll give him a chance but only one. I will not let that man hurt me again."

44

JJ

PRACTICE THIS MORNING WAS HARD. I DIDN'T GET MUCH SLEEP last night. I kept thinking about my dad. My mom. Lexi. The playoffs. How can Mom be so okay with me seeing Dad? He walked out on us. Why should I give him a second chance? He didn't give Mom or me a second thought. He doesn't deserve shit from me. Then I think how Lex gave me a second chance, and I wonder if I should do the same … once again bringing me back to confused.

"James, you're playing like shit," Coach berates me.

"Cut him some slack, Dad," Chelsea says to her dad, coming to my defense. "The last few days have been rough for him and Lex. You're lucky he's here at all."

"I know," Coach admits in defeat, "but—"

"It's no excuse for being a butthead," she throws back at him. Watching the two of them bicker causes a pang of jealousy to hit me. Could this be my dad and me if I give him a chance?

"When did you become so sassy?"

"You didn't raise no fool," she sasses and I can't help the chuckle that slips out. Coach glares at me and before he can yell at me, again, I skate away and decide to do some stick-handling drills on my own.

No one approaches me and I'm left to my own devices. I'm thankful for that.

"Jameson," Janice, Coach's assistant, calls out to me. It's not often she comes down to the ice, so I immediately know something is up.

"What's up, Janice?"

"There's a Chet James here to see you."

"My dad's here?" I ask her.

"If his name is Chet James, then yes, your dad is here. He's quite insistent that he needs to speak with you."

Looking up at the clock, I see that I still have an hour left of practice. "Tell him I'll be finished here in just over an hour."

"Sure thing, Jameson—" the sound of Rick bellowing, pauses her mid-sentence.

"James, get your ass out here. This is practice not a gossip session."

Nodding at Rick, I look back at Janice, but she beats me to it. "You better get back out there before he has you doing those suicide things." A laugh slips out and then she adds, "I'll tell your dad, one hour."

Nodding, I smile and head back out there, but I quickly spin back. "Janice," I call out. "Tell him he can come watch practice if he wants to."

"Can do," she states and she heads back the way she came.

My gaze keeps flicking to the stands, hoping to see my dad, but he doesn't come in.

Coach and Rick ride my ass for the rest of the session, but

it's warranted because my head isn't in it, and I'm playing like shit.

"If you wanna play tomorrow, James, you need to pull your head out of your ass," Rick berates me as we walk off the ice after practice. "Ella can do better than you and she's seven."

"I know, Rick. Just a lot going on right now."

He stops walking and turns to face me. He has his serious face on. "Anything I can help you with?"

Shaking my head, I run my hands through my hair. "Nah, all good, but thanks."

"Well, whatever it is that's on your mind, deal with it. We need this win tomorrow to secure our place in the playoffs."

"I know, Rick, I know. Tomorrow my game head will be on, promise."

"Good," he states, clapping me on the back. "Now get in the showers. You stink."

A laugh escapes me, but he's right. I do reek because I forgot my deodorant this morning. Walking over to my locker, I drop down onto the bench and go about removing my gear.

Arms slide around my neck and then there's a kiss on my cheek, but they quickly pull away, "Ugh, you stink, JJ. It smells like a skunk died."

"Tough session," I tell her. "I'm about to hit the showers." I waggle my eyebrows at her.

"As much as I'd love to. A. We're at work. B. We are not Chelsea and Kallen—"

"Hey, I heard that," Chelsea protests, but then she sees Kallen come out of the showers, his towel wrapped around his waist, and her eyes go all gaga.

"Case in point," Lexi throws toward her friend and then looks back at me. "And three, you stink."

"You went A, B, three."

"Whatevs, it's not happening. You'll just have to wait till tonight." She leans in. I can feel her heated breath on my neck and my cock twitches. "And I think we should order in. Then I'm going to give you a massage that has an ending I think you will be very, very happy with."

"Dammit, woman, I cannot meet my dad with a boner."

"Your dad?" she shouts.

"Yeah, Janice came down during practice. He was here to see me, and this time he didn't try accosting someone in the parking lot."

"How do you feel about that?"

"Well, I offered for him to come watch and he didn't, so I'm not really holding out hope."

"I'm sorry, babe. Do you want me to come with you?"

"Thanks, but no. I need to do this on my own, but I might need you when I'm finished."

"Just call me and I'll be there."

She gives me a kiss and heads off, leaving me to shower and then meet up with my dad.

After my shower, I wave bye to the guys and head toward the main entrance, guessing that's where my dad will be, but when I get there, it's empty. I check with security and they remember seeing my dad, but they don't know where he went.

Feeling dejected, I head out the main entrance doors and when I look up, I see my dad, leaning against a pillar having a smoke. He hasn't noticed my presence, so I take the moment to check him out. He looks old and I don't mean in a "it's been twenty years since I saw him last" old. It's in a "he's had a hard life" old.

His dark hair is sprinkled with gray and it looks greasy. His face is filled with wrinkles. He's wearing jeans, a tee, and boots, just like I remember. Unless he was in his work overalls, he was in jeans and a tee.

He must sense he's no longer alone and turns his head toward me. "Hey, Jay," he says by way of greeting.

"No one's called me Jay in years."

"Probably why no one knew who I was referring to when I asked around."

"You mean the times, plural, you accosted my girlfriend to get to me?"

"I didn't mean to scare her. I just wanted to see my son."

"I'm not your son," I snarl at him. "Why are you here, Dad?" I ask, my tone harsher than I intended it to be, but whatever, he doesn't really deserve pleasantries. "I haven't seen you in twenty years and suddenly you appear. The timing is kind of suspicious, if you ask me. I make it to the NHL and you come back into my life."

"I know how it looks, but, Jay, I've been looking for you for a while now. You and your mom left New York. I had no idea where you were."

"Well, if you hadn't taken off like you did, you would have known where we were, cause it would have also been where you were."

"Jay—"

"No," I shout, interrupting him. "You left us to fend for ourselves. Mom had to work several jobs just to make ends meet. She sacrificed everything so I could play hockey. Then one day, when I was almost seventeen, she got an amazing job opportunity and we moved."

"And it turned out fine. Look where you are." He throws his hand about at the stadium. "You have everything you ever dreamed of."

"Except a dad," I throw at him. "I was five-fucking-years old, Dad. Five." Lifting my hand, I thrust my fingers angrily at him. "I thought I did something wrong. It took me quite a while to realize that it wasn't me. It was you. You were the piece of shit who walked away from your family."

"I'm sorry, Jay. I just … I just couldn't do it anymore."

"Wow, Dad, way to make a guy feel wanted and loved."

"I never stopped loving you, Jay. If I had stayed, I would have made things worse."

"Yeah, 'cause it's all about you." Shaking my head, I breathe in deeply. "Look, I … I can't do this right now. I … I need to go."

Before he can say anything, I readjust my bag on my shoulder and walk past him. Luck is on my side and I manage to hail a taxi straightaway. That never happens in New York. Climbing in, I give the driver my address and he pulls out into traffic.

Looking out the window, I see Dad still standing there. He has his phone to his ear and he looks angry. Well, fuck him. I'm angry too. I never want to see him again.

Traffic is a nightmare and it takes almost an hour to get from the stadium to my place. I should have gotten out and walked, but, to be honest, it was nice to just sit back and think about nothing for a while.

Finally, the driver stops in front of my building and I hand over the fare. Grabbing my things, I climb out and head inside, waving to the doorman as I make my way to the elevator. Stepping in, I press the button for my floor and when I open the door to my apartment, I'm surprised by what I see before me.

45

LEXI

THE SOUND OF A KEY ENTERING THE LOCK ECHOES AROUND JJ'S apartment.

"Shit," I hiss. I'm not quite ready, but I quickly strip off my robe and throw it onto the sofa. Dropping to the rug, I lie down amongst the pillows and blankets I laid out earlier after moving his heavy sofa and coffee table out of the way. Readjusting the girls, I wriggle around and get comfy. I'm wearing a Monty's sheer baby doll in a pinky purple shade with a matching thong. Thongs aren't usually my jam 'cause who wants a piece of floss up their ass? But I'll give it to Peyton Montpellier. She sure knows how to design comfy butt floss.

When I hear the door swing open, I click play on the remote and "Never Tear Us Apart" the *Fifty Shades* version begins to play through the sound system.

"What the?" JJ utters when the music begins to play.

He drops his bag and kicks his shoes off, like he does every time he arrives home. "Lex?" he calls out my name like a question, but I stay silent. My heart begins to race. This is the sexiest thing I've ever done and now that I think about it, what if JJ has returned with his dad? That would be mortifying, but, thankfully, he's alone … I think.

Lifting one of my arms over my head, I put what I hope is a seductive look on my face and wait for him to find me.

He finds me pretty quickly and stops mid-step. His gaze roams over me and the scene before him. "What do we have here?"

"Surprise," I huskily purr. "Wanna join me?" I tap the spot next to me, flicking my gaze from him to where I'm tapping and back.

"Feel free to be like this when I get home anytime," he tells me as he begins to strip off his clothes. Like always, he does the one-handed shirt move I love and because he came from the stadium, he's in sweats, so he easily removes them too. Leaving him standing before me in nothing but his boxer briefs, my eyes skate over his body and I let out a hussy-like moan.

"Like what you see?"

Nodding, I bite my lip. "Very much so."

Pushing myself up, I get on all fours and crawl over to him. Resting on my heels at his feet, I lift my hands and hook them in the top of his briefs and tug them down his legs. His dick springs free and nearly takes my eye out. A chuckle slips past my lips.

"No guy wants to have his woman laugh when she pulls his underwear down."

"Sorry, but your massive cock nearly poked me in the eye."

"Massive, huh?"

"Mmmhmpf, and I cannot wait to have said massive cock in my mouth."

"By all means, suck away." He wiggles his hips, causing his cock to swing.

Leaning forward, I grip the base of his cock in my palm and dart my tongue out, swiping it over his glistening tip. He hisses at the contact and the hiss turns into a moan when I suck his shaft into my mouth. Up and down my head bobs and hearing him come undone has my pussy tingling. Reaching around, I cup and massage his balls as I continue to work his cock in and out of my mouth.

His dick hardens further and I know he's close.

Doubling down, I hollow my cheeks and relax my throat, I take him all the way to the back. Gagging a little, spit and precum dribble down my chin but seeing complete and utter ecstasy on JJ's face makes this all worth it.

His body stiffens and, giving his balls one last squeeze, he comes.

Releasing his seed into my mouth, I suck and swallow every last drop. Pulling back, I lick the last of his release off his dick and stare up at him.

Reaching out, he cups my cheek and runs the pad of his thumb over my bottom lip. Opening my mouth, he slips it in and I suck. "Fuck, babe, what are you doing to me?"

"I don't know what you mean," I playfully reply, waggling my eyebrows at him.

"You know exactly what you're doing. Now, lie back. It's my turn to devour you."

With my eyes locked on his, I lie back like he asks and strike a sexy pose.

"Fuck me, you're a vision, Lex. I don't know if I want to devour you with this sexy number still on or if I want to strip you bare."

"Why not both?" I suggest. "Eat me out while I'm

wearing it and then you can strip me naked and I'll ride you."

"I like your way of thinking, Lexi Knight. Now, spread those legs and let me have my appetizer."

Doing as he asks, I spread my legs and I notice the exact moment he sees the wet patch on my thong. "Did sucking my cock make you wet, baby?"

Nodding, I reach down and pull the material to the side, baring my freshly shaved pussy at him. The cool air feels amazing on my heated folds. Sliding my finger into my slit, I let out a guttural moan when I press it inside. Flicking my wrist, I slip my digit in and out. Pleasure shoots up my spine. My toes curl, but it's not enough. I can't quite get there. I need more.

"I need you, JJ," I pant like a hussy.

Dropping to his knees, he grabs my ankle and runs the tip of his finger up my leg. My skin thrums and breaks out in goose bumps the higher he gets.

Lowering himself down, he moves his head between my thighs and inhales. "You have the sweetest smelling pussy. I can't wait to have a taste."

"Yes," I mewl as I continue to finger myself. JJ just lies there, watching my finger enter my pussy. "Please," I beg.

He lifts his gaze to mine and throws me a wink. Gripping my wrist, he pulls my fingers out of me and brings them to his lips. Opening wide, he licks and sucks them clean, then turns his focus to my nether region.

Leaning forward, he drags his tongue over the material of my thong before sucking on my slit.

"Yesssssss," I hiss.

Gripping his head, I push him into my pussy as he continues to kiss me through the now soaked material of my panties. "Please," I beg again.

Pulling away, I miss the loss of his touch immediately, but when he hooks his fingers into the band of my thong, that want inside me increases because as soon as I'm bare, he's going to devour me and I cannot wait.

Shocking me, he pulls at the material of my thong and literally tears it from my body. Throwing the shredded material to the side, he lowers his head and hall-a-fucking-lu-jah he covers my pussy with his mouth and sucks. My back arches and when he inserts a finger, I see stars.

My body is thrumming with desire. I don't think I've ever been this turned on. JJ feasts on me like a starving man, and I love it.

Lifting my hands to my chest, I squeeze my breasts, thumbing my nipples through the sheer material of the teddy.

JJ presses another finger in, hooking it, hitting that magical spot that has me coming instantly.

Crying out, my body stiffens as my release explodes. Ecstasy courses through my veins. From head to toe I'm a pleasurable mess.

The feeling ebbs away and I relax into the makeshift bed.

Removing his fingers, he pulls away from my pussy and I miss his touch instantly. Like a tiger stalking its prey, he crawls up my body and covers my mouth with his. His tongue plunges into mine and I eagerly accept it. Our tongues slip and slide together and I'm so focused on his tongue, I don't realize what's happening down below. With a flick of his hips, he shoves his cock into me and I cry out into our kiss at the sudden intrusion. I didn't think I could take any more after that intense orgasm, but as he thrusts in and out, an orgasm hits out of nowhere and I scream. My cries echo around his apartment.

Kissing down the column of my neck, he makes his way

to my breasts. He bites my nipple through the teddy and I cry out in unimaginable pleasure. Freeing my breast from the confines of the sheer material, he sucks the tight, taut tip into his mouth, soothing the pain of his bite.

"Come for me, Lex," he demands and I shake my head.

"I can't," I protest.

My body is spent. I don't have another orgasm in me. The ones from before have sucked everything from my marrow.

"You can, and you will," he states.

Slipping his hand between us, he massages my clit. My body begins to shake and when he pinches my clit, it sets me off again. I scream as another orgasm rips through me. My walls clench down on him and it sets him off. His body stiffens and he begins to come, but at the last minute, he pushes himself up, pulls out, and finishes on my belly. White streams of cum paint my skin and teddy.

Watching him mark me is erotic in itself.

Collapsing onto the floor next to me, we both lie here panting. "That"—huff—"was"—huff—"a—"

"—mazing," I finish for him.

"Fucking amazing." He rolls to his side. "Thank you." He brushes a tendril of hair off my forehead and cups my cheek in his palm. Turning my head toward him, I smile and roll onto my side. Mirroring his position, I stare into his bright green eyes. "I've never seen your eyes so bright before," I tell him.

"Well, I've never seen you look so sexy. What did I do to deserve all of this?"

"Well, I thought you might need a release after meeting with your dad."

"And you'd be right." He sighs. "It didn't go well."

"Wanna talk about it?"

He shakes his head. "Not right now. Right now, I just want to lie here with the woman I love and forget that the outside world exists."

"That we can do," I tell him.

Pushing him to his back, I shimmy closer and snuggle into him from the side. He closes his eyes and pulls me in closer. Throwing my leg over, I scrunch my face up when I realize I just smooshed his release into him, but when I look up, he hasn't noticed because he's already fast asleep.

Resting my head on his shoulder, I close my eyes and drift off to sleep with him.

46

JJ

My alarm goes off at stupid a.m. and I reluctantly pull myself away from a sleeping Lex to silence it. Sometime in the middle of the night, we moved from the living room floor to the bedroom. I'm too old to be sleeping on the floor anymore, even if it is with a semi-naked Lexi.

As much as I'd rather roll back over and snuggle, I need to be at the stadium in an hour and with the playoffs coming up, I need to be in tip-top shape. Climbing out of bed, I stand up, stretch, and walk into the en suite to shower. There's dried cum on my side, but when I think back over the events of last night, I can't find myself giving a shit.

Turning the water on, I brush my teeth while I wait for the water to heat. As I'm brushing, I think over my time with Dad yesterday and I kind of hate how it turned out. Sure, he deserves my anger, but he is making an effort now, and I all but threw it in his face. Mom raised me better than that. As I step under the spray, I decide that if I see him again, I'll give him a chance.

Everyone deserves a second chance and he did go out of his way to see me, and he did help Lex with the Brandon issue.

Closing my eyes, I tip my head back and let the water wash over me.

A pair of hands slide around my waist and then I feel a kiss being pressed to my back. Turning around, I come face-to-face with the woman who holds my heart.

"Morning," I whisper.

"Morning. Did you sleep well?" she asks me.

"Very, very well, and you?"

"Like a baby. Who knew sex was such a good sleeping pill?"

"Maybe for scientific purposes we should test that theory again?" she suggests.

"Well, in the name of science, we must."

"Excellent." She traces her fingertip over my pecs and down my abs toward my cock, but I grip her wrist. "As much as I would love to start our experiment now, I have to get to practice, but tonight when I get home, we will experiment again."

"Game on," she seductively purrs.

Pushing me aside, she steps under the spray and I stand here watching as water sluices down her sexy as hell body. My cock twitches and as much as I want to spin her around, bend her over, and fuck her from behind, I think of fat, naked, old men because we don't have time for me to fuck her how she deserves to be fucked.

My cock instantly deflates and I rush through my shower to get away from the sexy, wet, and naked woman beside me.

Drying off, I glance into the shower and when I see Lex running her soap-covered hands over her tits, I let out an audible groan. She lifts her head and notices me staring at her.

"Like what you see?" she seductively asks, and then the minx that she is presses her soap-covered tits against the glass.

"You're a seductress and tonight, I'm going to fuck you in the shower as part of our experiment. Now, before I make myself late by climbing in there and fucking you, I'm going to go. I'll see you later."

She blows me a kiss and I pretend to catch it like the lovesick fool I am. Winking at her, I walk out of the bathroom and change into my workout clothes and pull on my running shoes. Grabbing my things, I head out and make my way to the stadium.

Coach rides our asses today—something different, not—and I'm surprised by how well I kept up with the rest of the guys after my extracurricular activities last night. After practice, Kal and I decide to head to Sushi Samurai together for a bite to eat. With full stomachs, we say our goodbyes and I head home. As I'm walking along the street, I bump into my dad coming out of the liquor store. "Dad, hey. Hi."

"Hey, Jay."

An awkward silence develops between us and then we both say sorry at the same time. "You go first," he says before I can tell him to go.

"Dad, I need to apologize for how I acted yesterday—"

"No, Jay, you don't," he interrupts. "You have every right to be angry. I could have handled things better back in the day, but we all make dumb decisions from time to time. Do I regret what I did? Every day, Jay, every-fucking-day." His eyes widen. "Ohhh, shit, sorry, I shouldn't swear around my kid."

A chuckle escapes me. "Dad, I'm twenty-five and I play

hockey professionally. I've heard all the swears and even on occasion, I've used them too."

"Thank fuck," he says. "I have a foul mouth at the best of times."

"Hopefully not around kids."

"You have a kid?" he asks me, shocked.

"God, no." I shake my head for emphasis. "I just manage to look after myself. I can't be responsible for another human being. Well, not yet anyway, but one day Lexi and I hope to have kids."

"So, it's serious between you and that girl?"

Nodding, I grin widely. "Yep, I'd ask her to marry me tomorrow if I thought she'd say yes, but I've just gotten her back."

"Gotten her back?"

"Long story, but she gave me a second chance and … and I think I need to give you one too."

"I'd like that, Jay. Maybe we can do dinner one night?"

"Yeah, sure. Maybe next week? The team flies to Toronto tomorrow and we'll be back early next week."

"Sounds like a plan."

Dad and I swap numbers and then I head home to work on experiment number two with Lexi.

47

LEXI

The guys smashed it in Toronto and they're one step closer to the playoffs. If they keep playing like this, the Cup will be theirs. I'd love for JJ to win the Cup in his rookie year.

The plane arrived earlier, but Doc and I had to head into the stadium because currently we're in talks with the NHL officials to implement our treatment plans across all teams in the league. After losing Brandon, we were a man down, but then Evie Salvatore came on board. Evie is an orthopedic surgeon who then did a fellowship in sports medicine, making her a brilliant addition to the Crushers and her six-year-old son, Tyler, is a delight. She has slipped into the dynamics of the team perfectly, even if she comes from a mafia family. I remember her family from when we were growing up. The Salvatores are a force to be reckoned with in Chicago. I went to school with her younger sister, Selene. There's a seven-year difference between the two of them, so I don't really remember Evie, but from first impression, it seems Evie is nothing like her sister—may she rest in peace. Selene was killed a year or so ago. Rumor has it, she was caught up in some Salvatore family drama, but from what I can gather, she has nothing to do with her parents or the Salvatore family anymore.

"Honey, I'm home," I call out as I let myself into JJ's place. I pretty much live here now. I usually only go to my place if I need an item of clothing or something, but I can't just invite myself to move in. I need to wait until he officially asks me.

"Hi," a voice I don't recognize says and when I look up, I see JJ's dad standing there.

"Hiiiii," I draw the word out.

"We haven't officially met. I'm Chet James. You're Lexi, right?"

"I know who you are," I mumble.

Memories of the day he accosted me in the parking lot at the stadium flash before my eyes and I take a step backward. My heart is racing. "What are you doing here?" I manage to get out.

"I ran into Jay last week and he invited me for dinner when he got back. He played so well in Toronto. Made me proud. I can see why he earns the big bucks. And what is it you do?"

"Hey, babe," JJ says before I have a chance to reply to Chet.

Just hearing his voice causes the fear gripping me to evaporate. As soon as I see him, I throw myself at him. Wrapping my arms tightly around him, I close my eyes and hold him close. He embraces me and I feel safe in his arms.

Opening my eyes, I see Chet over his shoulder, he's staring at us and I can't read him. I notice his eyes are darting around JJ's apartment. It's almost like he's scoping the place out.

JJ pulls away and laces our fingers together. "Lex, I want you to officially meet my dad, Chet. Dad, this is Lexi, my girlfriend."

"We just got acquainted when she let herself in. I didn't realize the two of you were living together."

"We're not," I tell him, "I have my own place downtown."

"She pretty much does live here. We just haven't made it official yet."

My gaze snaps toward JJ. "Is that your roundabout way of asking me to move in?"

"Sure, why not?" he says.

"Wow, feel the love there."

"Ohhh oh," Chet voices. "The lady isn't happy." The tone of his voice is anything but playful.

JJ laughs and then he turns to me and drops down to one knee. My eyes widen and he takes my hands. "Alexis Knight, will you officially move in with me?" I just stare at him in shock. For a moment there, I thought he was going to propose, which is stupid because we've only been back together for a few months. "Please, Lex. Please officially move in."

Nodding, I smile at him down on one knee. "Yes, JJ, yes. I'd love to."

Dropping to my knees before him, I take his cheeks in my palms and kiss him, cementing our new living arrangements.

"Seems tonight is a celebration," Chet says, interrupting our kiss.

Standing up, JJ takes my hand and we head farther into the apartment.

"Congrats to the two of you." He offers his hand to JJ and after they shake, he turns to me and opens his arms for a hug. Hugging him is the last thing I want to do, but I suck it up. Smiling at him, I step into his embrace, but I quickly pull back. "I'll start on dinner," I tell them and before either can protest, I head into the kitchen.

As I gather the ingredients to make creamy chicken gnocchi, I watch JJ with his dad. I really do not like that man and over the course of the evening, that feeling intensifies. I can't put my finger on it, but he's up to something, but what?

48

JJ

"YOU WERE QUIET LAST NIGHT ... AND TODAY," I STATE AS WE walk toward home hand in hand ... and I love being able to officially say that. It's a gorgeous spring day and since we finished midafternoon, we decided to take a stroll through the city together. She doesn't answer me, so I ask the one question I'm not sure I want the answer to. "Are you having second thoughts about moving in?"

"No," she refutes, vehemently shaking her head. "I just have a lot going on at the moment."

"Wanna talk about it?" Again, I get a headshake. "Well, I'm here for when you're ready to open up." We walk a few more blocks in silence and then it hits me. "Are you scared to tell your dad that we're moving in together?"

She laughs. "Oh My God, I hadn't even thought about telling him, but can you imagine how he's going to react when he finds out his princess is moving in with a boy ... and it's the boy who obliterated her heart when she was eighteen."

"I hate that I did that," I remind her.

"I know, and it's all in the past. This is a new adventure for us and regardless of what he says, I can't wait to be your roomie."

"You'll be barefoot and pregnant in no time," I tease, knowing exactly how she's going to react.

"Excuse me, Jameson James—"

"Ohhh, you full named me, but, babe, I'm joking. We're too young to have kids. Plus, I'm just starting my career, as are you. We each need to leave our mark on the world before we bring a mini-JJ into the world."

"God help us, there will be two of you," she jokes. Well, I hope she's joking. I know she is when she adds on, "Mind you, a mini-me will be just as bad. I was a super bitch when I hit puberty. The things I put my mom and dad through, I'm surprised they had kids of their own after me."

"I forget that Dr. Knight isn't your real dad."

"He is in every sense of the word, JJ. Just because my DNA isn't his doesn't change that fact. Look at you, you have your dad's DNA, but you aren't a family abandoning asshole like he is."

Her words shock me. "You think he's an asshole?"

"JJ, he up and left you and Lisa without so much as a goodbye. Rocking up twenty years later without so much as a sorry doesn't change that." She stops walking and turns to face me. "JJ, I want you to have a relationship with your dad, but something doesn't feel right. It feels like he's hiding something."

"Like what? And how can you say that? You haven't said hardly anything to him. In fact, whenever the two of you have been around each other, you've been rude and stand-offish to him."

"I have not," she shouts at me. "He doesn't give me the time of day, JJ. Do you want my honest opinion?"

"Yes," I hesitantly utter, but to be honest, I'm not sure I *do* want her opinion. Lexi never holds back when it comes to telling you what she thinks. It's one of the things I love about her, but what if she tells me a hard truth about my dad that I don't want to hear? Or what if she tells me something that makes me think poorly of her?

"I think he only wants your money and your connections. He's always asking how much you earn. What endorsement deals you have coming up. He scopes his eyes around the apartment like he's looking at what he can steal. He—"

"He does not," I interrupt her to defend him.

"And that's your opinion, but, JJ, I don't trust the man. At the end of the day, it's your life and he's your dad. I'll be by your side whatever you choose, but do one thing for me?" I nod. "I want you to be careful. I want you to hold your cards close to your chest because I don't want you to get hurt again."

"You really don't like him, do you?"

"It's not that I don't like him per se. I just … I don't know exactly what I feel, but I'm positive Chet is up to something."

"He's not," I defend my dad, and I hate he's coming between us on the sidewalk in the middle of the busiest city in the world. "I don't want to fight over this," I tell her.

"I don't want to fight either, so, from now on, I'll bite my tongue when it comes to your dad." Reaching out, I pull her into my arms and press a kiss to her temple. She slides her arms around my waist and rests her head on my pecs.

"Thank you," I whisper, even if in the back of my mind I think there might be some truth to what she's saying.

49

LEXI

How is it mid-April already?

It feels like just yesterday we were ringing in the new year, but nope, it's almost five months later and next week the playoffs start.

So much has happened this year and with another eight months to go, so much more is still to come, but I can already state this has been one of the best years in a long pucking time. *Damn you, Chelsea Maxwell, and making me say puck instead of fuck.*

JJ and I are a couple once again and we moved in together a few weeks ago. I moved into his apartment 'cause his is bigger than mine and also closer to the stadium. Plus, the security is much better than what was at mine ... and by better, I mean it has a doorman and you can only get up to our floor if you're on the approved list or we authorize you to come up.

This was the winning feature when we told my dad we were moving in together ...

. . .

"So, umm," I stammer while FaceTiming my parents for our weekly chat. "I have news ..."

"You came to your senses and got rid of that boy who broke your heart when you were eighteen?" my dad voices. His contempt for JJ is still there. Seems he cannot forgive like I can.

"No, not that and, Dad, that won't be happening ... ever because, umm, well, JJandIaremovingintogether," I run those last seven words into one long word.

"What?" he growls while my mom says, "I'm so happy for you, Lexi."

"Happy? What the hell, Cress? That boy broke my princess's heart and he'll do it again. Once a breaker always a breaker."

"Really, Dad? You don't think JJ has proved how sorry he is?"

"He. Broke. Your. Heart," he reiterates.

"We were young and dumb," I defend JJ. "And don't forget, he put on his big boy panties and called YOU when he was trying to win me back. That there proves he has big balls, but, Dad, I've loved JJ since I was sixteen. Yes, he was a bonehead, but we've moved past that and it's time you do too." I'm on a roll, so I continue, "Dad, I love him and he loves me, and we're moving in. And before you try to talk me out of it, I've made up my mind."

"What if his apartment isn't suitable? You are in New York, and with what happened the other week, your safety is paramount."

"Dad, his building is much safer and nicer than my current place—"

"Excuse me, Alexis Knight, I found that apartment for you. It's perfect."

"Dad, as much as I love my apartment, JJ's is better. It's closer to the park and work"—only a smidge, but I'm clutching at straws right now—"the laundry is in the apartment and the kitchen is to *die for. It has a doorman and you can only get up to our floor if you are on the approved list or we authorize you to come up."*

"That all sounds nice, but must you live with him? He's a boy."

"He's the boy I love, Dad, and I want this."

"Well, the fact it has a doorman is comforting ..."

New living situation aside, I'm smashing it as a PT and I love my job. I thought I'd learned everything I needed to know when I was at USC, but working alongside Doc Michels has been a game—pun intended—changer. The only kicker to this year is the return of JJ's dad, Chet James. He's a bone of contention when it comes to JJ and me. I don't trust the man. There's something about him that irks me and whenever I bring it up with JJ, we get into a fight. Even though, deep down, I think he agrees with me. Don't get me wrong. I hope I'm wrong and it's just my inner protectiveness of JJ coming out, but I don't think I am.

I'm sitting up on the second level in the stands, working on my notes, but my mind is all over the place right now. To tell you the truth, I'm nervous. To be associated with a Cup winning team would be awesome. The guys have played amazing all season and it all comes down to the next few games. They are up against the San Francisco Saints and it's going to be a fight till the end. The Saints will be tough contenders for the Crushers, but if the guys play like they have been, the Cup is theirs.

A smile appears on my face and when I look up, JJ is staring at me. How he knew I was here working is beyond me, but we seem to know when the other is around. Giving him a wave, he blows me a kiss, earning himself a round of

"Oooohs" and "Whipped" with an added sound of a whip cracking from his fellow teammates.

A laugh escapes me and I shake my head.

Putting my feet up on the chair in front of me, I get back to my notes. I really need to get these done in a more timely manner. That's the one part of this job I suck at.

I'm engrossed in my work when a raised voice from below garners my attention. Peeking over the edge, I see Chet standing in the walkway. He has his phone to his ear and from the look on his face, he's not happy.

"I'm working on it," he sneers into the phone.

Working on what? I ask myself.

"Look, Mr. S., I'll get you your money." He glances upward and I quickly duck out of sight. My heart stops beating, but I don't think he saw me because he continues his conversation. "I said I'll get it," he hisses as he walks farther into the stadium. "It's just taking longer than I anticipated."

Slinking back into my seat, I try and hide from view. This is clearly a conversation no one is meant to hear, but from the one side I can hear, Chet owes someone named Mr. S. money. And I can only assume that it's taking time because JJ isn't a fool and isn't throwing his money around. This man clearly doesn't know his son, but I do. If he just approached JJ, like a man, he'd probably hand it over without blinking an eye. That's the kind of guy he is, but instead of manning up, Chet is once again going to screw over his son.

Chet finishes up his phone call and walks out. I know I need to tell JJ what I overheard, but with the playoffs commencing in a couple of days, he needs his head in the game. He doesn't need his sperm donor messing with that, so for now, I'll keep this from him, but as soon as it's over, I'll tell him everything I know.

Trying to put what I heard out of my head, I get back to

work, but I can't concentrate, so a few minutes later, I pack up my things and head out.

Walking down the stairs, I exit into the atrium and when I turn the corner, I bump into someone and all my files go flying. Lifting my head, I come face-to-face with the last person I want to see.

"Hi, Chet," I utter, "what are you doing here?"

"JJ and I are meeting up for an early dinner."

"That's nice," I lie.

"Did you just come from in there?" He flicks his thumb toward the stadium where we both just came from.

My head moves up and down to say yes and I mumble a quiet, "Mmmhmpf," in confirmation.

"I guess you heard my call just now?" Again, I nod. He grips my upper arm, like he did the other month, and leans down. I can feel his heated breath on my face. Fear races up my spine, just like the day he approached me in the parking lot. "You listen here and you listen clearly, girlie. You will not fuck this up for me," he sneers in my face. "As soon as I get what I need, I'll be gone." He pauses for emphasis. "You hear me?"

I don't know where this surge of defiance comes from, but I wrench my arm free of his grasp and slam my palms into his chest. "I knew it," I snap. "You don't care about JJ at all. You only care about his money."

"It's more than that, little lady. My life is on the line."

"I don't give a flying fuck about you or that. I care about JJ. If you do this, he will never forgive you."

"Who do you think he'll believe? His dad? Or the girl he fucked over in the past?" He huffs, "You know, Jay is so much like me. One day, he'll tire of your sweet ass and he'll leave again. Once an asshole, always an asshole. I should know. I'm the king of assholes. It runs in the James genes and I have a feeling, my son and I are one and the same."

"You really are a piece of shit," I throw at him through clenched teeth. "I'm going to tell JJ what you're up to."

That was the wrong thing to say because he steps toward me again and this time, he wraps his hands around my neck and slams me into the wall. "You fuck this up for me and I will end you. Stay out of my business."

"JJ is my business," I manage to squeak out. He squeezes tighter, but the sound of heels clicking on the floor and a squeak of sneakers on the polished cement floor in the hallway has Chet quickly removing his hands from my neck and stepping away from me. He drops down into a squat and begins to pick up my things. I just stand here, with my back to the wall, holding my neck.

"You okay, Lexi?" Janice asks when she and Coach Maxwell step into the atrium.

"I'm," I begin to speak, but I stop when Chet growls at me from below and glares at me. "Yeah, I'm fine, Janice. Just a clumsy moment." My voice is rough from having my throat squeezed.

"Luckily, I was here to assist," Chet voices as if he's a fucking saint when, in fact, he's the devil in disguise.

Janice and Coach both flick their gazes between us. I smile, trying to reassure them everything is okay, but I'm not a very good actress and they both know something is up. Before they can ask any further questions, Chet stands up and hands me my things.

Taking them from him, I mumble my thanks and hightail it out of there. I race down the hallway and make a beeline for the locker room. The guys are still in the showers and right now JJ is singing an off-key version of "Tennessee Whiskey" by Chris Stapleton. Usually that would garner a smile from me, but not today. I race into my treatment room and close the door behind me.

Flicking the lock, I slide down the wood and draw my legs up to my chest and hug them.

He choked me.

He could have killed me.

Had Janice and Coach not interrupted, who knows what would have happened. I know I need to tell JJ, but I don't want him distracted. He needs to focus on his upcoming games. I can hold on for a little longer before I tell him. I mean, it's not like I see Chet all the time, right?

"IS LEXI OKAY?" COACH ASKS ME AFTER PRACTICE.

"Yeah, why?" I ask him, confused, because when I saw her just up in the stands earlier, she seemed fine.

"It's probably nothing, but she seemed rattled when I saw her just now. Maybe take her out tonight, have a night just the two of you before things get crazy with the playoffs and whatnot."

"What about practice this evening?"

"One night off won't hurt, but I expect you to bring your A-game bright and early tomorrow morning."

"Yes, sir." I nod. "Thank you."

"Just do me a favor?"

"Anything?"

"Stop singing in the showers. You sound like a dying cat in a blender."

"I'm not that bad of a singer," I refute, but a chorus of "You suck" and "Don't quit hockey" echoes through the dressing room and I can't help but chuckle. "You all love it when I sing. And you all love it when I sing 'Wonderwall' 'cause you all sing along with me." Jumping up onto the bench near my locker, I clear my throat, "Today is gonna be…" Soon enough the rest of the guys are singing along with me, even Doucheman joins in.

The door to Lexi's treatment room opens and when her gaze links with mine, she's shaking her head but grinning at the same time. Before long, she too is singing … as is Coach, Rick, and Evie.

Jumping off the bench, I walk over to Lex and pull her into my arms. Swaying from side to side, I sing the words just for her. "…one that saves me—"

"Saves me," she sings the last line of the song to me.

With my Grammy-winning rendition over, I lean back and stare at her. "You may not have saved me per se, but you did save me from falling for the wrong girl. You are it for me, Lexi Knight, and tonight, tonight I'm going to take you out and spoil you."

"What about practice?"

"Coach gave me the night off. He said you were a little off earlier and I need to treat my woman to a night out." He pauses. "You do look off. Are you okay?" Lifting my hand, I rest it on her forehead, but she doesn't seem to have a temperature.

"I was fine till you called me your woman."

"Okay, let me rephrase, Coach said I need to take my sexy, beautiful, gorgeous—and all the other amazing words out there—girlfriend out for the night and treat her before things get crazy 'cause you seemed rattled and off."

"I'm fine," she says, but a blind person can tell she's anything but.

"You know what fine stands for?"

"Do not *Italian Job* me, Jameson James."

"Ohhh, full name," I tease. "But seriously, are you okay?"

"Really, I'm fine, just tired, but a nice dinner with my man would be lovely."

"Sounds like a plan … and for the record, I like it when you call me 'your man' and you can do it all day every day."

"Fine," she throws back at me. "I'll get my things and we can head out. Meet you in the atrium in five?"

"It's a date." I waggle my eyebrows and earn myself another giggle.

Coach is on crack or something because she seems fine, but I'm not going to turn down a night out with Lex. She lifts to her toes and places a kiss on my cheek. Then she heads into her treatment room to get her stuff.

Heading back to my locker, I grab my things and just as I'm about to head out, Anton stops me and asks me a few questions about my latest endorsement deal with Monty's Lingerie. I give him all the deets and then he teases me about seeing my junk on a billboard in Times Square, to which I say, "You're just jealous my junk is bigger than your junk."

Saying bye to the team, I head out to the atrium to meet Lex. She's staring off into the distance and in her own world. When I reach her, I slide my hand around her neck. She flinches and retaliates with an elbow to the ribs. "Ouch," I hiss.

"Shit, JJ, I'm sorry, you startled me."

"Are you sure you're okay, Lex? You have never reacted like that before. You usually love a little choking."

"I … I'm fine, you just startled me. Come on, let's get an early dinner and then we can have dessert at home, if you get my drift."

"Lead the way, ma'am," I say before linking our fingers together. We step out in the hot summer afternoon. Going from the coolness of the arena to outside takes my breath away.

"Calling me ma'am is just as icky as you calling me 'your woman,' you know that, right?"

"My momma raised me to be a gentleman."

"And a fine job she did," a deep voice says and when I look up, I see my dad standing there.

"Dad, what are you doing here?"

"Hoping to spend some time with my son. I watched you practice earlier. You look really good out there."

"You were here?" I ask.

"Yeah, did Lexi not tell you?" he voices. "She and I had a lovely chat."

"You did?" I ask, not sure if it's to her or him, but if they did have a chat, it could explain why she's off since she's not a fan of my dad.

"We did," she says, "and I didn't tell you because it hasn't come up in the five minutes we've been together this afternoon, but we better get going, I'm starving."

"Where are you two lovebirds off to?" Dad asks.

"Early dinner followed by a night in."

"Mind if I join you?" he asks and I feel Lex stiffen beside me.

"Umm," I reply, but Lexi shakes her head and answers for me. "Sorry, Chet, this is our last chance for a date before the playoffs," she says.

"Ohhh," Dad dejectedly says, "I was hoping to spend some time with you."

My gaze flicks between Dad and Lexi. I really want to reconnect with my dad, but I know Lexi isn't a fan, and this is our last chance to have quality time together. Silence wraps around the three of us. Even the city feels quiet in this moment. I look from my dad back to Lexi. I can see that something is up. Even with how she feels about my dad, she's usually pushing me to see him, but, right now, she clearly needs me and Lexi will always come first. "Sorry, Dad, Lexi and I already have plans. Maybe after the play-offs," I suggest.

He doesn't seem so happy with my decision and it's confirmed when he snaps, "Fine. Whatever."

He takes off without another word to me, but the look he gives Lexi doesn't sit right, but before I can tell him off, he's gone. Storming off like a pissed-off bull. Muttering to himself, but it's too muffled and quiet to hear, but one thing's for sure, he's pissed off and angry.

"You sure you don't want to have dinner with your dad?" Lexi offers.

"Positive," I tell her. "Tonight is about us." Feeling cheeky, I add, "And my woman needs to be spoiled."

The 'my woman' comment earns me another smack in the stomach and then we head home to shower and change for dinner, but when I see Lexi naked and wet in the shower, it's game over.

We don't make it out for dinner. Instead, we make it to the bed and after three orgasms apiece, we order in and like I promised, I have her for dessert.

Tonight wasn't quite what I had in mind when Coach first suggested a night off to spoil my girl, but any time with Lexi is perfect and tonight was just that ... if only it stayed that way.

51

LEXI

We're in San Francisco for game six and the atmosphere in the stadium is electric. The guys are currently in the lead three to two. If they win against San Francisco tonight, it's game over and the Crushers will be this year's Stanley Cup winners. The home team is going to do their best to take it through to a seventh game, but the guys are fired up. They want the win tonight.

The roar of the crowd here in the locker room is just as loud as if I were in the arena. I'm doing a last minute massage on Jett's rotator cuff. "How's that feel?" I ask after rubbing my fingertips into the tissue around the side and toward the shoulder blade.

He rotates his shoulder, backward and forward, and from the grin on his face, it feels good.

"You have magic hands, Lex, my shoulder has never felt better."

"I aim to please," I tell him. "We can catch up when we're

back in New York and document what we did and pass it along to Doc."

"Sounds like a plan." He jumps off the table and pulls me into a hug.

"Get your grubby mitts off my woman, Jenson," JJ growls. You can tell he's joking, considering he's sporting a huge grin when I spin around and come face-to face with "my man."

"What have I told you about calling me woman?"

"What have I told you about letting other guys grope you?"

"It was a hug, not a grope, you thug." Walking over to him, I drape my arms over his shoulders. "And you know, the only person who can grope me is you, and I plan on doing a lot of groping after the game tonight."

"Shit, babe, you can't say shit like that before I take the ice. My dick is already hard thinking about taking the ice … and now it's hardening with thoughts of groping you later."

Biting my lip, I lean into him. "Win tonight and you can claim my ass again."

"You're a minx, you know that?"

Shrugging nonchalantly, I purr, "Think of it as extra incentive to win."

Before he can say anything else, it's go time.

The guys head toward the ice and I head up to the suite to meet up with Chels. She and I like to watch the game from up there because hearing what some of the puck bunnies say about our guys is disgusting and sometimes it's hard to hold back.

I'm standing by the buffet, chatting with Nessa, Coach Maxwell's wife, and Chelsea when the door to the suite opens and the smile on my face vanishes as the last person I expected to see walks in.

Chet saunters into the room as if he owns the place. I really pucking hate that man and now, each time he appears, I make myself scarce. JJ is becoming suspicious, but when he asks what's wrong, I brush him off and say, "I'm fine" or "I'm nervous about the playoffs." And that one's not a complete lie, but he knows something is up. I hate that he knows me so well sometimes.

"Ugh, JJ's dad is here," Chels quietly complains. "That man gives me the creeps."

"Girls, that's not a very nice thing to say," Nessa says, then she leans in and whispers, "but I agree."

"If only you knew the shit he's done," I add.

My eyes are locked on Chet as he makes his way over to the bar. He orders a Jack and Coke and once he has his drink in hand, he walks over to the buffet where we're standing. "If it isn't my daughter-in-law," he says by way of greeting.

"Chet," I tersely reply, "what are you doing here?"

"JJ offered to fly me out and here I am."

"Of course you are," I sneer, clenching my jaw and scrunching my fist by my side.

Chels picks up on my angst. "You need a new drink," she says.

I look at my soda glass and it's not empty and utter, "Umm." She notices my gaze, grabs my glass, and chugs it back.

"Do now," she states and before I can say anything, she loops her arm with mine and drags me away from Chet and over to the bar.

Placing my glass on the shiny bar top, the bartender asks Chels, "What can I get you, ladies?" I take a deep, calming breath and lower my head.

"Two wines, please," Chels replies, and the bartender gets to it before I can protest.

Turning my head, I look at her. "I can't drink. I'm technically on duty."

"Trust me, you need it."

Nodding, I take another deep breath, hoping to calm myself down, but it doesn't work. Lowering my head again, I sigh in frustration.

"You okay?" she asks and when I don't say anything, she tries again. "Lexi, what's going on?"

Without lifting my head, I let it all out. "I hate that man. He rubs me the wrong way. He's attacked me twice and JJ thinks the sun shines out of his pucking ass."

"Hold up. Time-out." She makes the time-out motion with her hands. "You said twice. What else has happened?" Opening my mouth, I go to tell her nothing, but she gives me 'the Chelsea' look and I close my mouth. "Don't even think about saying nothing. I know you, Lex. Nothing gets you down, but whenever that man is around, you fold in on yourself. I've noticed it on several occasions now."

Looking at my friend, I purse my lips, wondering what I can say without saying too much. Needing liquid courage, I pick up my wine glass and chug it back.

"Keep it coming," Chels says to our bartender, Marg.

With a new wine in hand, I tell Chelsea everything that's happened between Chet and me.

"Lex, you need to tell JJ."

"But the playoffs," I defend my decision.

"Playoffs, schmayoffs," she singsongs, waving her hand around. "You need to tell him, Lex."

"But—"

She presses her index finger to my lips, shushing me. "Do not even finish that sentence, Lexi Bernadette Knight."

"My middle name isn't Bernadette, it's Avery."

"Well, I didn't know what it was, but this called for a whole name."

"So you went with Bernadette?"

She shrugs. "But you get the importance. You need to tell him and you need to tell him now. What if he gets close to Chet? And before I go on, what kind of douchey name is that?" She doesn't give me a chance to reply and she continues on with her rant. "Think how JJ is going to feel if next time Douche Dad goes that one step further and physically hurts you. JJ will never forgive himself if that happens."

Staring at my friend, I process her words and from the corner of my eye, I see Chet with Nessa, and she looks really uncomfortable. For some reason, seeing her frightened sparks something inside of me, but before I can approach Chet, the puck drops and Game Six in the series commences.

San Francisco is out to win from the get-go and, unfortunately for the Crushers, the Saints win.

Tonight's game came down to a sudden death followed by a shoot-out. Unfortunately for us, Kal let the puck slip through, giving San Francisco the win. Meaning, we have another game, but to our advantage, the next one is in New York. In three days' time, we will be playing in front of a home crowd and hopefully winning the Cup.

52

JJ

THE PUCK IN THE FINAL GAME IN MY ROOKIE SEASON IS GOING to drop in less than twenty minutes and I'm pumped.

So.

Fucking.

Pumped.

Even if we don't win out there today, I'm proud of my efforts. I've trained hard, as has the team, and it all comes down to this.

We're all ready to head out and warm up and when Anton walks in after getting Lexi to look at his knee, everyone starts cheering and clapping for our captain. He's grinning like a mofo because not only is it Cup Day, but it's also his last game ever. He announced his retirement last week, so a win for him today would be the best kind of sendoff for one of the best captains I've ever had the privilege to play with.

"It's game day, boys," he shouts.

Walking around the room, he taps everyone affectionately on the head—with a not so affectionate tap for Doucheman—who rumor has it is officially being traded to the LA Legends next season. The two teams have done a player swap and we will be acquiring one of their players in return.

Kal drops onto the bench next to me and his smile is just as wide as mine. The announcer says something and it really gets the crowd going. We can hear the rumble of the crowd echo down the tunnel toward us here in the locker room. It adds to the already electric atmosphere and I have a good feeling about today.

My mom and dad are up in the family suite, along with Kal's sister and his nanna and pops. Even Lexi's family flew in for today's game. All those nearest and dearest are here to watch me and the team win this thing.

Lexi is going to hang down here today. She, Doc, and Evie will be on hand to assist with anything we need to keep our bodies in fine form for this last game.

Turning to Kal, I grin at him and slap him on the back. "Wanna make a bet?"

"I was wondering if you'd want to place one today," he says.

"I'm always up for it," I remind him.

"Up for losing again?" he teases, but it's not really teasing, it's fact. I can't remember the last time I won one of these, but Kal is my brother from another mother and I'd do anything for him … just like he and the guys did for me when I finally won Lexi back. "What you got in mind?"

"Why do I have to come up with it?" I know it was my idea, but to be honest, I hadn't thought beyond making the suggestion.

"Loser's choice," he replies with a shrug.

"Isn't it usually winner's choice?"

"Well, I was going to give you a go since you never get a chance to set them since you've lost the last..." Flipping him the bird, he just laughs at me. "Okay, so, you need to have an assist percentage higher than eighty-six for the game."

Hmmmm, a percentage-based bet, I like it. I'm obsessed with tracking my percentages because it helps me to become a better player. Each game I try and beat the last game's stats. If you ask me, it's a brilliant way to track and increase your skill level. "What's yours?" I ask.

He thinks for a moment. "Maximum of one goal for the Saints tonight."

"One goal, that's a good one, but what's at stake?"

"Loser has to shave his head for the entire off-season and grow a moustache. Style may change throughout, but you must always have a stash."

Shaking my head, I chuckle. "Deal."

We each spit on our palms and shake. "You're going down, Jones," I say as we shake.

"I highly doubt it, Jameson."

"You think first naming me is going to help you?"

He shrugs and before we can chat further, Coach walks in and we all cheer. He hushes us and gives a before game speech that lights a fire in all of us. With his speech over, he looks over the team and then says those magic words, "It's game time, boys, make me proud."

Three hours later and it's all over.

We won.

We.

Pucking.

Won.

And fuck me, what a game.

The final score is three to two, with a textbook assist from me to our outgoing captain in the last seconds of the game. The biscuit slid into the goal, sealing us the win.

After the Cup presentation and the endless interviews, we're finally back in the locker room. We're all sitting around, waiting for Coach to give another speech, but this time it's a season victory speech.

"I was impressed with everyone's performance out there today, and thanks to JJ and Anton in those last few seconds, we secured the win." The room erupts into a chorus of cheers and hoots and whistles. Once we all settle down, he continues, "You boys did us proud, we're Stanley Cup champs." Another round of cheers erupts and we begin to sing the team song and then it's Rick's turn.

"As an owner and assistant coach, I'm feeling pretty amazing right now. I've been in your skates, and I know exactly how each one of you feels right now. Don't let the win go to your heads. Enjoy it for tonight, but I want to retain that Cup again next season—"

"No pressure," Jett mumbles and we all chuckle.

"And we, as a team, need to put in the hard work once again. We say goodbye to Anton, who is headed off to retirement, and what a way to retire. You'll be missed around here, but know you're welcome to swing by anytime. With Anton leaving, we had a spot to fill and I think we've found someone who will fill the giant hole Anton is leaving. From the draft, we've secured Colton Bolton. He's—"

"I'm sorry," Anton interrupts, raising his hand in a stop motion. "Did you say his name is Colton Bolton?" He's trying to hold back a laugh as he says this.

"I did, but he prefers to go by Colt."

"I wonder why." Anton sniggers.

"Now, now," Rick growls, "we can't all have perfect names like you, Anton Seaton, but this kid out of Australia is going to give the rest of you boys a run for your money. He was the top goal scorer this season and he was one goal away from equaling my highest points in one game. He does, however, hold that title at a college level."

We all nod and are impressed with that. Sounds like Colton Bolton is going to be a major asset to the team and I cannot wait to meet him.

"One last point of business," Coach says. "By now, you all know that next season, Stefan is leaving us and is moving to LA to play with the Legends. We wish you the best in LA, Stefan." That's all he gets. No cheers. No applause. Nothing. To be honest, I think we're all inwardly cheering at this news. No one will be sad to see him go. "And as part of the trade deal with LA, Miller Wentworth will be joining us next season." My eyes widen at his name and I'm excited to play alongside him again. "With that said, go enjoy yourselves and I'll see you in a few days for the end of season team dinner."

With the speeches wrapped up, we all agree to head to Kallen's to celebrate since his place has a kick-ass terrace with breathtaking views of the Manhattan skyline and the Hudson River.

Once we are all changed, it's party time.

The sun is starting to peek over the horizon and we're still celebrating at Kallen's place. The table is littered with empty beer and liquor bottles, containers of food, half-eaten bowls of chips, and a bag of carrots. I have no clue where the carrots came from, but I do know, I'm ready for bed.

Looking up, I smile when Lexi steps out onto the terrace and makes her way over to me. There's a sway to her hips and a glint in her eye. She sits sidesaddle on my lap and hugs me.

Leaning in, she whispers into my ear, "We should get out of here and go celebrate, just the two of us."

"We should," I murmur, "but would it be rude to leave?" She shakes her head and bites her lip. "Okay, then, let's head home."

Nodding, she climbs off my lap and offers me her hand. Standing up, I take her offered hand in mine and tug her toward me. Sliding my arm around her waist, I dip her backward and cover her mouth. Passionately, I kiss her, earning us a few wolf whistles from the guys.

When I straighten us up, I give her a wink before I throw her over my shoulder and slap her delectable ass. With a wave, I sing out my goodbyes and take her home to celebrate, just the two of us.

53

LEXI

...three days later

HAND IN HAND, JJ AND I WALK OUT OF THE APARTMENT AND toward the elevators. JJ looks spiffy in his black pants, white button-down, and blazer. He leans into me as we wait for a car to arrive. "You look sexy as puck in this purple halter number. I'm really hoping there's no underwear underneath this silky dress."

"Question! Since you're the face of a lingerie company, should you not be wanting me to be wearing lingerie? Specifically a Monty's design."

"I'm the face of the male line, babe."

"I see, well, FYI, I'm not wearing a bra and I'm ... ohh look, the elevator is here. Shall we?" I say, stepping into the car.

"That wasn't fair." He pouts and he steps in beside me.

"Call it delayed gratification ... but since you like betting so much, if you can guess if I have panties on or not

WITHOUT touching or sliding your hand under my dress before we reach the dinner, I might let you have a preview."

"You have yourself a deal." I outstretch my hand to seal the deal and after we shake, he pulls me into his chest. "Ohh, and FYI, I play to win."

Looking up into his green eyes that are as vibrant as the sparkliest of emeralds, I lean into his ear and whisper, "Game on."

And because I'm a tease, I squeeze his dick through his slacks, taking his mind off our deal. The elevator doors open and I step into the lobby. Glancing backward, I notice him subtly adjusting his dick.

"You coming?" I playfully ask him.

"You don't play fair," he grumbles.

With a laugh, I shrug and keep walking. JJ catches up to me and snatches up my hand. He laces our fingers together and we exit the building. Normally, we'd walk, but in these heels, this dress, and not wearing panties—Shhhh, don't tell JJ—we grab a taxi instead.

JJ sits next to me, tracing his fingertip over my thigh. It's not anything seductive, but from the satin of my dress pressing against my bare nipples, it's turning me on.

Thankfully, before I make a fool of myself and leave a wet patch on the seat of the taxi, we arrive. JJ climbs out first and ever so carefully, I slide out behind him, making sure not to flash anyone.

JJ pouts when I keep my legs tightly closed.

"You don't play fair," he whines as we walk toward the entrance of his building.

"I'm playing to win," I toss back at him.

"Well, wouldn't letting me win really be letting us both win?"

"Nice try, dude, and yes, your logic is correct, buuuuuut you and I will still win when we get home."

He stops in the middle of the corridor. "Home," he utters that one word with a huge smile on his face. "I love that we're living together. Both of us working in the jobs we dreamed of when we were seventeen. My life is complete and with you by my side, Lex, I feel like I can conquer whatever is thrown my way."

"JJ," I sniffle, "that was beautiful."

Stepping closer to him, I grip his cheeks in my palms and press my lips to his. As always when I kiss him, everything around me fades into the background. It's just JJ and me and our unfiltered love for one another.

"Get a room, you two," Jett calls out as he arrives with Margot. Those two have this fake dating thing going on, but I guarantee you, it's real. The chemistry between the two of them is off the charts. I wonder how long it will be before the two of them get their act together?

We all say our hellos and head to the bar. We order drinks and I look around the room. "Umm, why does Kallen look like he's ready to vomit? This thing only started like five minutes ago. Surely he's not hammered already?"

"So, you know how he and I like to make bets?" I nod. "Well, we made a bet for the last game. I had to have an assist percentage higher than eighty-six for the game and he was to allow a max of one goal for the Saints."

"So Kal obviously lost. What was at stake?"

"Loser has to shave his head for the entire off-season and grow a mustache."

"Oh My God, I cannot wait to see pics of Kal with a bald head and a stash."

"You and me both ... now, if you excuse me, I have a

wager to claim." He orders two more beers before heading over to his best friend.

Leaning against the bar, I sip my cocktail and glance around the room. This is a great team to work with, and next season I cannot wait to work closer with Evie. She's a wealth of knowledge and so fun to be around.

Finishing my drink, I duck to the ladies' and when I return, I stop mid-step when I see Chet is here. He's standing with an uncomfortable looking Evie, Nessa, and Rachelle.

"What the puck?" I mumble to myself. A small laugh escapes me and I shake my head when I realize I'm turning into Chelsea and saying puck all the time.

After our run-in in LA a few days ago, I haven't seen Chet since. I know JJ has caught up with him, but we never discuss Chet. He's like Bruno—we don't talk about him. I hate that I feel like this about his dad and I hope I'm wrong with my assumptions, but seeing him here when he wasn't invited has pissed me off.

JJ is still with Kallen and Coach, so I hope I can get rid of Chet before he makes a scene and embarrasses JJ.

Marching over to them, I squeeze in between the girls and *him*, blocking them from Chet. "You need to leave, Chet," I sneer at the man through clenched teeth. "This is a closed, invite-only event and I guarantee you don't have an invitation."

"You can't tell me what to do and like I'd listen to a little bitch like you. As I've said, as soon as I get what I want. I'll be gone."

"Just go," I plead again. "You aren't wanted here."

"Says who?" he throws back at me.

"Me," I snap. He chuckles an evil laugh and the sound causes me to inwardly shudder. He's like a villain from a cartoon and I'm hoping like in the cartoons that he loses. Inhaling deeply, I take a deep breath and step into his space. "You are done threatening me. I don't give a flying fuck that you owe some goon money."

"The Salvatores will kill me," he pleads.

"Did you say Salvatores?" Evie voices from behind me, her eyes wide and full of fear.

"Mmmhmpf," he replies.

"For fuck's sake," she mumbles, then says, "Excuse me," and quickly walks away from us. I furrow my brows at her sudden departure.

"Please," Chet begs, "I need Jay."

"You don't need Jay, you need his money, but I promise you, you will not get a dime from him. You're going to turn around, walk out that door, and never look back. Go face whatever it is that you've gotten yourself into and leave JJ out of it."

"I'm not leaving until I get what I came for."

Over his shoulder, I see JJ coming our way. I know this is a real bitchy thing to do, but I goad him. "And what exactly did you come here for, Chet? Tell us why you returned from wherever the hell you were."

"Money," he hisses. "I need money."

"You need money?" I repeat. My tone gives away exactly how I feel about the situation.

"You know I need money, you little bitch. I'm in deep with the Salvatores and my dear son, the millionaire hockey player, is the one who can get that for me, and I'm not letting a bitch like you stop me from getting my money."

"Is that so?" JJ voices from behind him. His eyes widen in shock and in the blink of an eye, they turn to anger, and that anger is directed at me.

"You little fucking bitch," Chet sneers when he realizes I just set him up.

In the blink of an eye, he lunges for me and wraps his hands around my neck, just like he did the other week. As quickly as they latch on to me, they're quickly removed when JJ pulls his dad off me and throws him to the floor.

Standing here frozen, my gaze flicks between the two men. JJ saved me from his dad. He didn't hesitate. He just jumped in and removed his dad's grasp on me.

Stepping over Chet, he cups my cheeks in his palms, turning my head from side to side to check me over. "Lex, babe, are you okay?"

"I'm fine," I tell him, covering his hands with mine and when I look into his green eyes, I see nothing but concern and love for me. "I'm just a little rattled, but physically, I'm fine. You saved me."

"And I always will," he states. His words warm my heart. "I'm sorry I didn't believe you. I just wanted my dad back. I ... I wanted to believe he cared. I—"

"I do care, Jay," Chet pleads.

JJ spins around and stares down at his father, who's still sitting on the floor. "Yeah, you cared about my money. You never cared about me or rebuilding our relationship." He shakes his head. "Get the fuck out, Chet."

"But I'm your father," Chet cries, pushing himself up to stand before JJ and me.

"Sperm donor, you're my sperm donor. Nothing more. I never want to see you again, Chet. Forget you have a son and do what you do best, leave."

Before Chet can leave of his own accord, the police arrive and they haul him away. JJ's shoulders drop as he watches his dad be escorted out.

"You okay?" I ask, resting my hand on his shoulder. He

nods, but I can tell he's really bummed right now. However, I have an idea on how I can cheer him up. Leaning into him, I whisper, "Wanna find out if I'm wearing panties?"

Turning his head toward me, he smirks. "I pucking love you, Lexi Knight."

"And I pucking love you too, Jameson James. Now, let's go find out if I am or am not wearing any panties."

...eighteen months later

"HE'S SUCH A DOUCHEHOLE PUCKWIT," KALLEN COMPLAINS TO me for the millionth time today. Today he and Doucheman have to give a speech on team bonding and how to deal with big personalities at the annual Christmas fundraiser for underprivileged kids. Normally, it's just the Crushers, but due to the incident the other week, Coach Maxwell and Coach Feldman from the LA Legends decided to join forces and try to mend this rift once and for all. The incident I'm referring to is when the two of them got into a scuffle at Squires, resulting in the both of them getting arrested. As well as this team bonding speech, they were both scratched for three games and fined ten grand.

It's ironic and funny when you think about it, but I'm hoping this is finally the end to the feud between them. Yes, we all like a bit of competition on the ice, but this thing between the two of them has bubbled over and things off-ice are arctic.

"And you're acting like said douchehole puckwit," I tell him, shaking my head at how he's acting. I give him the eye for emphasis, but he ignores me. "Come on, man, you're better than this, and him. Three more hours and you're done."

"We still need to give our talk," he whines like a three-year-old who doesn't want to leave the park. "How can I talk about being all buddy-buddy with him when all I want to do is kick him in the nuts?"

"Fake it 'til you make it," I offer with a shrug and this time, he eyes me. "Look, you can either suck it up or face the wrath of Coach, your wife, and an indefinite suspension. I know what choice I'd make."

"When did you become the levelheaded one?" Kal huffs.

"About the same time I pulled my head out of my ass, manned up, and faced my feelings for Lex."

"Pussy-whipped." He sniggers, but there's also a smile on his face.

My eyes find Lex in the crowd, like they always do, and as my gaze roams over her, a giddy feeling develops inside me. Yes, I sound like a douche, but I'm a douche in love, who got a second chance. Now that I have her back in my arms where she belongs, I'm never letting her go. I'm never going to do anything stupid again. Well, maybe not that last part. I do stupid stuff all the time … but not stupid enough to get arrested and have to do a talk with my nemesis.

"Too right I am. Have you seen my sexy as sin girlfriend?"

He ignores that question because we all know it's an opening for a punch. "When you going to put a ring on that?" he throws back at me instead.

"I've been thinking about it, but when's the right time?"

"When you know, you know," he matter-of-factly tells me.

"That's not very helpful," I voice.

"Well, Christmas is coming up. An engagement ring would be a pretty amazing Christmas gift."

"Yeah, but then I puck myself over for future Christmases." *Oh My God,* puck? Really? I've been hanging around Chelsea too much lately.

"New Year's?" he suggests.

"Too cliché."

"Valentine's Day,"

"See previous comment," I reply, rolling my eyes.

"Fuck, you're picky … How about January third?"

"Why that date?"

"I just picked a date. You can't pick one, so I did it for you."

"I kinda want to do it this year."

"Then December twenty-eighth?"

"But that date has no meaning."

"Puck me, JJ, you're so annoying. Just pick a date and slap a ring on it."

"I need to ask her dad first, but he's a scary dude and I'm kinda scared he'll say no."

"If I can ask Coach for Chelsea's hand, you can ask Mr. Knight for Lexi's hand in marriage."

"Dr. Knight."

"Whatever, just man up, ask him, and then ask her … on December twenty-first."

"I thought you said December twenty-eighth?"

"Pucking hell, just do it."

Staring at my best friend, I consider doing it and then I think *puck it.* "Fine, I'll call Dr. Knight now."

"Good luck, but I'm sure the good doctor will be happy to give his blessing to the man who broke his little girl's heart before he finally grew a pair and swept her off her feet."

"You're a real piece of work sometimes, Jones. Go back to pucking Canada."

"I will, next month when we play Toronto."

Rolling my eyes at him and resisting the urge to flip him off, I turn and walk away. Pulling my phone out of my pocket, I take a deep breath and hit call. Bringing it to my ear, I wait for him to pick up. It feels like it rings and rings and rings, but in actual fact, it only rings a couple of times before Dr. Knight answers.

"Jameson," he booms down the line.

"Dr. Knight, how are you, sir?"

"Good. What can I do for you?"

"I … umm, sir, I'd like your permission to ask Lexi to marry me." I'm so nervous. After the question passes my lips, I hold my breath and I feel like I want to vomit … especially when nothing happens.

I'm met with silence.

Pulling the phone from my ear, I look at the screen, wondering if maybe the line disconnected, but it's still connected.

"Sir—" I say just as he says, "JJ—"

Holy fuck, he called me JJ. "JJ, son, I've been waiting for this call since you called me and asked for her flight details all those months ago. Then again, I knew it would take time because my princess didn't forgive you just like that. She made you work for it and then when needed, you stepped in and saved her. For which her mother and I are extremely grateful."

Nodding, I remember the moment like it was yesterday. I

still can't believe my father did that, but then again, what kind of man walks out on his family?

"And aside from the fact my daughter loves you unconditionally, I will allow you to ask her."

"Really?" I question, kinda in shock that he said yes.

"Yes, really," he confirms. "I could not think of a better man for my little girl."

As I process his words, a Ronald-freakin'-McDonald-worthy smile graces my face, I'm McSmiling. I catch Kallen's eye across the way and I offer him a thumbs-up. He smiles back and then I remember I'm on the phone.

"Thank you, sir. I promise to love and cherish and spoil Lexi for as long as I shall live."

"Save that for the vows, but remember—"

"That you know how to inject me with something that will kill me and it won't show up on an autopsy, allowing you to get away with murdering your daughter's husband."

"Well, yes, there's that, but I was going to say, I'm proud of you, JJ. You owned your mistakes and you won back the love of my daughter. That in itself is a feat and now, now she's yours to look after forever."

"Forever. I like the sound of that."

"Good, now when are you going to propose?"

That's the next dilemma, but for now, I'm going to watch Kallen and Stefan play nice and then I have an epic proposal to plan.

55

LEXI

JJ HAS BEEN ACTING WEIRD EVER SINCE THE CHARITY THING FOR underprivileged kids the other day. He keeps brushing me off, saying things are fine, but I don't believe him. And we all know what they say about people who say they're fine. They're anything but fine.

We're flying home for Christmas since we have three days off and I cannot wait to see my family. It's been a few weeks since we've seen each other in person and I've missed them. I may be almost twenty-seven, but I'm a Mommy and Daddy's girl at heart, more a Daddy's girl, but don't tell my mom that.

With our luggage in hand, we exit the terminal and I smile when I see my dad waiting at the curb. "Go," JJ says from next to me and he outstretches his hand and nods toward my suitcase in a silent 'give that to me and go hug your dad' kind of way.

Smiling at him, I hand my suitcase off to him. I blow him

a kiss and race over to my dad, leaping into his outstretched arms. "Hey, Princess, I missed you."

"Missed you too, Dad."

A few moments later, JJ joins us and I pull away from my dad. He outstretches his hand to JJ and JJ takes it, just as he says, "Good game last night." That's a dad greeting, in lieu of a hello.

"Thanks, Dr. Knight—"

"I think after all this time, you can call me Preston."

My eyes widen at Dad's words and I mouth, "What the puck" to JJ. Even though JJ and I have been back together for nearly two years now, Dad is still very protective of me. I love him for it, but he really needs to calm the farm. JJ and I are a done thing. I just need the ring and then hopefully Dad will relax. But in all honesty, I don't need the ring or the big, fancy wedding and a piece of paper to prove my love. I know deep in my heart that I love JJ and I always will.

We climb into the car and Dad drives us home. Like always when I come home, all the family—blood and chosen —congregate at Mom and Dad's for a catch-up.

As soon as we walk in from the garage, I hear Mom and Aunty Bay arguing about the upcoming arrival of their grandbaby.

Yep, my little brother knocked up Lily Cox, the daughter of Mom's sworn enemy. The two of them have been sneaking around since the Halloween before last. She got pregnant and the two of them in their infinite eighteen-year-old minds decided to elope and become a family.

Now, Mom and Aunty Bay will be bonded together forever due to a surprise pregnancy and an elopement.

"You're glowing," I tell Lily when she enters the room.

"Thanks, Lex." She smiles at me and rests her hand on her baby bump. "Your nephew is kicking up a storm."

"It's a boy?" I cry out.

CJ nods brightly as he slides his hands around Lily's waist and rests his hands on hers. "Yep, wee lil'—"

"Noooooooooooooo," Mom and Aunty Bay sing out together.

"We don't want to know the name," Aunty Bay says. "You already ruined the sex surprise. I don't want to know the name."

"And neither do I," Mom adds.

My eyes widen. "Am I in *The Twilight Zone*?"

"What? Why?" JJ asks.

"Mom and Aunty Bay just agreed on something. I can count on one hand the number of times that's happened in my life."

"This is something we agree on," Mom states as she walks over to me and pulls me in for a hug. "Welcome home, Lex."

"Thanks, Nana," I mumble.

"See, I should be called Nana. Even Lex agrees."

"What did I agree to?" I furrow my brows in confusion.

"I want to be called Nana and so does Bay, but I called it first, so I should get the title."

"And I keep saying Mom can be Nana and Aunty Bay can be Nanny B," CJ voices, earning a chorus of "I agree" from *everyone* in the room.

"I like that too," JJ agrees and I just nod.

"See?" Mom hisses at Aunty Bay, and the two of them get into it again over who gets to be called Nana.

JJ tugs on my hand. "Come with me," he whispers.

Nodding, I lace my fingers with his and we leave them debating who's going to be called what—FYI, Mom won, much to Aunty Bay's disgust.

He hands me my coat and helps me into it. Then he slips

his on and we walk out the back. He leads me to the base of the treehouse. "For old times' sake?"

"JJ, it's pucking cold out here. Can we do this another time?"

"Nope." He shakes his head and begins to climb up. Sliding into the treehouse, he pokes his head out, "You coming up?"

"Fine," I relent and then I begin the climb.

When my head pops over the edge, my eyes widen when I see the scene before me. Pulling myself the rest of the way into the treehouse, I rest on my knees and look around the treehouse.

Littered around the small space must be hundreds of mason jars with candles lit inside. Fairy lights adorn the ceiling of the treehouse and there, in the middle, down on bended knee is JJ.

"Lex, I've been in love with you from the moment your head appeared in that window there." He points to the window to the right of him. "I did a bonehead thing when I was eighteen, but Fate believed in us and she gave us a second chance. I love you more than I ever thought I could love another person, and I want to spend the rest of my life with you. So, Alexis Avery Knight, will you do me the absolute honor and marry me? Make me the happiest man in the world?"

Words elude me as I stare at the man who has owned my heart since I was a teenager.

"Lex?" he hesitantly says my name as a question and at the sound of his voice, my head begins to bobble up and down.

"Yes, JJ, yes, a million times yes."

"Thank fuck," he utters.

We shuffle toward one another and he takes my left hand

and slides a gorgeous princess cut diamond onto my ring finger. Lifting my hand up, I gaze at the bling on my finger and then I look over at my fiancé. "Kiss me, fiancé," I demand.

"As you wish, fiancée," he replies.

Gripping my cheeks in his palms, he covers my mouth with his. We fall to the makeshift bed in the corner, but before we can get to the good stuff, Dad yells out, "Did she say yes?"

"Yes," I call out, "I sure did."

"Then get down here and celebrate with your family … besides, it's pucking cold out here."

"Did you just say pucking?" I call out to my dad.

"Yes, that friend of yours is very persuasive when it comes to that word."

JJ and I chuckle. "Be right there," I shout back. Then I look at my fiancé lying beside me looking all sexy like. "Rain check?"

He nods then adds, "I'd say for old times' sake we head back here once everyone is asleep, but by then it'll be below freezing, and I like my cock hard but not frozen hard."

An unladylike snort escapes me. "I agree with that, but it does mean you will need to sneak past my parents' room and into mine."

"You think now that we're engaged your dad will let me sleep in your room?"

"I have no idea, but you're allowed to call him Preston now, so anything is possible."

"Yeah, that shocked the shit out of me when he said that at the airport."

"You and me both, but I'm guessing he knew about this." I wave my hand around the treehouse.

"Actually, it was your mom and sister who helped with

this, but I did ask for his permission to ask you when we were at the underprivileged kids event the other week."

"You did?"

He nods.

"Guuuuuuys," CJ calls out, "hurry up, 'cause we can't eat till you guys get inside. Lil is ready to eat me if she doesn't get real food, and we all know Lisa's cob thingy is tastier than me."

Another snort slips out. "Coming," I sing out.

JJ and I make our way back inside and as soon as I step into the house, I sigh. It's pucking cold outside right now, but the sigh of relief turns into a yelp because when JJ joins me, party poppers are popped and everyone sings out "Congratulations."

We spend the rest of the afternoon with our families, celebrating our engagement and cooing over Lily and CJ's upcoming baby's arrival … And stuffing our faces with food and wine.

Lily and CJ are the first ones to head to bed after everyone has left. When I notice the two of them head to the one room, I get my hopes up that JJ and I will be able to sleep in my room, but the thought is squashed when Dad says, "JJ, help me make up your bed in the den."

"Why can't he stay in my room?"

"Because you're not married," Dad replies.

"We're engaged, which is pretty much the same thing."

"Lex, you know the rules when it comes to boys," Dad enforces as if I'm seventeen. Looking at my dad, I raise my eyebrows. "Sorry, Princess," he adds as if that'll fix everything.

Resting my hands on my hips, I stare intently at my dad and then I pull out my smoking gun and I utter one word, "Lollipop."

Both his and mom's eyes widen, and Pepper bursts out laughing. "Oh My God," she cries, slapping her thigh. "You did not just pull that card out."

"You know too?" Mom asks my sister, embarrassment written all over her face.

"Please," Pepper scoffs, "what do you expect to happen when you get down and dirty in the media room?"

"Hmmmpf," I add, "so your antics aren't just confined to the kitchen?"

"Hell no," Pepper adds, "Kitchen. Media room. The back deck."

"Oh My God," Mom mumbles into Dad's shoulder. "Kill me now."

"Sleep wherever you want just … never mind." He looks to Mom. "Come on, let's go to bed. The kids can clean up."

Mom nods and calls out "Good night" as she hightails it down the hallway to their bedroom. Dad is hot on her heels.

Pepper and I are laughing our asses off as we clean up the kitchen. "You know," she says to me as she turns the dishwasher on, "I think that was the last time we will ever be able to play the lollipop card."

"I think you're right," I agree, "but what a lollipopping good way to go out."

That causes us to both laugh again. We say good night and then I head into the media room and join JJ.

Straddling his thighs, I stare into his eyes. "So, everyone is asleep." Gripping the hem of my sweater, I lift it over my head, leaving me in my fuzzy socks, jeans, and a bra. "If we do it here, you won't have to sneak past my mom and dad's room."

He slides his hands up my back and makes quick work of unclasping my bra. The straps fall down my arms and I flick it to the side. Leaning forward, he takes one of my nipples into his mouth and sucks. "I don't have to sneak since you lollipopped me into your bedroom, but I do like this."

"Like what?" I pant as he massages my breast, rolling the tip he just sucked between his fingers.

"The possibility that your mom or dad could bust us."

Freezing in his lap, my eyes widen. My reaction causes JJ to chuckle. "How about we take this into the bedroom, and then I can worship your body the way you're meant to be worshipped."

"Yes," I moan like a wanton hussy.

JJ scoops me up into his arms bridal style and heads to my bedroom. He shows me three times how much he loves me and in the wee hours of the morning with our legs entwined, I look up at my fiancé. "I pucking hated that you still loved me, but now, I pucking love that you still loved me. I cannot wait to become Mrs. Lexi James because, JJ, I pucking love you. Now and forever."

He rolls me to my back and shows me one more time just how much he never stopped loving me. I'm one lucky woman and I could not be any pucking happier.

EPILOGUE - JJ

...seven months later

WE'RE ONCE AGAIN STANLEY CUP CHAMPIONS, MAKING THAT three in a row for the Crushers. This win was that much sweeter because we beat the LA Legends four to one. They won the first game of the playoffs, but we smashed them in the next four games, sealing our win.

As usual, Kal and I made a bet and I lost. My penance, Lexi and I had to fly to Vegas to get married, so here we are. In Vegas. About to get married at *The Little Vegas Chapel*. Kal and Chelsea have FaceTimed in because she's in the final weeks of her pregnancy and can't fly right now.

"You nervous?" Kal asks as we wait our turn.

"Not at all. I cannot wait to marry Lex."

"And I can't wait to marry you either. I'll officially be Mrs. Lexi James," my bride-to-be coos. She's wearing a simple, off-white strappy dress that's tight across her tits and falls down her body in layers and layers of silky soft material. She has a veil pinned into her hair that's been curled. It flows in luscious waves around her shoulders, and on her feet, a killer pair of heels that elongate her sexy calves.

"I like the sound of that." Pulling her to me, I cover her mouth with mine and kiss her deeply.

"That comes later," Chelsea says, just as the doors to the chapel swing open and my eyes widen when I see who stumbles out the door.

"Congratulations, Mr. and Mrs. Däuchmen," the attendant says.

With wide eyes, I stare at Doucheman and Wren as they exit the chapel hand in hand. She's wearing a white, figure-hugging strapless dress and Doucheman is dressed like me in black slacks with a white button-down. She's holding a bouquet of flowers and I notice matching rings on their left hands.

"Holy-pucking-shit," I hiss and the sound of my voice has the newly married couple turning toward us. Both their eyes pop open when they see Lexi and me sitting here.

No one utters a word as we silently stare at one another.

"What's going on?" Chelsea asks, her voice echoing around the little reception area.

Lexi reaches over and flips the phone screen so she can see what we see.

"Puck me," she mumbles, but before anyone can say anything to the happy couple, Wren drops Doucheman's hand and races out of the chapel. Leaving her new husband behind.

"Go after her," Chelsea shouts and that spurs him into action. He chases after her and waves over his shoulder just as Chels calls out, "Congratulations, Stefan."

"Holy shit, I did not see that coming," Kallen says. "I thought they hated each other?"

"Kal, you're so dim when it comes to love," I tell him. "Those two are your classic enemies-to-lovers trope."

"Someone's been listening at book club," Lexi teases me.

"I think you mean wine club," I throw back at her.

"Whatever," she nonchalantly says. "Besides, you love book slash wine club 'cause you get the benefits of said schmexy books with a tipsy me when I get home." She winks at me and that little eye movement has my cock twitching.

Down, boy, we need to get hitched first, I internally tell my dick.

"That I do," I reply. Lexi gets so amped up when she reads sometimes that she literally attacks me. I wonder what it's like for the author writing? Their husbands must be pretty lucky guys.

"Jameson and Lexi, you're up," the attendant announces.

"That's us," I shout and jump up.

"Someone's excited," she says to me.

"Hell yeah, I am, I'm marrying the woman I've been in love with since I was sixteen."

"Aww," the lady coos, "that's so sweet. Well, let's get you two lovebirds married."

Lexi and I follow the lady into the chapel. We place the phone with Kal and Chelsea on a stand specifically for scenarios like this and the officiant begins.

"We are here today to join Jameson James and Alexis Knight—"

"Sorry," I interrupt her, "can you call us JJ and Lexi? It feels like we're in trouble when you use those names."

Kal and Chels laugh and Lexi just shakes her head, but her smile agrees with me.

"Of course." She smiles brightly. "Let's try that again."

She takes a deep breath. "We are here today to join JJ and Lexi in holy matrimony."

Lexi and I decided to go with a standard ceremony. Neither one of us are wordy people and the standard ceremony has been around long enough and it gets the point across.

Less than ten minutes later and the officiant utters the most perfect words, "I now pronounce you husband and wife." She looks at me. "You may kiss your bride."

Gripping Lexi's cheeks, I cover her mouth with mine, sealing our vows with a kiss.

"I pucking love you, Mrs. James."

"And I pucking love you, Mr. James."

"Now, it's time for the fu—"

Lexi shuts me up with another hot and heavy kiss, and then we head back to the hotel where we get to the fucking … and it was so pucking good. I cannot wait to spend the rest of my life with this woman. I lost her once. That was a hell I never want to endure the again, but now that we're married, no one and nothing will tear as apart.

It's endgame.

Game over … and she's the best win of my life.

THE PUCKING END!

If you want to read what happens after the chapel back in the hotel room, click this link to download the bonus scene … but I warn you, it's pucking hot!

BONUS SCENE - JJ

THE DOOR TO OUR SUITE CLICKS CLOSED AND IT'S A FRENZY OF hands and teeth as we attack one another. "You, Mrs. James, are wearing too many clothes."

"Well, you better help me with that, Mr. James."

Lex spins around and lifts her hair over her shoulder, offering me an unobstructed view of her from the back. The silky material flows down her body and I cannot wait to see what's underneath.

Stepping to her, I lean down and press a kiss to her shoulder blade. Lifting my hand, I grip the zipper and ever so slowly, I slide it down. Inch by inch it falls open, exposing her naked back to me. "No bra," I muse.

She looks back at me. "Or panties."

Shaking my head, she just smiles and shimmies the straps down her arms. Pulling her arms free, she wiggles her hips and the material floats to the carpet, leaving her naked except for her heels.

"Fuck me, Lex, you're a vision."

"And you, husband, are way overdressed."

"Well, wife, you better help me get undressed then."

She spins around to face me and a groan slips out. She was sexy from the back, but from the front, I have no words. Her tits are perky. Her stomach flat. Her mound is hair-free and glistening in the low light reflecting in the room. She steps out of her dress and walks over to me.

Leaning into me, she presses her lips to mine, but before it gets too far, she pulls back. "Let's see about removing some of these clothes. I want to ogle my husband."

"Have at it."

Pulling my shirt free of my pants, she starts on the buttons. One by one, they pop open, but it's clearly taking too long because Lex grips the material and tears. The rest of the buttons fly through the air. She pushes the material over my shoulders and down my arms. It flutters to the floor and joins her dress.

Licking her lips, she leans into my chest and kisses my pecs. She sucks on my nipple and the sensation is surprising. She nips and kisses her way down my abs, dropping to her knees before me.

With nimble fingers, she makes quick work of opening my belt. The button pops open and then she lowers my fly. Sliding her hands into my open pants, her eyes widen. "No briefs?"

"I'm taking a leaf out of my wife's book … Plus, letting it all hang free is kinda comfortable."

"Aaaaand, it gives your wife easy access to do this." She pulls my dick free and licks the weeping tip, her tongue sliding through the slit.

"That is an added bonus," I say on a moan.

Circling her tongue around the head, she slides my shaft into her mouth and sucks. Her lips wrap around my dick as it slips in and out of her mouth. Running my hands through her hair, I guide her head back and forth. My cock hits the back of her throat with each motion.

My balls begin to tingle and I'm on the verge of coming, but I step back, my dick popping out of her mouth with an audible pop. "As much as I want to come down your throat, Lex, I want the first time I come after becoming your husband to be in your cunt."

"Ugh, way to ruin the moment with *that* word."

"I bet I can make it up to you," I tell her.

"Yeah, what did you have in mind?"

"Well, I'd splay you out on the massive bed in the bedroom. Spreading your legs, you'd play with your clit as I kiss, nip, and suck at your inner thigh."

"And then what?"

"Once you've worked yourself up, I'd push your hand out of the way and I'd feast on your cun—I mean, pussy, until you're a quivering, incoherent mess. After giving you an orgasm with my mouth, I'd flip you over and slap you on the ass. Then I'd grip your hips and shove my dick into you. I'd bottom out and you'd press back into me. Back and forth we'd rock and when you're screaming my name, I'd lift you up and cover your tits with my hands. I'd pull on your nipples as I continue to fuck you from behind."

"Yes," she mewls and I notice her hand is between her thighs.

Gripping my cock, with my eyes on her, I continue my sexy story. "When you're just about to explode, I'd pull out and spin you around. I'd cover your mouth with mine and then we'd fall to the mattress. You'd spread your legs—"

"And your cock would slide back in and we'd fuck," she interrupts. "Now, less talking and more actioning ... please."

"How can I say no to that?"

"You can't," she teases.

Standing up, she walks over to the bed and splays herself out, just like in my story, but seeing her spread open, willing and waiting, sparks my inner desire and I pounce on her.

My dick effortlessly slides into her and she moans in that sexy way that has my dick stiffening further. I didn't know I could get any harder, but when Lex is naked beneath me, anything is possible.

With our eyes locked on one another, I fuck her.

It's fast.

It's hard.

It's carnal.

It's perfect.

Just like my wife.

"You are perfect, Mrs. James, and I'm one lucky son of a bitch."

"I'm the lucky one," she hisses out, "but shut up and kiss me."

Leaning down, I press my lips to hers. My tongue plunges into her mouth in sync with my dick in her pussy. Back and forth we rock. My balls begin to tingle, but I can't come until she has. Sliding my hands between us, I press on her clit and circle the pad of my finger over the sensitive bud.

That's the detonation she needs. Her walls clamp down on my shaft and she explodes. Her juices coat my dick and I soon follow. My body stiffens and I spill inside her, no need for condoms anymore. I can fuck my wife bare anytime I want now, and it's glorious, so fucking glorious.

"I love you," I whisper into her neck when I collapse on top of her.

"I love you too, JJ. I have since I was sixteen years old. Even when I hated you, I still loved you, and I will continue to love you until my dying breath. You're it for me, Jameson James, and now that your ring is on my finger, I'm not going anywhere unless you are by my side."

"Ditto," I tell her because that's exactly how I feel. Lexi James is my Stanley Cup and I've just won the best thing ever, her heart and love.

Want more from the Pucking Love series?
Stefan and Wren's story is coming mid 2024.

*I pucking hate
to love you*

I vowed I'd never get involved with someone I worked with again. I learned that lesson the hard way. When I'm assigned Stefan Däuchman aka Doucheman, I realize I have a huge problem.

Not only is he a douche. He's also my client, my very attractive client. My number one rule is "never date someone from work" … "or a douche." Especially a high-profile douche client.

It doesn't matter how good-looking he is with his rich as chocolate eyes, washboard abs, and heart of gold which he keeps hidden under his douchey exterior. He's my client and I'm not going there. But the more time I spend with the douche, the deeper I fall.

I pucking hate to love him, but I can't help it … I'm so pucking screwed.

Preorder I Pucking Hate To Love You now.

PLAYLIST

We Used To Be Friends - The Dandy Warhols
Natural - Imagine Dragon
High Hopes - Panic! At The Disco
Don't Look Back In Anger - Oasis
Half of My Heart 0 John Mayer
I Hate Everything About You - Three Days Grace
Thnks fr th Mmrs - Fall Out Boy
How Far We've Come - Matchbox Twenty
Welcome to the Back Parade - My Chemical Romance
This Is War - Thirty Seconds To Mars
Perfect - Ed Sheeran, Beyoncé
If You Love Her - Forest Black
10,000 Hours - Dan + Shay (with Justin Bieber)
My Girl - The Temptations
Tennessee Whiskey - Chris Stapleton
Yours - Russell Dickerson
Complicated - Avril Lavigne
War of Hearts - Ruelle
Fuck it I love you (E) - gnash, Olivia O'Brien
Bleeding Love - Leona Lewis

Easy to Love You - Theory of a Deadman
Hurts So Good - Astrid S
Two Is Better Than One - BOYS LIKE GIRLS feat. Taylor
Swift
Far Away - Nickelback
Memories - Maroon 5
The One That Got Away (acoustic) - Katy Perry
Back for Good - Take That
What About Us - P!nk
Wonderwall - Oasis
I'm Gonna Be (500 Miles) - The Proclaimers
Bad Habits - Ed Sheeran
I Don't Wanna Live Forever - ZAYN, Taylor Swift
Waves - Dean Lewis
Water Under the Bridge - Adele
Mercy - Shaun Mendes
Hey There Delilah - Plain White T's
I See Red - Everybody Loves an Outlaw
Never Tear Us Apart - Bishop Briggs

This playlist can be found on Spotify.

ACKNOWLEDGMENTS

These things never get any easier and after many many books they become harder and harder to write.

Karen Hrdlicka from **Barren Acres Editing**; thank you for everything you do for me. So glad to have you on Team DL and so glad that I finally got to hug you in person in 2023.

Emily; thank you for checking all my I's are dotted, my T's are crossed and there's no extra e's or s's

Renae from **R.L. Cover Designs**; thank you for brining JJ to life, it's one pucking hot cover.

And I cannot forget **Kristie** from **Vanilla Lily** for the alternate cover. As soon as I saw that pre-made series, I had to have them and I just love them.

Sam from **Honey + Sin**; thanks for all of the amazing teasers and countdown images. You always nail it and I love working with you.

Lainey from **DS Promotions** and all of the bloggers, thank you for helping me share IPHTYLM with the world.

My beta babes **Bec, Margaret, Rhi Rhi, Sarah and Vi;** I would be lost without you ladies. You give me advice when I second guess everything and you help me bring each story to life. Thank you from the bottom of my heart.

Troy, my husband, my everything. You really are awesome at what you do and you are an even better husband and father. Love you long-time dude.

To my munchkins, **Piper** and **Kade**. You two are my

greatest achievement and I'm so lucky to have you both in my life. Love you long-time guys and I look forward to the day when you are forty and can finally read my books.

And finally, **you, my reader**. Thanks for joining me on the pucking journey. What was a standalone, is now a seven, yes seven book series and I cannot wait for you to meet each of the players and their ladies.

Cheers,

Dana XoXoX

ALSO BY DL GALLIE

STAND ALONES

Antecedent

Doc Steel

Oops

Off the Books

Fractured:A driven world novel

Deck…the Balls

Secrets and Sunrises

Always in the Cards

Out of Nowhere

Before the Ashes

After the Ashes

Love Me Like You Do

Never Let Me Go

Seven Nights

Seven Kisses

PUCKING NOVELS

I Pucking Hate That I Love You

A Pucking Good Christmas

It's Pucking Fake (appearing in Fake It Till You Make It)

I Pucking Hate That You Love Me

I Pucking That To Love You

…and a few pucking more

FALLING NOVELS

These men make it hard not to fall for them

Falling for Dr. Kelly

Falling for Dr. Knight

Falling for Agent Cox

Falling for Agent Cruz

Falling: The Complete Collection

LORDS OF CRESTWOOD PREP

Co-write with Tara Lee

Thatcher

Reign

Hendrix

Saint

THE UNEXPECTED SERIES

When it comes to love, expect the unexpected

The Unexpected Gift

The Unexpected Letter

The Unexpected Package

The Unexpected Connection

The Unexpected series: The Complete Collection

THE CASTAWAY GROVE COLLECTION

Love has arrived in the Grove

Oasis

Unequivocal Love

Five Words

Broken Rules

…and a few more to come.

The Castaway Grove Collection, Vol 1

THE LIQUOR CABINET SERIES

Liquor has never been so disturbingly saucy

Malt Me (Book 1)

Tequila Healing (Book 2)

Wine Not (Book 3)

The Final Shot (Book 4)

The Liquor Cabinet: Series boxset

All of these books are available on Amazon.

ABOUT THE AUTHOR

DL Gallie is from Queensland, Australia, but she's lived in many different places all over the world, including the UK and Canada. She currently resides in Central Queensland with her husband and two munchkins. She and her husband have been together since she was sixteen, and although they drive each other crazy at times, she couldn't imagine her life without him.

Shortly after her son was born, DL began reading again. With encouragement from her husband, she picked up the pen and started writing, and now the voices in her head won't shut up.

DL enjoys listening to music, drinking white wine in the summer, red wine in the winter, and beer all year round. She's also never been known to turn down a cocktail, especially a margarita.

FACEBOOK ~ INSTAGRAM ~ BOOKBUB

GOODREADS ~ WEBSITE

dlgallieauthor@outlook.com

Sign up to my newsletter

DL GALLIE

ROMANCE WITH A SHOT OF SUSPENSE
AND A DASH OF COMEDY

Milton Keynes UK
Ingram Content Group UK Ltd.
UKHW010645010324
438562UK00001B/30

9 780975 640913